TIME
IN
TIME

TIME IN TIME

Short Poems, Long Poems, and the Rhetoric of North American Avant-Gardism, 1963–2008

EDITED BY J. MARK SMITH

McGILL-QUEEN'S UNIVERSITY PRESS
Montreal & Kingston • London • Ithaca

ISBN 978-0-7735-4083-5

Legal deposit first quarter 2013
Bibliothèque nationale du Québec

Printed in Canada on acid-free paper that is 100% ancient forest free (100% post-consumer recycled), processed chlorine free

This book has been published with the help of a grant from the Canadian Federation for the Humanities and Social Sciences, through the Awards to Scholarly Publications Program, using funds provided by the Social Sciences and Humanities Research Council of Canada.

McGill-Queen's University Press acknowledges the support of the Canada Council for the Arts for our publishing program. We also acknowledge the financial support of the Government of Canada through the Canada Book Fund for our publishing activities.

Library and Archives Canada Cataloguing in Publication

Time in time : short poems, long poems, and the rhetoric of North American avant-gardism, 1963–2008 / edited by J. Mark Smith.

Includes bibliographical references and index.
ISBN 978-0-7735-4083-5

1. Experimental poetry, American–20th century–History and criticism. 2. Experimental poetry, American–21st century–History and criticism. 3. Experimental poetry, Canadian (English)–20th century–History and criticism. 4. Experimental poetry, Canadian (English)–21st century–History and criticism. I. Smith, J. Mark

PS325.T54 2013 811'.540911 C2012-906297-9

Contents

Acknowledgments

"Lyric and Experimental Long Poems: Intersections": "A Poem for Painters" by John Wieners from *The Hotel Wentley Poems: Original Versions* (San Francisco: David Haselwood, 1965) © 1958, 1965, renewed 1984, is used by permission of the John Wieners Literary Trust, Raymond Foye, executor. Lines from "An Impossible Poem" by George Oppen from *New Collected Poems* (New York: New Directions, 2002) © Linda Oppen, has been quoted with permission. Some of the analysis of Zukofsky's work in this essay also appears in Rachel Blau DuPlessis, *Purple Passages: Pound, Eliot, Zukofsky, Olson, Creeley, and the Ends of Patriarchal Poetry* (Iowa City: University of Iowa Press, 2012). With thanks to The University of Iowa Press.

"More Apparent than Real: The Lyric/Avant-Garde Divide": section iii of "Notes Toward a Supreme Fiction," *The Collected Poems of Wallace Stevens* (New York: Vintage / Random House, 1990), is used by permission of Random House.

"Hannah Weiner's Book In Air: *Clairvoyant Journal* and the Clair-Style Poems": excerpts and images from pages 1, 16, 29, 34, 48, 54 of Hannah Weiner's *Clairvoyant Journal*; and 63, 127 of *Hannah Weiner's Open House* (Berkeley: Kenning Editions, 2007) are used by permission of Charles Bernstein for Hannah Weiner in trust.

"The Lyric Turn: A Poetics of Falling" by Erín Moure was first published (as "*O Cadoiro*: The Cataract") in *My Beloved Wager: Essays from a*

Writing Practice (Edmonton: NeWest Press, 2009), 271–8. Reprinted by permission of NeWest.

"By the Numbers: Jackson Mac Low's Light Poems and Algorithmic Digraphism": excerpts from pages 19 and 76 of *22 Light Poems* by Jackson Mac Low (Los Angeles: Black Sparrow Press, 1968); excerpts from pages 208–9, 220, 222–3, 228, and 230 of Mac Low's *Thing of Beauty: New and Selected Works* (Berkeley: University of California Press, 2008); and an image of "Jackson Mac Low's light chart" from page 41 of *22 Light Poems* are used by permission of Anne Tardos for Jackson Mac Low in trust.

"Getting Every Word In: A.R. Ammons's *Garbage* and the Corpora": Excerpts from pages 22, 25–6, 49, 55, 63–4, and 78 of *Garbage* by A.R. Ammons (New York and London: W.W. Norton, 1993) are used by permission of W.W. Norton.

An early version of "*Day* Labour" by Steve McCaffery was first published as "From Muse to Mousepad: Informatics and the Avant-Garde," in *Phrasis: Studies in Language and Literature*, 49.1 (Fall 2008): 179–97.

I would like to thank David Higgins, Dean of the Faculty of Arts and Science at Grant MacEwan University, for crucial financial and moral support of this project at various steps along the way; the Awards to Scholarly Publication Program (ASPP) of the Canadian Federation for the Humanities and Social Sciences for generously subsidizing the publication of the book; Roger Davis, my former colleague at Grant MacEwan University for co-organizing with me the 2009 conference on contemporary poetry and poetics that was the book's beginning point; Jonathan Crago at McGill-Queen's University Press for his astute and well-timed editorial advice; the three anonymous readers of the initial version of the manuscript for their critical suggestions; Anita Parker for her assistance in preparing the manuscript; and Susan Glickman, who copy-edited it. Much love to Jen and Gabe – yes, Papa's book is finished now!

Abbreviations

ACF	Hugh Kenner, "Art in a Closed Field," 1982.
AL	Jacques Derrida, *Acts of Literature*, 1992.
B	Jesper Hoffmeyer, *Biosemiotics*, 2008.
BSP	The Black Sparrow Press archive, Bruce Peel Special Collections Library, University of Alberta.
BW	Hannah Weiner, "Big Words," 1974.
CJ	Hannah Weiner, *Clairvoyant Journal*, 1974.
DI	M.M. Bakhtin, *The Dialogic Imagination*, 1981.
DOI	Marjorie Perloff, *Dance of the Intellect*, 1985.
EWN	Timothy Morton, *Ecology without Nature*, 2007.
G	A.R. Ammons, *Garbage*, 1993.
IN	Alain Badiou, *Handbook of Inaesthetics*, 2005.
JB	Jack Spicer, *Collected Lectures*, 1998.
KR	Julia Kristeva, *The Kristeva Reader*, 1986.
LD	Louis Zukofsky, "Interview by L.S. Dembo," 1969.
LP	Jackson Mac Low, *22 Light Poems*, 1968.
MBM	Benoit Mandelbrot and Richard L. Hudson, *The (Mis)Behaviour of Markets*, 2004.
MM	Gérard Genette, *Mimologics*, 1994.
NCP	George Oppen, *New Collected Poems*, 2002.
NI	Steve McCaffery, *North of Intention*, 1986.

NLH	Charles Altieri, "Taking Lyrics Literally," 2001.
OEW	Helen Vendler, *On Extended Wings*, 1969.
OH	Hannah Weiner, *Hannah Weiner's Open House*, 2007.
P	William Carlos Williams, *Paterson*, 1992.
PE	Hannah Weiner, "Pictures and Early Words," 1972.
PCO	Charles Olson, *Collected Prose*, 1997.
PM	Raymond Williams, *Politics of Modernism*, 2007.
PMC	Jean-François Lyotard, *The Postmodern Condition*, 1984.
RA	Marjorie Perloff, *Radical Artifice*, 1991.
RC	Marjorie Perloff, "Revolving in Crystal," 1985.
SCA	Jakob von Uexküll, "The Theory of Meaning," 1982.
SD	Rick Smith and Bruce Lourie, *Slow Death by Rubber Duck*, 2009.
SG	M.M. Bakhtin, *Speech Genres and Other Late Essays*, 1986.
SiM	A.R. Ammons, *Set in Motion*, 1996.
SM	Jesper Hoffmeyer, *Signs of Meaning in the Universe*, 1996.
SP	Charles Bernstein, "Sounds Physical," 2005.
ST	Hannah Weiner, "Silent Teacher," 1994.
TA	Gérard Genette, *The Architext: An Introduction*, 1992.
TB	Jackson Mac Low, *Thing of Beauty*, 2008.
TCM	Marjorie Perloff, *21st Century Modernism*, 2002.
TE	Dana Phillips, *The Truth of Ecology*, 2003.
TI	Jean-François Lyotard, *The Inhuman*, 1991.
TRG	Toronto Research Group, *Rational Geomancy*, 1992.
UG	Marjorie Perloff, *Unoriginal Genius*, 2010.
WCW	William Carlos Williams, *Collected Poems, Vol. II*, 1988.
WS	Wallace Stevens, *Collected Poems*, 1990.

TIME IN TIME

1

Introduction: Poetic Form and the Rhetoric of North American Avant-Gardism, 1963–2008

J. MARK SMITH

The goal of this collection is to construct a representative English language history of recent North American ways in which one or another idea of the lyric poem has figured in, or been conceived as standing against, the effort to realize a more "open" poetic form. While the writers whose work is gathered here acknowledge the existence of something like a late twentieth-century battle of the books waged between practitioners and proponents of avant-gardist and of more traditional poetries, our emphasis is on what has actually been done in this 1963–2008 period to reconceive, reframe, or (in some cases) interknit the possibilities of short and long poetic forms. In essays of criticism and excursions into theory and poetics, the six Canadian and two American contributors to this volume carry out sustained analyses of poems and/or works of criticism by Louis Zukofsky, W.C. Williams, Jackson Mac Low, Hannah Weiner, George Oppen, Marjorie Perloff, A.R. Ammons, Ron Silliman, Erín Moure, and Kenneth Goldsmith.

Since the early 1980s, critics and practitioners of diverse ideological commitments have asserted that important literary and indeed political possibilities might belong to an "anti-lyric" poetics.[1] A caricatural view of lyric and its meanings has gained some hold as well. The conventions of lyric poetry, it has been said, are not only tired: they are intellectually dishonest, even ethically suspect (in that they promote a false picture of the self in relation to language and sociality). Among anti-lyric critics, Marjorie Perloff is probably the best known. Her critical and polemical efforts can be given a fair share of credit for repopularizing the word "avant-garde" and in firming up a binary ("lyric" vs. "avant-garde") that over the last twenty years has become surprisingly entrenched within the broader literary culture of the English-speaking world. In part of what follows, I will advance some criticisms of Perloff's most frequently employed instrument – her identification of most post-World War II short poems with "Romantic lyric," and her finding in any and all contemporary resistance to diverse avant-garde poetic practices a stubbornly persistent "Romantic lyric paradigm."[2] I should hasten to add that there would be little point in testing out the weight-bearing qualities of Perloff's critical judgments if the signs of her influence as a literary taste-maker were not widely evident both inside and outside of the academy. She has been, for instance, Kenneth Goldsmith's pre-eminent critical supporter, and her championing of his conceptual poetics has played no small part in giving it prominence enough to justify the two essays devoted to his work in this volume.

In several important ways, moreover, this volume aligns itself with, and is indebted to Perloff's thinking: first, in her concluding that the term "postmodernism" can be of little help in coming to grips with the most interesting poets of the late twentieth century; second, in her claim that "avant-garde" is not an anachronistic or defunct term of literary history; and third, in her argument that a second wave of modernism arrived in the late twentieth century.[3] Perloff's work should not be confused with the definitive academic scholarship – produced by critics such as Peter Bürger, Renato Poggioli, and Hal Foster – of the early twentieth-century avant-garde. It is in support of the recuperative and ongoing avant-gardist movements that her work has been aimed and broadly disseminated. Perloff herself has made inconsistent use of the term "avant-garde" over the years, as Kerry Doyle points out in her essay in this volume.

By the umbrella term "avant-gardism" – given chronological limits by the date-range of 1963–2008 – I mean to indicate innovative/experimental/non-traditional poetries of the late twentieth century. I include in this category long non-narrative poems. I also include the "radical modernism," Language poetry, and conceptual poetry that Perloff has serially championed. By "avant-gardism," I do *not* refer to the early twentieth-century avant-gardes. All of the essays and essayists in this collection are tied together by their engagement with this background discourse of second wave or recuperative literary avant-gardism. Some contributors (DuPlessis, Dickinson, Russo, Moure) are working in its train, furthering it, refining it; others (McCaffery, Doyle, O'Driscoll, Smith) are skeptical or running at cross-currents to it – but for none are the claims of a contemporary avant-gardism or experimentalism unheard of or ignored or beyond weighing.

As for "North American," the scope of this collection is limited to English language poems (hence we cannot consider the poetries of the continent's third nation-state, Mexico). While the analytic focus of the majority of the volume's essays is on poems by citizens of the USA, the works of Canadian poets are prominent here too. Moreover, the affiliative networks and inter-generational lines of avant-gardism on the continent in this period have been noticeably unconstrained by the US-Canadian border. During the 60s and 70s, for instance, Jack Spicer's work shook the world of many a young poet – on both sides of the 49th parallel.[4] In 1966, Robin Blaser moved from the Bay Area to teach at Simon Fraser University, and remained in Vancouver until his death in 2009. Another influential poet served well by our relatively porous border has been the Canadianized Englishman Steve McCaffery, a long-time resident of Toronto who currently holds an endowed chair in poetry and poetics at SUNY Buffalo. If one takes into account as well contemporary criticism and poetics written by Canadians, it becomes clear that there has been a North American avant-gardism quite distinct from, though not necessarily hostile towards, the organs and institutions of literary nationalism in both countries.

By "rhetoric" I mean the literary and conceptual moves and strategies of, as well as the promotional and polemical discourse around, this North American literary moment, its works and networks.[5] One public effect of literary avant-gardism in the 1963–2008 period has been to set the extrinsic, ideological values of short (lyric) poems and long (non-narrative) poems against one another – with the former almost always found to be "conservative," "humanist," or "Romantic." Sustained factional polemics can, of course, have a coarsening effect on literary critical evaluation and discernment. So, here, too – if reductive point-scoring had been the sum of it. But a signal achievement of North American literary avant-gardism in this period has also been, practically and publicly, and in a great range of works, to re-imagine the function and interplay of short and long poetic forms.

The phrase "time in time" encapsulates a number of the main claims of the essay by Rachel Blau DuPlessis that anchors our volume. If short poems constitute one sort of poetic time and long poems constitute another sort, neither of these is "out" of time (i.e. ahistorical). One of the starting points for DuPlessis's discussion is time as duration, the length or measure of time that it takes to read or to write a poem (following on Edgar Allan Poe's declaration that there is no such thing as a long *poem*). Another is her Zukofskian observation that "there is no difference between a short and a long poem except length, which is a measure of time." And a good part of DuPlessis's essay considers the way that a certain sort of long poem may "envelop and present" a very short poem "inside" itself: "one kind of poetic time inside another kind of poetic time."

Until the early eighteenth century, a long poem was as a matter of course epic, or for a time mock-epic – but, in any case, narrative. In the decades following, lyric (or some combination of the lyric and the prophetic) swallowed epic whole. Things came to such a pass that Poe could speak for most in declaring that the long poem was "simply a flat contradiction in terms."[6] Robert Browning did not noticeably shift this consensus, nor Walt Whitman. But Ezra Pound's *Cantos*, admitted by all, even Pound, to be a failure, somehow did – with the improbable consequence that Pound has dominated mid-twentieth through early twenty-first-century poetry as John Milton did mid-eighteenth through early nineteenth. To put it another way, self-conscious announcement of failure is in effect a convention of the long poem after Pound. Another is the willingness to *include*, using various poetic means but not, except in patches, narrative. Pound's *Cantos* "include history," and much else that would not once have been considered material amenable to being placed, or worth the effort of placing, in a recognizably poetic frame. Among contemporary literary forms, only the long poem has allowed, and only the long poem still seems to allow, such a loosening or decompressing of readerly expectation.

The characteristic long poem, since Pound, expands and spreads, jumps channels, and continues on unpredictably and seemingly without end, all the while implying, sometimes announcing, its inability to capture or represent a whole or a totality. Sometimes it declares an unwillingness to do so: as DuPlessis puts it, "the modern/contemporary long poem often exists to put an unassimilable mound of writing between yourself and culture as usual."[7] Much of the work considered in this volume is non-miniaturist, if not necessarily anti-lyric: Goldsmith's *Day*, an 866-page large-format book of "truly sumo proportions," or his *No. 111 2.7.93-10.20-96*, a 600-page compendium of "schwa" sounds; Hannah Weiner's *Big Words*, a "sprawling, stuttering, messy, never-published, 200-pg manuscript"; Jackson Mac Low's "pluriform and multitudinous corpus" including various poetic series extended upon numerical principles (*Asymmetries 1-260*; *Twenties: 100 Poems*; etc.); and A.R. Ammons's *Garbage*, a poem that acknowledges and mocks at once the fantasy of "get[ting] every word in."

But short poems, or series of short poems, feature as prominently as objects of analysis in several of the essays collected here. Moreover, it is not assumed in these analyses that a short poem is by necessity a closed form. Michael O'Driscoll's study of Jackson Mac Low's *Light Poems* demonstrates one of this collection's major contentions, which is that we would do better to understand "lyric" as a mode of enunciation rather than as a genre defined and walled off by what it is most commonly taken to represent (i.e., the thoughts and feelings of an individual subject). Likewise, Erín Moure's essay in poetics finds a place in this book because her creative and critical engagement with medieval Portuguese/Galician troubadour poems has bearing not only on her own work but on other North American efforts to write short – as opposed to long – poems that are (in DuPlessis's words) "disunified, heterogeneous, self-inconsistent."[8]

"The Lyric Turn: A Poetics of Falling," an essay first published as a prose afterword to Moure's 2007 collection *O Cadoiro*, introduces the not-so-well-known troubadour tradition of medieval Iberia, an alternate starting point of European lyric. The poems in *O Cadoiro* are improvisations upon the medieval Iberian songs archived in the Ajuda Codex and the *Cancioneiro da Biblioteca Nacional*. In an appendix, Moure lists the names of 161 troubadour poets, unattached to works, in a manner reminiscent of a scene late in Saramago's *All the Names*. It is the moment when Senhor José meets a shepherd in the General Cemetery who, after the interment of each body but before the delivery of stones and inscription, alters the plot numbers identifying the whereabouts of the new suicides.[9]

Even if one had all the names, that is, and they were all correctly attached to a text or texts, one would not have the origin of the poems. *Razo*, a word cognate with "reason," refers to a biographical prose narrative that accompanies many of the troubadour poems, and that purports to explain each of those poems' origins. *Trobar* is to compose poetry. The

Provençal verb means most simply "to find." The beginning point of any poem is always being lost, hence always open to being found again in the time of reading. The *razo de trobar*, Giorgio Agamben asserts (in the essay Moure quotes a long passage from), is "neither a biographical nor a linguistic event." It is an experience of speech itself, of the possibility of speech, and so of knowledge, "as an inexhaustible experience of love." This "taking place" of, this falling into, language appears as theme in the troubadour poems of both Occitan and the Iberian Peninsula.[10] The enigma of the *razo de trobar* is at the heart of the trove of short poems found and invented by Moure. Each in their own way, Hannah Weiner's and Jackson Mac Low's quasi-lyric works also explore the taking place of language as a strange sort of dictation.

The most reflective avant-gardist poetries have never simply embargoed the traditional virtues of lyric. When Louis Zukofsky turned to the phrase "more of a good thing" in a 1968 interview with L.S. Dembo, he seems to have meant that his sort of long poem belongs to the same formal category as does lyric. Zukofsky had used the same phrase almost two decades earlier in "A Statement for Poetry" (1950): "The length of a poem has nothing to do with its merits as composition in which each sound of a word is weighed, though obviously it is possible to have more of a good thing – a wider range of things felt, known, and conveyed."[11] DuPlessis reminds us of the first part of this sentence repeatedly through her essay: "*A*" is long but it is through-composed. It is "composition in which each sound of a word is weighed." In that demanding and limited sense, there is no essential difference between lyric and long poem. But even in the broader and more loosely discursive contexts in which, as DuPlessis puts it, one might give thought to "our individual subject presences and subjected present-tenses," a simple opposition of lyric and long poem will be critically unfruitful.[12]

It is, of course, partly in tribute to Zukofsky that DuPlessis insists there is no such (ahistorical) thing as *the* lyric.[13] But where there is singular embodied existence, there will be the "irreducible, implacable, impenetrable IS-ness" of lyric materials.[14] And correlative to such being, DuPlessis writes, there is *lyricism*, which shows itself in poems marked by intensity, contradiction, and pan-erotic force.[15] (Musicality, according to DuPlessis, is not definitive.) Lyricism has outlasted and will outlast, though at no time does it float entirely free of, the historical contingencies that mark the emergences and disappearances of literary notions such as lyric, epic, genius, and author. Short poems are not the exclusive texts of lyricism. While DuPlessis's essay in this volume is a veritable encyclopedia of late twentieth-century North American experiments in the long poem, Zukofsky's *"A"* and William Carlos Williams's *Paterson* provide her best examples of what she calls "allusive use" of lyric materials. In *"A,"* she finds a still more remarkable instance of a very short form set within a long poem in counterpoint to the broader stream of non-poetic discourses the text opens itself to.

A key theoretical contention of this volume is that, while it is possible to distinguish between contemporary "short," "shortish," "long," and "longish" poems, short and long forms are not inherently different literary phenomena. Another is that the conventions usually taken to be "lyric" belong to a mode of enunciation and not to a distinct literary genre or to a particular set of theoretical commitments regarding the nature of the self. Another is that "creativity" will appear differently in both short and long poems at different historical moments, and that the digital technologies of the present moment – more than any particular authorial ideology – make available, but also limit, certain possibilities for the long poem. The eight essays all take up one or more of these three contentions.

Rachel Blau DuPlessis, as we have seen, attacks the idea that a trans-historical literary entity named "the lyric" really exists. Kerry Doyle calls into question "the lyric/avant-garde divide" by showing how the same model of lyric – one that takes lyric to be genre rather than mode of enunciation – is operative in Perloff's and Helen Vendler's seemingly antithetical mid-1980s readings of a poem by Wallace Stevens. Jennifer Russo investigates the quasi-confessional poetics of Weiner and analyzes the long poem *Clairvoyant Journal* in relation to the fractured lyric fields of Weiner's other "clair-style" works of the early 1970s. Erín Moure contemplates the "shiver of the archive" that informs and inhabits not only her own translated troubadour lyrics but any radically conceived short poem. Michael O'Driscoll explores how intentional, "lyric" expression seeps into the chance-generated compositions of a series of short poems by Mac Low. I interpret A.R. Ammons's long poem *Garbage* in relation to Romantic philosophy of language as well as to the findings of the databases of current usage known as the corpora. And both Adam Dickinson and Steve McCaffery, though with very different critical armatures, approach

Kenneth Goldsmith's long poems and the radical challenge those works present to the idea of literary creativity.

▲●▲

Why the stretch of years 1963–2008? As Rachel DuPlessis says about her own proposition concerning lyric and long poems, this box of time may have a use-by date. Nevertheless, our start date is 1963, the year of President Kennedy's assassination and the *de facto* beginning of the decade now known as the sixties. It was the moment of the Vancouver Poetry Festival, when prominent US and Canadian poets gathered and sent forth the rhizomes of a cross-border avant-gardist nexus. The year 1963 was an important one as well in the publishing history of two very influential poems that figure prominently in DuPlessis's essay. Sections 16 and 17 of Zukofsky's "*A*" were published in 1963: "A"-16, a 3-line lyric; "A"-17, a twelve-page homage to Williams Carlos Williams. In 1963, the five books of *Paterson* were first published together as a whole. The popular and long-lived Williams (who died in March of the same year, just short of his eightieth birthday) had emerged as the most celebrated American modernist, a unifying figure in the early years of this decade of Romantic and modernist reprise, and of rapid transformation in popular and literary culture. It is surely noteworthy that Williams has been a hero to *both* the experimental poets and to the reputedly more domesticated poets of the creative writing programs of North America. The young A.R. Ammons, a follower of Williams (and, by less obvious or more diffuse lines of transmission, of John Cage), wrote *Tape for the Turn of the Year* in 1963.[16] It was his first long poem to be both constrained and opened up by a no-going-back method of composition; he used it again in a number of later works (including *Garbage*, published in 1993). Jackson Mac Low, who in the late 1950s attended a seminar in experimental composition given by Cage at New York's New School for Social Research, was from 1962–67 composing his *Light Poems*. In 1970, Hannah Weiner, looking to Jack Spicer's example, began to take the "dictation" that would result in her clair-style journals.

In 2008, at the other end of the period we have delimited, with Williams's reputation as strong and non-polarizing as at its beginning, Cage's name thoroughly non-marginal, and Zukofsky's work as obscure and difficult as ever, critics can look back – as DuPlessis does – to the surprising number of experimental long poems produced, as well as to challenging collections of short poems. Books from the end of this period that feature prominently in this volume include Goldsmith's *Day* (published 2003), Erín Moure's *O Cadoiro* (2007), and Ron Silliman's *The Alphabet* (completed version, 2008).

In an apparent exception to our date range, Doyle's essay pivots upon an analysis of Wallace Stevens's "Notes Toward a Supreme Fiction," first published in 1950. The critical legacy Doyle considers most closely, however, is that of Perloff, who, between 1981 and 1985, published the books and articles that forcefully propounded her claims concerning the "Pound" and "Stevens" traditions.[17] Perloff, in the mid-1990s, aptly observed that modernism "remains, at the end of the century, our Primal Scene."[18] That is, the literary and cultural implications of modernism, as well as the duration and extent of this period – even the question of whether a concept of periodicity captures its essence, whether modernism is in fact over and done with – continue to be contested by those who follow and hope to inherit its possibilities. For that reason, though modernism in poetry can indeed be divided into historical phases for the purposes of study, few labels are widely accepted. Tyrus Miller, in his 2009 book *Singular Examples,* writes somewhat archly of "latter day modernists."[19] The subtitle of that book refers to the "neo-avant-garde," which he takes to include diverse poets and artists including Mac Low, Gilbert Sorrentino, David Tudor, Stan Brakhage, and (from an earlier generation) Beckett and Cage. A term such as "neo-avant-garde," though I do not take it up, has a certain usefulness: it acknowledges that late twentieth-century and early twenty-first-century avant-gardists are most recognizable by their attempt to recuperate the energies of certain modernist forebears. Or, as Charles Altieri put it recently, "Our contemporary literary culture has to work through the apparent contradiction of treating avant-garde ambitions as part of a continuing tradition."[20] Strictly speaking, "avant-garde" implies a militancy, a hostility to bourgeois culture and the high art tradition, and would seem to apply to only a few of the figures touched upon in this volume. Some would call it a complete misnomer.[21]

According to Alain Badiou's analysis in *A Handbook of Inaesthetics,* the early twentieth-century European avant-gardes (a plurality) were stymied by their own internal contradictions: "The avant-gardes were didactic in their desire to put an end to art in their condemnation of its alienated and inauthentic character. But they were also Romantic in their conviction that art must be reborn immediately as absolute – as the undivided awareness of its operations or as its own immediately legible truth."[22] Though there are traces of these contradictory tendencies in the work of an artist such as Goldsmith, the particular historical matrix that gave rise to avant-garde modernism has vanished. Badiou's accounting of the (exhausted) twentieth-century schemata that link art and philosophy would be illuminating in any context. For instance, his diagnosis of "a brand of aesthetic voluntarism" (*IN*, 8) in avant-garde modernism gives us gives us some insight into why contributor Steve McCaffery has come to prefer the term "emergent poetries."[23] Badiou's account of literary history, like Lyotard's, should provide a tonic to those persuaded by Perloff's repeated insistence over the years (in slightly differently phrased formulations) that the only "quintessentially modern" poetry is that which is separated from Romanticism by a "rupture."[24]

Nevertheless, the invidious comparison of any given "modern" work to naïve, self-absorbed, and played-out instances of Romanticism (especially of Romantic lyric) has been a reliable standby of Perloff's over the decades, even when not in the midst of polemic: "Those who denigrate Language poetry and related avant-garde practices invariably claim that these are aberrations from the true lyric impulse as it has come down from the Romantics ..." (*TCM*, 4). Against Pound's radical modernism, she set the "Romantic" inheritor Stevens; against the Language poets of the 1980s she set "the first-person lyric or lyric sequence" of the 1960s and 1970s; and against the twenty-first-century poets of "unoriginality," of copying, collating, and reframing, she now sets – in a startling reversal – the Language poets, whose makers trusted too much in the Romantic value of "verbal originality."[25]

Doyle's study of the "lyric/avant-garde divide" does the criticism of modern poetry a service by drawing attention to Gérard Genette's erudite and little-known essay "Introduction á l'architexte" (1979). Genette's analytic target is the late eighteenth-century refiguring of lyric as one of the three genres. That was the moment lyric ceased to be, as it had been for Plato and Aristotle, a mode of enunciation alone. Friedrich Schlegel, Genette says, fired the first shot in 1797. It is in the light of Genette's critical analysis that we should consider Perloff's long campaign to put behind us the genre of lyric poetry *along with* all other Romantic conceptions of poetry. What Genette's analysis implies is that Romantic thought itself has supplied Perloff with the generic straw man of her anti-lyric polemic.[26] It follows as well that avant-gardism, at least as Perloff understands it, has made anything but a definitive break with Romantic thought. Doyle's essay convincingly dismantles the factitious opposition between Vendler's untroubled reception of the lyric tradition and Perloff's somewhat belligerent championing of anti-lyric avant-gardism by pointing out that both critics rely on the same implicit model of lyric as genre rather than mode of enunciation.

In his essay on Mac Low, O'Driscoll recalls Douglas Barbour's comment that "lyric/anti-lyric ... definitions can only occur in contrast to a rather sentimental definition of lyric."[27] Similarly, we might ask how Perloff, a critic of such boldness and discernment in the arena of late twentieth-century American poetry, arrived at such a caricatural picture of "the Romantic lyric." Perloff's remarkable autobiography, *The Vienna Paradox*, gives a partial answer. It relates a family history of wealthy and cultured Viennese Jews abandoned to the Nazis by the same refined people with whom they had upheld the ideals of *Bildung* and High Culture. Perloff's father, by her account, "was given to dramatic recitations" of "Kennst du das Land," the lyric sung by Mignon in *Wilhelm Meister* and "would explain to us children that Mignon's song was the touchstone of poetry, that here Genius with a capital G was to be found."[28] Her father and his contemporaries were seduced by a lie, Perloff writes. The high Germanic post-Romantic tradition; *Bildung* (as a civilizing doctrine); lyric (the literary genre most expressive of *Bildung*) – this interwoven cultural inheritance, she concludes, "went hand in hand with the mendacity of the war years."[29] Hence "radical modernism," a term Perloff coined and employed polemically, with striking success, to designate a line of American poets whose formal innovations were the more welcome for breaking with middlingly high-brow cultural hypocrisy. Taking only what she needed from Pound's long poem experiments (while judging his rabble-rousing radio broadcasts to be less toxic than genteel versions of anti-semitism), Perloff has weathered the historical ironies by understanding this Pound tradition to be above all hostile to ideals involving cultivation of individual sensibility and responsiveness to art. The possibility that open form (the "collage" technique, for instance) in twentieth-century long poems might itself owe much to the Romantic inheritance remains submerged at best in Perloff's ongoing critical project.

Most recently, Perloff has argued that radical modernism continues – and continues to discomfit all unexamined Romantic assumptions – in works that catalogue, collect, and cite without regard for values such as originality, uniqueness, or individual inventiveness. In this line, she asserts, Walter Benjamin's hard-to-classify, quotation-heavy *Arcades Project* [*Das Passagen-Werk*] of 1935–39 assumes the position of avant-gardist forerunner, "look[ing] ahead to the cataloguing of such recent long poems as Kenneth Goldsmith's *No. 111 2.7.93-10.20.96* with its constraint-generated, alphabetically organized syllable lists" (*UG*, 37).[30]

▲●▲

In a rather different formulation, Steve McCaffery declares that Goldsmith's long poems belong to a body of work that "signals the revenge of the *Dunciad*." The antepenultimate line of Pope's poem – "Light dies before the uncreating word" – sits as epigraph to his essay in this volume.[31] *Day*, a book-length, page by page transcription of all the words and numbers in the Friday 1 September 2001 edition of the *New York Times*, is the Goldsmith poem that McCaffery considers. Pope, of course, used the participle "uncreating," with "creating" its implied opposite; he did not use the words "creat*ive*" or "creat*ivity*" (nor negative forms of these with an "un-" prefix). These forms' moment comes a few decades later, in sentences composed by the poets of sensibility and the Romantic writers.[32] The "Creating word," to follow Pope's implied antithesis, spoke the *fiat lux*. The creating word, the poetic word, is, according to this theological philosophy of language, an echo of the divine Logos. It creates by ordering well-formed sentences and lines so as to express thought. The "uncreating word," its opposite, has no access to reason, and hence is incapable of form or thought. Moreover, the "uncreating word" that Pope imagines in the *Dunciad* is, as opposed to mere individual incapacity or lack, the cosmic agency itself of "Dullness," Chaos, and is only ever temporarily instantiated in its writerly instruments (however worthy of satirical contempt those particular persons and their aspirations may also be). Not long after the time of Pope but long before that of Kenneth Goldsmith fell the epochal upheaval that we call Romanticism. And yet, curiously, a presupposition of works such as *The Weather* or *Soliloquy* is that the chaos of the linguistic moment is an agency more broadly generative than the verbal inventiveness temporally instantiated in any particular person. The "Creating word" for Pope is divine light itself: "creativity" would be a preposterous conceit. Nor for Goldsmith are "creative" and "uncreative" terms to be used in good faith. Nevertheless, his conceptual poetics proceeds from a confidence (if not a faith) in the productive workings of a collectively distributed *logos*. The crucial difference – and it is again a textbook instance of the before and the after of Romantic transvaluation – is that the *logos* of Pope's philosophy is a rational Word. In contrast, a wanderer through Goldsmith's works and the partly ordered regions they draw upon will chance upon discursive crossings of language and reason but not upon the source of linguistic abundance.

Goldsmith (b. 1961) was first trained as a sculptor and came to "conceptual" work via an interest in concrete poetry. The effects he aims for – some coded as literary, some as visual art – are reminiscent of Duchamp's, of whose ready-made works Jean-François Lyotard noted that they do nothing but signify "[the] constant process of dispossession of the craft of painting or even of being an artist."[33] Like Andy Warhol's productions, Goldsmith works such as *Day* or *The Weather* deliberately court the suspicion of artistic charlatanry. It might be less provocative, then, to call Goldsmith a collector of words – other people's words as well as his own. When working on *No. 111 2.7.93-10.20.96*, he collected words and vocables ending in variants of the short, squashed "a" sound known to phonologists as "schwa." By his own account, he recorded instances of overheard sounds "from conversations, the newspaper, television, books – anywhere that there was language. I was constantly scribbling down things or speaking into a tape recorder."[34] Another of Goldsmith's collections – "found and insane poetry off the streets of New York City," gathered over three decades – has attracted art-world attention.[35] Collecting is an activity that in the era of Google and searchable databases sounds quaintly of (and can be framed as belonging to) another era, close to the practice that Walter Benjamin expresses admiration and nostalgia for in his *Arcades Project*.[36] Goldsmith's procedures, devoid of nostalgia if not of allusiveness, have availed themselves freely of internet-era technologies of mechanical reproduction and information storage.[37] A near-simultaneous historical development was the recognition by public-realm archivists as well as by Google that all of the old books in existence could, in practice, be digitized. Goldsmith's procedures also happen to be historically coeval with the early years of the linguistic corpora, those digital stores of tens of millions of published or otherwise recorded examples of non-literary usage.

While Goldsmith's conceptual poetry relies upon digital technologies to bring into being collections where collecting would seem uncalled for, UbuWeb, the on-line archive founded in 1996 (by Goldsmith and others) and "dedicated to all strains of the avant-garde, ethnopoetics, and outsider arts," collects more neutrally, curatorially.[38] Although its virtual space has been challenged with regard to intellectual property law, the assemblage of texts, sound recordings, images, and videos at UbuWeb is uncontroversially and unenigmatically (in contrast, say, to Benjamin's *Arcades Project*) a collection. Only the mode of access for the curious is something quite new.

A collection brought into being where collecting would seem uncalled for is one way, then, to characterize long contemporary poems, and not only Goldsmith's. Such works, at the very least, illuminate "the dialectic" – in poet Jackson Mac Low's words – "between making and letting be."[39] Adam Dickinson, in his reading of Goldsmith's poetics, provides another handle by which to take hold of the creative/non-creative crux. He gives it an environmentalist inflection, arguing that we should let go of our inherited notions of individual aesthetic response, since an information management model that looks to biosemiotic flows, interchanges, and membranes is truer to what we are and what we should become. Dickinson looks to Uexküll's quasi-phenomenological, quasi-Romantic concept of organismal *Umwelten* for an early theory of "multiple singularities." With Peirce and the biosemioticians, Dickinson supposes that signs give a dimension of ideality to a realm that empiricists and Kantians have taken to be a space of purely physical necessity. Not exactly utopian in any modern political sense, this vision of the semiosphere as a multitudinously and harmoniously interconnected system hearkens back to pre-Romantic conceptions of natural order. The higher ordering that biosemiotics moves toward is an ever more complex communicative system, which enables in turn an expansion and liberation of semiotic activity. All human languages, and all poetries, are according to this view but a layer upon the fundamental creativity of living systems. Dickinson finds in Goldsmith's long poems not so much the revenge of the *Dunciad* as of the "Essay on Man" – its "great chain" become membranous web.[40]

If Pope's philosophy of man and nature comes across as antique compared to that of the biosemioticians, late eighteenth-century aesthetics is not so easy to dispense with, particularly the still philosophically authoritative concept of the sublime. Granted, no contemporary work of art elicited such a reflective judgment – it was mostly the "works" of the natural world that were judged sublime. Nevertheless this concept, with a refitting of emphases, remains our best model for thinking about how the long aggregative poems of the digital era, failures all, have come to seem emblematic of twenty-first-century conundrums: a steady expansion of the discourse of knowledge and a concomitant recession of the knowable; a global dissemination of several millennia of artistic production and a universal deformation and destabilization of taste. Jean-François Lyotard, in his essays collected as *The Inhuman*, says little about modern poems but draws out affinities between the American abstract expressionist painters of the post-WW II period (such as Barnett Newman) and his own part Burkean, part Kantian concept of the sublime. More broadly, his formulation in the appendix to *The Postmodern Condition* positions the sublime as the key concept for understanding modern art and literature:

> The sublime takes place … when the imagination fails to present an object which might, if only in principle, come to match a concept. We have the Idea of the world (the totality of what is), but we do not have the capacity to show an example of it. We have the Idea of the simple (that which cannot be broken down, decomposed), but we cannot illustrate it with a sensible object which would be a 'case' of it. We can conceive the infinitely great, the infinitely powerful, but every presentation of an object destined to 'make visible' this absolute greatness or power appears to us painfully inadequate. Those are Ideas of which no presentation is possible. Therefore, they impart no knowledge about reality (experience); they also prevent the free union of the faculties which gives rise to the sentiment of the beautiful; and they prevent the formation and stabilization of taste. They can be said to be unpresentable (PMC, 78).

The Romantic theorists found the sublime to reside in "an over there, in another word, or another time" (*TI*, 93). The sublime of painters such as Newman, Lyotard argues, resides in the event, the occurrence: "that (something) happens" (*TI*, 93). Goldsmith encapsulates the point of *Soliloquy* this way: "If every word spoken in New York City daily were somehow to materialize as a snowflake, each day there would be a blizzard."[41] Because there is no way to present that totality of words in a way that would make it "visible" or even "audible," the Idea is sublime. But this unpresentable happening does not belong to an "over there" or "another time"; it is (as McCaffery remarks in a slightly different context) a sublime of the quotidian.

Day sets in play another Idea: not the comparatively innocent snowflake infinity of freely spoken utterances in the present moment, but the totality of verbal information stored in the data banks and computer memory repositories of the world. Thomas De Quincey, in 1823, felt the pain of the mathematical sublime as he set his own insatiable desire to read against the temporal limits of a human life and his estimate of the 1,200,000 books in print "over and above what the presses of Europe are still disemboguing into the ocean of literature, many of them immense folios or quartos."[42] McCaffery, thinking of how information accumulates in the global techno-capitalist economy, seems to recollect De Quincey's choice of participle when he writes of "a vast disemboguing of commodities and language into irreducible and inescapable sedimentation."[43] This ocean of information (and what it sediments) is discouragingly more vast, and what De Quincey called the *non*-publication of everything nominally "published" can be news only to the very naïve or the blissfully unreflective among us. If one considers how the instantaneous dissemination of information made possible by communication technologies inflicts an overwhelming multiplication of instances much more than it elicits a pleasurable feeling of sensory privation in combination with intellectual mastery, Kant's or Burke's aesthetic judgment of the sublime must give way to Lyotard's account of clashings and disharmonies that "prevent the formation and stabilization of taste."

I have already mentioned an instrument available to the twenty-first-century philologist, the corpus (pl. corpora) – a linguistic database that records spoken and written utterance and makes it possible to analyze the frequency of occurrence of particular words and phrases. If, for instance, you were to search the fields of representative data archived between 1990 and 2009 in the *Corpus of Contemporary American English* (COCA) for the phrase "more of a good thing," you would find that it was not a very common expression, but not unheard of either.[44] You would find, in another instance, that "epiphany" saw an upswing in frequency of use in popular American magazines during the second decade of this period. You might notice that "epiphany" was almost always used in ignorance, without precision or awareness of its history. (Admirers of dictionaries such as the OED or *Webster's Third* that cite sentences illustrative of usage largely from literary or otherwise exemplary texts will find the corpora dispiriting in this way.)

But let me return to that blizzard of words spoken daily. Setting aside for a moment discipline-sanctioned applications, the most valuable function of COCA or any other corpus of contemporary utterance may be as an aid to meditation on the sublime. This hybrid of computing technology and lexicographical method, for all its speed and apparent comprehensiveness, confirms Goldsmith's, as well as Ammons's, intimation that the synchronic whole of contemporary utterance cannot be presented. It is only possible to comprehend the present moment of speech by means of an Idea of it. For however large the data-base becomes, however much representative material it archives, the corpus cannot be a complete or total archive. In but a single "one of man's dialects" (American English), the totality of actual utterances at any given moment, though presumably not an infinite number, nevertheless exceeds the possibilities of representation and of archive.[45] The linguistic moment is, in its totality, unrepresentable.

Lyotard, in the essay appended to *The Postmodern Condition*, adduced several ways or moods of proceeding in twentieth-century art and literature: one melancholic and nostalgic in its emphasis on "the powerlessness of the faculty of presentation" (e.g. Proust); another "inhuman" in its emphasis on the power of conception (e.g. Apollinaire); another jubilant about the possibilities of "assay," "increase of being," and "the invention of new rules of the game" (e.g. Joyce; see PMC, 79–80). Showing a preference for the power of conception over all shaping or making or creating, Goldsmith's works of language management perhaps fit best under Lyotard's mood of the "inhuman" in modern art. And, tellingly, they slip free of the label "experimental," which came during the mid-twentieth century to be applied to the realms of both avant-garde art and institutional science. The jubilant sort of modern art is turned towards endless assay, while technoscience supposes the infinite to be at play "in the dialectic of research" (*TI*, 128). For this reason, Lyotard argues, experimental art and poetry cannot help but be "in accord with the contemporary world of industrial techno-sciences at the same time as it disavows it." (*TI*, 127)

Lyotard also points, darkly, to "a kind of collusion between capital and the avant-garde," a collusion whose main exhibit is technical or formal innovation: innovation everywhere sought, frequently produced, and endlessly proclaimed (*TI*, 105). It is a basic assumption of the capitalist economy that nothing valuable emerges without great waste and loss (of time, energy, labour, wealth, and so on). One place we currently see the monstrous or shadow side of creativity, McCaffery argues, is in that "irreducible and inescapable" sedimentation of information and commodity garbage. Another is in the "accursed share" of contemporary poetic productivity (McCaffery's allusion is to Georges Bataille's mid-century writings on the role of surplus or waste in all economies). Out of undifferentiated excess comes more of what is good, which is to say new. Anti-capitalism *and* common sense argue otherwise. In order to abandon the dream of innovation, McCaffery suggests, the sort of gathering traditionally named *poiesis* might be of some aid. As collecting is a ritual gesture that removes the commodity from all relations of utility, so Goldsmith's information management is a ritual gesture towards "uncreating" the oceanic accumulations of text and data stored in a digital limbo of not-yet or no-more.

There is an almost aggressive lack of innovation in *Day* – a book-length poem meant to be contemplated as Idea rather than read. Moreover, this is a work that (in Lyotard's words) does not "forget the possibility of nothing happening, of words, colours, forms or sounds not coming; of this sentence being the last, of bread not coming daily" (*TI*, 91). One might even claim that *Day* fulfils the "avant-gardist task" as Lyotard formulated it in a 1983 lecture: to undo "the presumption of the mind with respect to time" (*TI*, 107). By composing no new sentences, Goldsmith certainly avoids the presumption of the maker or innovator. He gives to the work such form as it has by "transposition, transcription and enlarging" but *not* by writing.[46] McCaffery finds, even so, that Goldsmith insinuates one of the effects of *poiesis* into the unliterary act of repetition that is *Day*: namely, that the work solicits, or petitions, *dianoia* – "the thought that links and deduces."[47] It is a kind of offering to thought. McCaffery reads *Day* "against a broader poetics of desertion and return."[48] In this imagining, poetry itself has been abandoned not only by any sort of "I" that might see, understand, create, but by thought itself. Rather than waiting for that near mythic return, he observes, Goldsmith welcomes the occasion of abandonment "as the time and space for mundane labour."[49]

Day labour, in the fields of information. What counts as – what for a couple of hundred years has been called – creativity does not stay constant, though the poet one supposes must have always left his or her procedures open to a favourable working out of the "dialectic between making and letting be." The word creativity could fall entirely out of use, and the word *poiesis* too: "making and letting be" would nevertheless continue their *pas de deux* into the future. As for short and long – and shortish and longish – the forms of poetry are rhetorical, their meanings changeable. If the contemporary long poem is beset or distracted or tinged in lurid hues by the sublime possibilities of twenty-first-century information technology, the contemporary short poem seems more and more free of the ideological load that for some while burdened "the lyric." What is the difference (now) between short poems and long? There are various ways a critic might go to begin to answer that question, as the essays in this volume demonstrate. An answer premised without hesitation upon the concept of genre, however, would properly belong to another time – or another book.

2

Lyric and Experimental Long Poems: Intersections

RACHEL BLAU DuPLESSIS

A long *poem* is merely more of a good thing, shall I put it that way?
Louis Zukofsky, interview with L.S. Dembo

This essay concerns some points of contact between long poems/experimentalist poems and lyric poetries, something that has interested me over the years as a writer of a long poem who has claimed polemically to "resist the lyric."[1] Already I feel double, duplicitous, and I haven't even begun. My essay presents a peculiar proposition (wary of being a thesis), and one I might also abjure under pressure, as it is an odd or quirky finding. The proposition may also have a use-by date: it seems to emerge at our mid-century and be operable currently, thus also susceptible to other further shifts. The proposition is somewhat Zukofskian, that is, paradoxical: There is no difference between the lyric and the long poem – except length. But that doesn't mean the long poem is a lyric. "A long *poem*," to cite Zukofsky's sly, possibly antic comment, "is merely more of a good thing."[2] In practice this means two features of long poems on which I will comment. One is the aesthetic necessity of through-composed long poems that may take certain, though not all, elements of lyricism, but not "the lyric," as important elements. The other is the intentional contrastative marking of the length of the long poem by enveloping and presenting a lyric poem, or a very short poem, inside it.

In his 1968 interview with L.S. Dembo, Zukofsky alludes to Edgar Allan Poe's considered finding on the long poem. If we believe Poe, a long poem is impossible. "It does not exist." It is "simply a flat contradiction in terms."[3] It can't be a poem if it's long. The intensity of poetry as a yearning artifact seems to be at odds with the scale of the long poem. This is logical in its own obsessive terms; Poe bases his opinion on a sense of how much excitement a reader can stand; this leads to many scientistic rules and assumptions about readership and poetry, rules couched universally, but that offer amusing data for the historical reconstruction of reader behavior. A poem should be (rule) consumed in one sitting, and the exact budget (rule) of soul-elevating emotion and visceral intensity cannot be sustained (rule) for more than – he is wonderfully exact about attention span – (rule) one half-hour. So the situation of poetry conceptually deliquesces into the longish lyric (often the Pindaric/Horatian ode or the philosophic meditation) as the master genre.

The impossibility of the long poem for Poe was based on a particularly rigid sense of what attention meant. It was like Aristotle on drama – anything too long disobeyed the unities of time/place (one sitting to consume) and of intention or focus (one impact, no change-ups, just greater intensity to climax). So a poem was reasonably short, focused, to be read in one sitting, and emotionally, viscerally intense. The opposite situation exists for Poe as well, though this is less emphasized; there can be a poem too short, too slight and epigrammatic.[4] Poe might have sounded as if he were laying down the law for all time, but he makes this principle from his own "fancy" to account for "some few of those minor English or American poems which best suit my own taste."[5] I should repeat that caution about my essay.

Poe's proud refusal of the possibility of the long seems based in a literary historical debate with the flaccid nationalist epics of *his* time. Like most rules, it's historical, situated, impermanent, and not a norm like a fixed star. One sympathizes, given what he is responding to in the way of American poems: the early nineteenth-century epic is nationalist, aggrandizing, didactic, and a bit historically faked. Poe claimed no alternative to this mode in poetry other than the lyric (yet he actually invented another alternative – the prose poem – what is UP with him?). Curiously, Poe's interest in intense effect could lead to something like Mallarmé's Book – a long, synoptic, total, performative, and encyclopedic (if also imaginary) work. At the very least, the use of that term capital B Book (itself idealizing and evanescent) as the long genre, rather than epic, breaks the question of length open, by offering series, long poem, book-length works, as well as epic as some appropriate genre terms. A related argument comes from Robert Creeley in praise of the poetics of Charles Olson: "Valéry, in *The Art of Poetry*, qualifies as *lyric* that mode of poetry in which the content and the form are realized simultaneously. Neither one can precede the other as a possibility. It is this sense, then, which Olson extends to all occasions of writing in verse [that is, to large forms]."[6]

However, and this is a big caveat, the proposition of "no difference" but "more-ness" – size (or amount) – depends upon a critique of the most common, conventional definitions of the lyric. It also raises the question (not considered here) what "amount" or "scale" means, how it functions for any writer, how it is registered by readers. That is, if you define the lyric without looking too hard at the terms you use, you will have a pretty big distinction between lyric and long. But if you make what I consider a proper critique of conventional definitions of the lyric, this differently focused sense of lyric has a variety of pertinent relationships to the long poem.

Part One: Defining "a Lyric" Equals Debunking "the Lyric"

What is the lyric? The lyric is a collection of former definitions of the lyric, most of which are obsolete or wrong. When we speak about the persistence of the lyric, we should really ask why we persist in talking of *the* lyric, as though it were trans-historical. How to face down a formulation asserted as a mode of continuity down the centuries? To understand these stakes, we need thoroughly to examine those former definitions of "the lyric" – since most of its definitions are inadequate.

1. *There is no "the lyric."* J.W. Johnson has a notably debunking paragraph in his article called "Lyric" in *The New Princeton Encyclopedia* (1993). "Though the attributes of brevity, metrical coherence, subjectivity, passion, sensuality, and particularity of image are frequently ascribed to the lyric," the rest of the paragraph is spent in counter examples that puncture the applicability of these traits.[7] For brevity, his counter example is Milton's "Il Penseroso"; for metrical coherence, imagist and free verse work; for romantic passion, the counter example is metaphysical wit; for individualized subjectivity the counter is the impersonality/generality characteristic of

Elizabethan love-lyric. Johnson also penetratingly announces that it is impossible to find the boundary between lyric and non-lyric "on a metaphoric or thematic basis."[8]

Where a lyric is bounded and how is it defined are evidently questions with different answers at different moments. Definitions of this mode are unstable historically. What genres are "in" the lyric vary a good deal. Here is one bundling issue and boundary issue: in the OED in an 1879 usage, the noun "lyric" is extended to include "[Wordsworth's] odes, his sonnets, and some narrative poems in stanzas." The same point is shown in George Puttenham's 1589 *The Arte of English Poesie* (from which the OED takes its first example of "lirique" [adj.]). Puttenham suggests that "lyric" is a catch-all rubric under which other more defined kinds of poems are found – specifically song, carol, ballad, ditty, all of which are sung. At any rate, according to this first OED definition, lyric includes what we would now call pop music, show tunes, country and western, rock, art song, *lieder*, song cycles, even opera arias (in recital, taken out of their narrative context): all strophic, feeling-laden words (poetry) set to music.

2. "*The*" *lyric is an elective affinity*. There are implicit claims in some lyric criticism that the construction of Western subjectivity in Sappho – the frankness, the emotional climaxes and stakes, the "high moments" (*akra*), the intensity, the sensual intimacy, the apparent judgment of or distancing from epic, the subjective center – have leaped forward to our time, as if nothing had changed in subjectivity, eros, gender, or war between then and now.[9] This seems implausible; at very least one would have to argue that there is authorial choice in participating in a tradition whose varying terms we re-evoke, part of *our* desire for evocative continuity, not "the lyric's persistence." *It* has no agency; we do. While there are bedrock universals in human experience (like death and historical accidents), it is still we who have to elect in any instance to focus, discuss, and interpret them. (There are different kinds of death, different attitudes toward its inevitability, different ways of understanding it and accounting for it, different delusions about afterwards. There are also different historical accidents – wrong place/wrong time/bad luck is one; poverty and corruption leading to poor buildings and their collapse in an earthquake are quite another.)[10] To say this again, there is no "the lyric"; rather there is an author's choice of mode. Poetry's authors have some reasons to claim trans-historicalness; sometimes critics of poetry do also.

That is, in writing any work, one draws on historically maintained rhetorics and discursive practices, and alludes approvingly, analytically, or critically to an accumulated storehouse of poetic and language conventions as well as to findings and themes that may be time-honored, but from which one re-selects or which one chooses to reaffirm.[11] This storehouse is hardly static – it is mutable, with differential attentions paid to varying parts of general human heritage and to heritages from a variety of cultures. In this way, I am trying to account for poetic agency and authorial choices, which may be propelled and compelled by any number of assumptions as well as by individual analyses and subjective situations.

3. *"The" lyric is a schooled entity.* We have learned, in school, to read things called lyrics and to respond to them under this rubric. Indeed, schooling helps to establish what the literary is at any given moment of its uses. Schooling is a way both of helping and of policing the uses of poetry and (approved/disapproved) ways of reading it. Curiously "the" lyric might also be a reading effect of what constitutes "the teachable" vs. "the unteachable" poem. A sonnet or a set of quatrains, or various shorter "anthology" poems, whatever their other virtues, seem readymade for fifty minutes of class time, particularly in the regime of close textual reading. A long poem takes a different pedagogic calculus.

4. *Personal presence in lyric is a humanist ideology, and like all ideologies, a partial view.* Lyrics are short poems that we value highly because they appear (to us) to be "expressive" of the poet's, a person's (or a speaking subject's) feelings. The most authentic feeling (we feel) is that this poet AS a real person is really speaking to you – creating your own best thoughts heightened and improved. The humanist illusion of a speaking-to-you personal presence or expressive voice was consolidated at a particular moment in the history of subjectivity (according to Antony Easthope, who made this point in 1983).[12] For when the OED on "lyric" is read down the ages, it's not until John Ruskin in 1873 that we get this articulated: "lyric poetry is the expression by a poet of his [*sic*, obviously] own feelings," as if secretly overheard by others. However, a poem – even a lyric – is a more complex mechanism or artifact with more social meanings than can be summed up by this touchingly voyeuristic postulate.

Think, further, of the poetic and linguistic conventions involved to convince you of this "illusion of presence." This moment depends on a constructed confluence of the inside speaker (as a "character" or pronoun inside the poem) and the imagined speaker *of* the poem as amalgamated textual practices (tone, form, genre) – that is, the subjectivity of the enounced and the subjectivity of the enunciation coincide (also Easthope via Émile Benveniste). These two constructs are fused in the humanist lyric, and are further stabilized by the poet's biography as consumable terrain (the "announced," in my neologism). Further this "humanist presence" is particularly strong only in some lyrics. Other lyrics are more *im*personal, transpersonal, persona-laden, or insincere/masked, stagy, even mordant on the question of sincerity and presence (like Raymond Queneau's 1961 remixable sonnets in strips of lines, making up *A Hundred Thousand Billion Poems* or *One hundred million million poems* – the original French title is *Cent mille milliards de poèmes*). No matter, the word "presence" and *our* senses of heightened or ennobling connotations of "individual," our investments in personhood and "expression," are still ideologically pre-mixed with the word "lyric," and quite hard to disentangle.

5. *Writer, speaker, characters: Divided or united or variously mixed.* "Expressive" (heart to heart) readings of poetry in general and lyric in particular are incredibly naïve about poetry. They overlook any use (i.e. motivated manipulation) of the medium, any particular or selective stagings of subjectivity and its interior clashes, the performances of authenticity, folksiness, seriousness, realness by the writer as the "announced"; they overlook the potential splits among enunciation (textual practices, via the imagined "speaker" of the poem), enounced (semantic, content-laden statement, made by the characters, if any, inside the poem), and the "announced" or the subjective and social agency of the writer as existing person.[13] Think, to cite *Blue Studios*, of the "personages/characters/pronouns" running around inside a poem as paper dolls played with by the speaker of the enunciation, a warm puppet created by the author or by some part of her, that I call the "announced." Therefore there are fantastic, powerful possibilities for disjunction, contradictions, and combinations among announced, enunciation, enounced/enoncé that have implications for our sense of a disunified, heterogeneous, self-inconsistent "lyric" rather than an authentic expression of a real soul speaking to you.[14]

A reader needs to calibrate splits and unities of the speaker and of imagined character(s) inside the poem. An example of lyric dialogism is William Carlos Williams, writing poems of multiple, interlocutor-laden, and even self-rupturing voices, such as "Portrait of a Lady": "Which shore? / Agh, petals maybe. How / should I know?"[15] Here some voice(s) interrupt each other in a way that sets writer, "speaker," maybe character at odds over the very question of the lyric (and its traditional female object), with self-critical questions interrupting a paean to prettiness. This certainly is a lyric critical of itself as well as foolish/fond of those petals.[16] One might also imagine a lyric (short poem) that "calls voice out" impersonally, creating a focused but unmoored discursive play of congruent incongruity as an intervention, not an expression. *O Cadoiro* by Erín Moure produces poems of a great lyric intensity (often about love) distanced from authenticity by the paratextual materials she has set in her text-folio numbers, the (imagined) ascription of authorship, and the illusion that these are translations from medieval Galician-Portuguese. In her work "the lyric" is revealed as a construct – at the same time that the urgency of feeling is also honored.

Flarf, conceptual poetry, and related Oulipean-inflected practices also resist simple notions of "subjectivity" in lyric. These are composed of heterodox materials whose discursive palette is set up or set in motion by the author but who (in a contraposto'd evacuation of personal agency) employs an impersonal prosthetic entity, a search engine, with access to many more lexicons and discourses than any one individual can command. The combination of the elements may also de-personalize the results even if one might solemnly aver, with Tristan Tzara in a last ditch – or an ironized – staging of humanist subjectivity, that "The poem will resemble you"/"Le poème vous ressemblera."[17] It is also true that even conceptual work may still be subjectively oriented. If you open every fifth book on your bookshelf and pick every fifth sentence and write it down – still, these are the books on *your* bookshelf and they expose and refract, if they do not express, something about you.

If I write a short or "lyric" poem, the me as the "announced" (a historical subject with some wobbling agency) is making an object of words, traditions, rhetorical and always-already literary conventions, textual materials, and thinking (including some thinking about the construction of the artifact). Some of this is authenticated by how well I channel or deploy traditions that do not "express" all of or much of me; indeed, I may only ventriloquize them helplessly, or they may be pre-selected in ways that seriously distort the possibilities I have. Thus to write a lyric is to fight *the* lyric. (Think of the work of Paul Celan – or even Emily Dickinson.)

6. *The criterion of music or the musical.* People sometimes say a lyric is a short-ish poem imaginatively "sung" without music. It's true that before long-modernity, the melos of stanzas to be sung, with their near-similar vowel quantity and strophic organization did indeed define "the lyric." Yet most of the OED's historical definitions of lyric rest on a ruse, a claim of strophes *as if* the work could be sung, whether or not it was intended to be. That *as if* is very cunning indeed, because it makes a historical bridge instead of emphasizing a major discontinuity in literary history, the separation of poem-songs (lyrics) from sheer poems (lyrics). Two now-different situations are covered by the same word.

The fall-back adjective "musical" brings in gigantic, compromising problems – for (aside from strophic organization, which means approximate evenness of the warbled numbers) what is "musicality" in poetry, after all? For lyric and musical/lyrical are not synonymous. Presumably any poem can be musical/lyrical – with some of the following: a quality of *melos* on all scales from pleasant to aggressive, rhythmic understanding, the smart management of effects of sound, often by placement of syntactic emphasis along the line. (Milton is quite musical, but not necessarily a writer of the lyric.) It is very important to me, as a poetic practitioner as well as a poet-critic, to acknowledge that sound effects occur in all types, modes, genres, kinds of poems. No type of poem has a corner on sound.[18] Since all words have a sound, and all ways of putting sounds together create some sonority, rhythm, pattern, phoneme sequence, and a relationship of syntax to line, all poetry is musical. "Musical" is about as useful as the term "personal voice" or "expressive" for defining the lyric – that is, it's not.

Further, "musical" is often reduced to sounding nice, prone to smooth sounds. (Would this be high, open vowels, no consonant clusters, and buckets of alliteration?) There are a lot of reasons why evoking musical "smoothness" or pleasant sounds is unhelpful; it can only be an ideological criterion that blands the lyric down to a custard-y consistency. Some moments of *melos* in poetry – G.M. Hopkins's mouthy lyrics, Basil Bunting's *Briggflatts* – have harsh or aggressive music. Is such music not to be called musical? Is musical an ideological category for the mellifluous only? Do we want "lyricism" reduced to "prettiness"? This would be an example of poetry ideology, and its nice, consoling functions. The terms "musical" or "mellifluous" or even "flow" have to be evacuated within definitions of "the lyric"; even with the limited notion of "smoothness in the mouth speaking our language with an educated accent" [note the social qualifiers], these terms may be true descriptors of individual works, but they are useless as definitions of a category.[19]

It's also true that the category "musical" rarely exists in a semantic vacuum. We depend on meaning and consistency to help read – nay, even to anchor – poetic musicalness or sonority. You all know the famous limit case of this, John Crowe Ransom's jerking of dewy-eyed readings of Tennyson, by his changing "murmuring of innumerable bees" to "murdering of innumerable beeves." This far less soothing semantic content contains almost the same "soothing" phonemes (a *jeu d'esprit* cited, even if with a shiver of disapproval, by Wellek and Warren).[20]

Following those dead beeves wherever they lead, one could also postulate (parallel to the way Flarf and Oulipo exaggerate, explode, and recode subjectivity) transgressive poems that are excessively "musical." Certain poems by Poe or by the two Charleses, Swinburne and Bernstein, offer sound flowing in an almost complete semantic vacuum, with a content so barely paraphrasable and a syntax so unfixable that we are shocked at the force field set up by "de la musique avant toute chose."[21] Swinburnean "lushness" (high proportion of shimmery sound, low proportion of discursive clarity) produces "feminine" excess – no balance, just slither (as Pound might have said).

7. *Pronouns and gender in lyric.* First, we haven't comprehended the pronouns we do have in poetry. Conventionally, the book of lyric pronouns has been all too short. We have been too transfixed by "I/you" pronouns in poetry fully to notice the range of inter-subjectivities created in poetry. This would include not only the relations of scale and power among subjectivities of the enunciation and enounced but also the unspoken subjectivities (others, "ears"?) to whom the speakers address themselves. Further, we (readers) are among the listeners, and have some special roles to play. Our critical senses of identification and the inter-subjective are not wide enough yet to account for the evocative callings poems make. (Of course, as in John Ashbery's *Three Poems*, "you" can be wonderfully indeterminate – anything from the self through the lover to the reader to the vaguely divine, even to the dead. Ashbery makes this clear, but it is not unfamiliar as a situation of poetry in general.)

And thus we arrive at gender and the lyric. Conventionally, the speaking subject ("I") is often male; the addressee of "the lyric" is often an imagined female ("you" = "she"). The residual <me Tarzan, you Jane> configuration may make one squirm, but it reverberates all too strongly in our sense of lyric poetry. For "I-you" relations and the intimacies implied between speaking subjects and viewed objects have had some play in lyric, after all. And there is an irony here – more than one – that by talking of stereotyped gender words, I am reverting to a personalized or humanist critical zone.

In fact, critiques of the lyric in our time have used conventional gender notions of the lyric to establish a new kind of lyric. This is articulated with some noble tendentiousness by John Wieners in "A Poem for Painters":

> My poems contain no
> wilde beestes, no
> lady of the lake, music
> of the spheres, or organ chants,
>
> Only the score of a man's
> struggle to stay with
> what is his own, what
> lies within him to do[22]

Score is (at least) both a musical composition written down, the tally of naming, a scoring or slashing mark, an advantage or sexual conquest, and the number of points in a game. This is the statement of an Olsonic or projective lyric, made valid by individualist action, dependent on a person (man *is* Wieners' word) to find unique, self-validated terms for activity and honesty. The self is treated as an exemplary force, not as a spokesperson for conventional emotions or modes (at least two former writers are adduced critically – Walter Scott and perhaps Dryden). These lines are notably dependent on a gender-evocative binary – man versus lady; struggle versus stasis; subject versus object; contemporary "score" versus antique/antiquated music. This lyric is a symptom of the gender terms in poetry at the same time that it makes a critique of mere lyric formalism in the name of manhood.[23]

The self in this lyric does not speak as an authentic transcendent subjectivity, but rather is depicted in the midst of a continuous action that constitutes itself continually. So the self is becoming – in motion, volatile, split, suspicious, and resistant. The self that speaks seems perpetually in formation, not finally made, but always struggling (yet still with the social authorization that "man" offers, which is not a small fact). "A Poem for Painters" provides a useful sense of a genre in some self-debate.

If John Wieners constructs a subjectivity to defeminize lyric (or to put it in motion), George Oppen constructs a subjectivity to pluralize lyric: the "I" becomes "we." In "Of Being Numerous" (1968), George Oppen, along with Creeley, Olson, and Wieners, delineates a shift mid-twentieth-century in the relationship of lyric (the singular) and quantity, amount, masses (numerousness) – a shift with political and formal implications. "Singular" is helpful; it avoids "man" as such, at least until sections 9 and 10 of that poem. This poem marks a crisis both ontological and epistemological for Oppen – it appears that only the singular vision of the outstanding man (or person), or the repeated plural pronoun "we" can adequately see or produce the necessary "intensity of seeing," and yet that sightedness distances him from "them, the People" (numerousness) and from certain political commitments of populist loyalty involving directed slogans rallying a reader. Historical embeddedness is, instead, very complexly represented. Singularity is a mode of double resistance – to the bounded self, and to excessive, crippling, social bonding with others. Selfhood or subjectivity in community thus becomes a very fraught and narrow place. I link this to the shifts of post-World War II discoveries – "the simple ego in a lyric" becomes "A strange one in war. / To a body anything may happen."[24]

Although he talks of "the lyric valuables," Oppen uses lyric materials along with philosophic materials, historical materials from the news of the day or the endless war to construct an amalgam that stretches "lyric" (*NCP*, 50). In Oppen, the personal and erotic intermingles with the ontological and social:

> Now in the helicopters the casual will
> Is atrocious
>
> Insanity in high places,

If it is true we must do these things
We must cut our throats (*NCP*, 173)

Oppen allows us to appreciate the crisis of (the inadequacy of) a pure "the lyric." Inadequate, that is, to the modern practitioners who attempt historically to mix awe and subjective wonder with historical dilemma, rather than treating lyric as moments of separable ecstasy and pleasure, or consolidation and focus. The modern or contemporary long poem (like "Of Being Numerous") has had to "do something" – has indeed "done" something – with lyric, with the lyric poem. It has taken lyric materials as irreducible, implacable, impenetrable IS-ness – as a mix of ontology, epistemology and ethics – and lost most of the rest of what we used to define as "the lyric."[25]

Yet we are not finished with gender materials yet. As Barbara Johnson reminds us about Baudelaire, there is in poetry a "male privilege" – "the right to play femininity."[26] So under many regimes, male poets can indeed appropriate stances and attitudes that are culturally coded as the feminine (or the semiotic for Julia Kristeva, or the general economy of waste and unfocused excess for Steve McCaffery out of Georges Bataille). If a male poet moves into this realm, praise may result from his crossing into the semiotic in a reasonably male body.

We are just beginning to examine the potential for female privilege in poetry – it is exciting to be part of this period of exploration – whether it goes to querying the assumptions of genders we are familiar with or goes to a queer position of "post-gender." Females have just (have they just?) emerged from a period of being culturally confusing whether found dissolved into the semiotic (cf. some H.D. and Stein – Caution: delays in reception may result) or boldly logopoetically stalking the intellectualized semantic (as Loy and Moore do – Caution: delays in reception may result). It remains true that when a male poet was too tempted by this lush realm, certain compensatory moves have been a logical result – at least in modernism. One might, for instance, as both Eliot and Pound did, guard the borders against women poets, or dump on "Swishful Swinburniania."[27] But we are, of course, finished with all that, now.

8. *Ideology, world view, and "the lyric."* Epiphany is a goal, we used to be taught, of lyric poems.[28] Strong closure, heightening, a sudden realization of the essence, a revelation at the end of a short poem – but these terms,

though apparently formalist, are not culturally neutral. May we call this Christian textuality? Such a mode may belong to all of us, but such a critical terminology reveals the inflection from "fulfillment" theologically postulated by Christianity. Epiphany is, after all, a moment on the Christian calendar that honors the baby Messiah, the manifest of God in human form. This word seems to have been fore-grounded under the pedagogic regime of New Criticism as the goal of the lyric – clarity/illumination and sense of heightened presence, a paradoxical unity of disparate elements, as also exemplified by the paradoxes of the Trinity. This terminology for the lyric was part of the loose Christianizing in post-War literary critical culture (with T.S. Eliot playing a leadership role).

What is an alternative to the aura of Christian theological textuality in the lyric or in any poem? It would be a deferral of fulfillment, stiff-necked resistance to any culturally hegemonic revelation. It would be like that "curious" open-ended conclusion such as Oppen provides to "Of Being Numerous," or some cacophonous excessive ending, as of Zukofsky's "*A*." It is, in short, a textuality drawing upon rabbinical hermeneutics or endless interpretation, not Christian stories of fulfillment that offer a limit term for all discussion. (I am informed by, and applying, Susan Handelman's work.) Neither of these interpretive frames is necessarily attached to particular religious adhesions nor to the religious culture of the poets. I am indicating a rhetorical and hermeneutic attitude that one may identify with by authorial choice; it is not an identity or an essence that's being expressed.

What tactics would we critically foreground then? Perhaps continuous glossing – the midrashic work of reading as writing. Works that play aggressively with the letter, that use paragrammic materials, the pleasures of anagrammatic mysteries that find names within other names, words hidden in words; numerological proceduralism and unfinished texts: bpNichol, Jackson Mac Low, Christian Bök might be some of the poets to mention in this context.

What about modernist *condensare* – the clarity of "spare, specific, no excessive word" (I imagine you can now predict the gender narratives here, so I won't say anything more). This too is not a neutral, all-purpose, always deployable criterion for the lyric with no historical strings attached. Indeed, as is now clear, no rhetorical choice is unmarked by its own history of use. As Charles Bernstein argues: "There is no wholly intrinsic meaning to any form, nor are there a priori superior forms. Devices and techniques – the tools and styles of the past – shift in their meaning and value over time, requiring continuing reassessment. Yet forms do have extrinsic, social meanings that are forged through a contestation of values from which it is impossible to withhold judgment."[29] Pound's *condensare* is marked by motifs of cleansing as well as condensing; his rhetoric on this topic would come to have a serious political undercarriage. *Condensare* is, in some ways, a knife of light. It made the coy subject position "the weeder [of] the Garden of the Muses" as important to the beginning of *ABC of Reading* as the very Poundean stinking fish of Agassiz's student.[30] This desire for excision, cutting away, cauterizing the rot of culture and society as *he* defined it led Pound eventually to unrepentant, insistent justifications for ethnic cleansing.[31] Pound also had an interest in condensing the amount of material that should be carried forward, culturally speaking. This too is less benign than it looked at first glance – because he thereupon became the cultural commissar, dictating what was important, what was to be retained, and what was not. By destroying social rot and condensing culture, he was the controller, acting against alternative, multiple paths for cultural access and cultural importance.

So social location (here, gender, religious culture, political assumptions) and related historical attitudes play in ways we have defined the lyric after all. Hence, the lyric and any criteria used to try to define it are going to present historical and ideological marks in its practices.

9. *Poem/lyric – are they synonyms*? Finally, even the best-regulated critics can, do, and will eventually use the words *lyric* and *poem* interchangeably. This will conceal – even from themselves – their own polemical and tendentious move between the terms. For these words are not synonymous.

While any formal modes of poems might superficially look the same over time, they are invested with different contexts and meanings and implications. No term is neutral or trans-historical. It is always filled with the content, affect, and social uses specific to the moment of its use. So after all that debunking, is it possible to define "a lyric," after all? (Not "the lyric" – this is an obvious distinction.) I will affirm *intensity* (a learned reading effect) but try as well to account for the structure of meaning Theodor Adorno proposes, with his gnomic assurance that "the lyric work is always the subjective expression of a social antagonism," an antagonism hidden by hegemonic practices that read from a work the eternal, the trans-historical.[32]

A lyric is a shortish poem designed intensely to deliver a sense of socio-cultural contradictions as these poise, fold, or abut. The contradictions that might be identified are as potentially endless as the social itself, but each exists in form, voices, and diction, each can be identified in a historically mediated manner, and each is susceptible of socio-poetical analysis. Some contradictions are individual subjectivity and community; inter-subjectivity and loneliness; skepticism and belief; social homage and social suspicion; grief and consolation; appropriation and resistance; now time and eternal time; immediacy and distance; ecstasy and fear; fixity and change; presence and ghostliness; plenitude and void; longing and satiation; *odi et amo*; power and powerlessness; singularity and numerousness; the representable and the unrepresentable; the vocation of writing and its impossibility. However, any intense contradiction that might emerge at any historical juncture could be imagined in a short poem. A lyric poem may offer both sides in the unresolved dialectical phase of the negative, or second term, or it may "resolve" them. In some short poems, the second term of the dialectic lies in an unspoken zone just outside the poem; sometimes only half of the contradiction is given, but both sides are apprehended. What we call "lyric" is a poem in which these allusive and contradictory yearnings are focused in a short-ish space. Hence relative length (relative formal compactness) and time of unrolling are important for impact/intensity of the contradictions abutting.

While mine is not an explicitly functionalist definition, a recent discussion by Charles Altieri offers a related definition of the lyric that does emphasize its use. Lyric is a mode that accomplishes certain aesthetic-and-psychological tasks, takes on certain functions, notably encouraging emotional growth in its readers.[33] Altieri analyzes the affective elements of lyric. He has proposed that the lyric "composes our energies" via three values: intensity (of patterning, evoking the here and now in ways that also raise our sense of absolute ontological conditions); involvedness (or inter-subjectivity, both between others and the self, the natural world and the self, and the poem and the self [NLH, 268–70]); and plasticity (which is also involved with expanded horizons, and the infusion, into the secular world, of the speculative horizon that religion once satisfied, or at least claimed to [NLH, 278]). The poem tunes or "contours" us in our reading (NLH, 270). This emphasis on the training of the emotions via reading practices is a well-articulated didactic claim. It is also a discussion that again shows how absolutely difficult it is to define this kind of work in any absolute (a-historical) ways.

With all this, one begins to see the pertinence of a definition that looks ridiculously over-simplified, such as a "short, generally non-narrative poem" a.k.a. "a lyric." Or it's a lyric if people said it was at that time. Or it's a shortish poem necessitating intensity of attention in a short-ish reading time, and leading to some kind of satisfying impact. Back, that is, to Poe. At any rate, there is no such thing as "the lyric" across time; there are iterations of lyric claims.

Part Two: A Lyric Object and a Long Poem

Here I want to entertain what is implied in Zukofsky's droll, provocative, paradoxical remark, "A long *poem* is merely more of a good thing, shall I put it that way?" – a remark that goes a long way to erasing any distinction between a short poem (lyric) and a long poem, by saying that a long poem is also intricately composed. By this remark he suggests that a long poem "merely" extends the "lyric" and, to stretch this a bit, that a mark or trace element of lyric enters the long poem (the trace of high intensity, the trace of the short, the trace of condensed and locally identifiable contradictions). Most of the surface terms of the definition of lyric that I have just debunked (like flowing or smooth musicality, epiphany, the expressive, single focus on I, and perhaps on I-you relations) are over-passed by what happens in the long poem, although both sublimity and intensity are certainly part of its potential.

Certainly, these two modes of practice (genres?) have somewhat different goals. The modern/contemporary experimental long poem often exists to put an unassimilable mound of writing between yourself and culture as usual; a large realignment of what you know and what you see takes shape in it. (That is, it is negative, while the epic is generally affirmative.) The lyric may be positioned as the inheritor of a civilization that the writer of a long poem prefers to anatomize, scrutinize, and criticize. (Here's where you forget about Paul Celan and Emily Dickinson – neither is "inheritor." But, arguably, their lyrics are imploded odes – long poems condensed to black hole intensity.) The long poem, especially the very long poem, is often excessive, unclear, unmanaged, intertwined with a life and a life-time. The long poem might change course and purpose as it is being written – some emphatically do (*The Maximus Poems* might be an example), some (perhaps the ones more quickly finished) don't. The lyric may have changes in it, but the changes are often staged as *voltas*, not great heavings of scale and rupture. The lyric, by design, is contained, and some would say "out" of time. Under what terms can these two modes possibly intersect? The generalization *is* droll – is there NO difference between a short and a long poem except length? which is a measure of time – of writing time and reading time … and therefore a measure of some kind of synoptic cultural investment …

Let me offer a couple of positions along this "more of a good thing" spectrum, proposing that that at least some long poems that we know have some relations to lyric shortness and lyric intensity and contradictions worth anatomizing.

1. *The extension of lyric materials or tropes into a long work via seriality.* In Oppen's "The Impossible Poem" (in "Some San Francisco Poems") there are allusions to lyric materials: an opening with the loved woman and her "naked eyes," a "shining" at the site of the city and on the bay, but this eros or an "Archangel" is only one beautiful part of a time also implacably called "clumsy" with an explicit questioning of a poet's task (*NCP*, 222, 223, and 231, 228, 232).[34] Oppen seems hyper-saturated with the kinds of contradictions just listed: at least individual subjectivity and community; inter-subjectivity and loneliness; skepticism and belief; social homage and social suspicion.

In the lucid towns paralyzed
Under the truck tires
Shall we relinquish

Sanity to redeem
Fragments and fragmentary
Histories in the towns and the temperate streets
Too shallow still to drown in or to mourn
The courageous and precarious children (*NCP*, 232).

This is poetry *in extremis* and doubting its own vocation. The work turns lyric poem against and into long, while writing both.

A description of seriality: the intimacy and particularity of tacking from notion to notion without necessary self-consistency of argument nor any telos, but only vectors, eventually to gain scope and a sense of overview.[35] Oppen's oeuvre is centered by serial poems oriented toward unresolvable ambiguities in which were presented "the social and historical dimensions of our innermost selves."[36] Seriality as a mode of practice is one way of extending a lyric into a long poem but without grandeur, without any necessary continuous narrative nor any *systematizing* philosophical position, and even without conclusion/ resolution. Formally the sections and the clashes of position between sections dramatize the dilemmas to which they testify. For instance, Oppen's poems use the serial form to articulate a radical political and ontological skepticism. He uses the modular mode of a serial poem as a way of breaking attention to one finished, composed, poised lyric icon. And he uses linebreak as a vector within seriality to create shadowing double and triple ways of reading, a strategic, epistemologically unsettling use of parataxis and anacoluthon. So contradictions in Oppen – at least between that which is numerous and that which is singular – and the clash of different outcomes from these positions are expressed exactly by extending the shorter poem into a longer poem with the shorter units as modules. It is a particular version of part/whole relations that renounces the (lyric) telos of a totalized or unitary "whole."

The transformation of "empirically true" yet plausibly contradictory lyric modules into long poems by the tactic of serial (often paratactic) linking is one key mode interleaving or intersecting lyric and long poem. Achieving lyric intensity and contradictions with long-poem scope is something worked on, not only by Oppen in the serial poem, but variously by T.S. Eliot in *The Waste Land*, H.D. in *Trilogy* and *Helen in Egypt*, Charles Olson in *Maximus* 3, Robin Blaser in *Image-Nations*, Lyn Hejinian in *The Cell*, Harryette Mullen in *Muse and Drudge*, Nathaniel Mackey in the twining of *Song of Andoumboulou* and *Mu* (two serial works, joined in *Splay Anthem*), even Alice Notley in (a narrative work) *Descent of Alette* – to think of just a few obvious (mainly US) examples. Perhaps the experimental long poem of our era smashes the epic into lyric shards as a social critique precisely of the totalizing ethos of the epic, which is installed in our time in corporations, the military, and nationalist claims to control minority populations, including sexual minorities, and women. It is interesting that none of the distinctive modern and contemporary long poems can work for very long with the "epic" as background thought (although some critics were interested in that term for a while).[37] Indeed, one word that almost never crosses the lips of the contemporary long poem writer is "epic." Unless to deny it. Nathaniel Mackey in *Splay Anthem* makes such a declaration overtly: "It wasn't / an epic we were in."[38] An exception here are works (by Eliot, H.D., Notley, Ashbery, among others) that consciously stage themselves as epic *spiritual* journeys – in the zone of Dante, and barely in the zone of Homer/Virgil except for the *nekuia* section of epic.

So one might argue that certain modes of long poem offer ways of bending/extending lyric (intensity and poised contradictions) into length via continuous activity (the objective becomes the projective, and vice versa). If constructed as serial poems, long poems retain as modular units shorter materials at the general length of a lyric, with all that this implies in concision and focus, but not necessarily in subjectivity and "musicality," which veer variously. Serial works construct an interesting third path between lyric and long modes. Further, by extending short sections into length by vectors of position-staking and position-altering argument, a long poem definitely annuls short poem temporality. So by absorbing lyric, a long poem is also making a critique of the short and all that it implies in poetry ideology and in the use of closure in poems.

2. *Critique of Genre – a depth charge.* Yet now we have to ask why we are talking about genre as if this term has defined boundaries? We are acting as if Jacques Derrida had not written the essay (1979/1980; rev. 1986) called "The Law of Genre." If ever there were a genre of the "modern and contemporary long poem" or of "the lyric" as a "law," that law of genre has been mooted – as is true of any genre, according to the slide-y sort of "law" illegally handed down in Derrida's essay. Any genre can only be self-different, contaminated, and parasitic.[39] These glissades between individual text and intertextuality and among genres are fundamental to the literary act. Because of its scale, it's arguable that there are as many generic traces in a long poem as there are genres one might name. But if this is true of *any* genre, this finding, though quite suggestive for the contemporary long poem, cannot distinguish our genre particularly, except perhaps by more intense hybridity, because of length. "More of a good thing." If all genres

are, in Bakhtin's terms for novels, "heteroglossic" and "heterogeneric," in Derrida's terms "heterogeneous" and "hybrid," we still don't have a definition of anything. Except to say these texts are long, they long for themselves (as Peter Middleton once quipped) and have generally taken a lot of time to do, even a lifetime.[40]

Derrida is making a critique or a dialectical absorption of Bakhtin, applying to all genres what Bakhtin sees as proper to the novel exclusively. Bakhtin is of the highest interest here, as he attempts against modernity itself, to segregate "poetic style" and "poetic genres" from "any mutual interaction with alien discourse"; any "hetero – and polyglossia."[41] That is, according to Bakhtin, the *poetic* work is cleared of/purged of the social in world views, sense of jargons, linguistic specificity, and typical voices (DI, 297). His most rigid statement is "the poet is a poet insofar as he accepts the idea of a unitary and singular language and a unitary, monologically sealed-off utterance. These ideas are immanent in the poetic genres with which he works" (DI, 296–7). Bakhtin speaks about a "Lethe" effect in heightened italics; to write a poem, one must *forget* historical and social saturations, in a studied duplicity about one's otherwise socially formed subjectivity: "Everything that enters the [poetic] work must immerse itself in Lethe, and forget its previous life in any other contexts: language may remember only its life in poetic contexts (in such contexts, however, even concrete reminiscences are possible)" (DI, 297). In contrast, one might argue that this untenable position limits poetry to "the lyric" – precisely with a "THE" and that it makes poetry a marginalized, inflexible, and unresponsive medium (this in tendentious contrast, of course, to our Bakhtinian hero, the Novel). That bizarre codicil about social meanings displaced at a temporal distance recurs in the politically correct reminder, "of course, even the poetic word is social, but poetic forms reflect lengthier social processes, i.e., those tendencies in social life requiring centuries to unfold" (DI, 300). It is a frustrating discussion, as the modern poem, particularly the modern long poem has often been written in a generative relationship with the social and heteroglossic. Nevertheless, there is a grain of truth in Bakhtin's exaggerations.

The more striking postulate in Derrida's mobile and debunking essay on fixed genre is that any genre can only be constituted in our critical imagination comparatively – only by existing alongside the shadow of its opposite, only by presenting phantom alternatives, only by articulating the markable presence of a "counter-law," or alternatives never totally swallowed by any crude majoritarian claim of generic boundaries (AL, 225).

I will borrow this idea as my second position along a spectrum of intersections between lyric and experimental long poem. By this calculus, long poem is – must necessarily be – marked by its opposite (short poem); and short poem by maybe another opposite – drama, or poetic dialogue, or the narrative poem. This claim of multiple generic intersections may simply re-multiply the notion of generic plurality and is another way of stating Derrida's original point. Yet we can postulate/select a *key* "counter-law" playing a definitional role in understanding any genre (AL, 225, 226). Based on Derrida's suggestion, we might mark the presence of the short poem as the main counter-law among a plurality of hybrid and multiple generic allusions characterizing the long poem. We could say that a lyric poem haunts the long poem even as the long poem surrounds it, trumps it, smashes it, and envelops it (these moves are different of course). Even when it is made to disappear, or to become untenable, the ghost of lyric may haunt the long poem.[42] Thus spake theory, or at least my "fools rush in" paraphrase. Is there any evidence of this haunting presence of short poem as a counter-law to long?[43]

3. *The Mark of "a" Lyric in the long poem.* Yes. Williams's *Paterson* is a long poem that sometimes deliberately envelops the lyric, presenting it in a framed way, as if lyric were an ekphrastic figure depicted within a long poem.[44] *Paterson* is, of course, a strikingly anti-monologic poem, to cite Bakhtin against himself. It is fully juiced up with multiple discourses in voices placed helter-skelter on the page; some of the work is meditative descriptive, some is like a masque, some has a general narrative base with a rolling repetition (like the walk through the park, or the fire burning through the city that create intersections of material, allowing the reader to discover nodules of thematic findings). We can barely list the dialogized and documentary genres of this poem: actual letters of a rare intensity and urgency, a speech by a preacher, antiquarian documents of local history, snippets of recorded conversation, a geological strata chart, a political tract ... But amid this plethora of discourses, a visible, repeated element in *Paterson* is the enfolding of lyric. At several junctures in the poem, the incorporation of one genre into its "opposite" dismantles the (Potemkin village) wall between monologic and dialogic. Indeed, the allusive use of lyric materials in heteroglossic counterpoint with other dis-

courses, and the modular inclusion of many fragments of lyric materials left deliberately incomplete, streaming into other non- or less-lyric sounds is characteristic of *Paterson*. As a long poem, *Paterson* is in full dialogue with this counter-law called lyric.

One strategy in *Paterson* is the literal embedding of an extant short poem in a long one as a citation. *Paterson* cites the Sappho poem (#31) about sexual arousal and desire (Book V, ii; 215; it also appears as "Sappho" in WCW, 348 suggesting precisely that it may stand as an autonomous short poem).[45] In *Paterson*, it is a moment that recognizes the importance of female figures, desire, sexuality as a root of the energy and urgency of this long poem. The citation of Sappho #31 is ekphrastic in that it "depicts," or gives a textual frame to, an exemplary short poem. The author sets a well-known lyric inside a long poem; the reader notes how that lyric "represents" themes of interest. Similarly, in *Sweeney Agonistes*, T.S. Eliot cites the Bob Cole and the Johnson brothers' minstrel pop song "Under the Bamboo Tree" as a complicated tribute to African-American makers whose cultural impact he both envies and deplores.[46] And if "Patriarchal Poetry" by Gertrude Stein is a long poem – what else does one want to call it? – one sees in it the embedded "A SONNET / To the wife of my bosom" that praises womanly virtues with satiric élan.[47]

A related event of embedding does not use citation but a cunning variation; it is a version of this ekphrastic framing of an intact lyric in a long poem. Ashbery's *Flow Chart* incorporates a rewriting of a Swinburne double sestina (base of 12, not 6); the same end-words are used as in "Complaint of Lisa" but a new poem is built.[48] This thick allusion to an intricate lyric form is nonetheless almost indistinguishable from the rest of the long poem in tone and manner. Part-whole relations here reveal the small unit as miniature version of the large, like a doll's house built to look like your house, or the architectural mockup of a building housed in that building. The double sestina focuses on death in a parallel line with love – and how they intertwine – lyric themes if ever there were. The provocation to the writing this long poem (Ashbery's mother's death, his own dangerous illness in 1987, and then death in general) and the ways this theme is concentrated in the double sestina suggest that this embedded lyric is a holographic summary of the whole work. Both sestina and the long poem in which it is set contribute to the elegiac trace and affirmatively pleasant nobility of *Flow Chart*.[49] The two modes are not at odds.[50]

In *Paterson* there are lots of lyric moments. In *Flow Chart* there is one marked, yet camouflaged lyric. An even more extreme case of the presence of a lyric counter-law is Louis Zukofsky's "A"-16, which stands as a separate section in a work whose other sections massively exceed it in length.[51] This studied gesture by Louis Zukofsky (is there any other kind from this most Duchampian of poets?) consists of a three line, four-word poem, taking one-half page yet with a lot of white space, a shock in contrast to "A"-15 (16 pages in length) and to "A"-17, "A Coronal … for Floss," (11 pages).[52] "A"-17 eulogizes Williams, indexically and chronologically, cataloguing and citing the many times, in Zukofsky's career, at which Williams has been palpable: as an intervening figure, as a goad, as sometimes secretly motivating certain words or poems. Zukofsky draws on citations from letters exchanged between the poets. And "A"-15, while incorporating many things, including a homophonic translation of part of the Book of Job, ends with the shock of the assassination of US President Kennedy in November 1963. In any event, Zukofsky places his hyper-short, hyper-oblique poem between these two. The lyric gesture has been made; it is outrageously disproportionate to the rest of the poem.

The actual four-word text of "A"-16 should be consulted in any convenient edition of "*A*."[53] This tiny work is excessive precisely by being so tiny. Something tendentiously unequal to other sections – very short among very long – has been created. One can make this section a literal illustration of what Derrida would say much more allegorically: the long poem contains, or is marked by, its opposite, or by one of its key opposites, in this case, an obscure notational a-syntactic lyric. (It is notational because it lacks any punctuation.) As well, the placement of this singular section between two markedly elegiac sections of much greater length further suggests that words are always unequal to the tasks of elegy.

The very conventional natural images in this small section suggest something conventionally poetic, a small thing being overwhelmed by a larger natural force. However, the page space separating the words creates an unconventional textual blankness, particularly as there is no apparent verb linking the phrases. Yet conversely, the latter two words, read initially as adjective and noun (or compound noun) could also be two verbs. The suggestiveness of "A"-16's four words are unequal to their simplicity and bareness.

The gesture seems engineered precisely to place lyric materials inside the long poem, to allow that haunting, that disturbance. Zukofsky engineers an eruption from a lyric temporality, an abstract generalization from a lyric marker – plausibly, but not necessarily, a flower blown by the wind – between two sections that concern contemporary and personal history. This could be read (somewhat sentimentally) as beauty destroyed, or flower hardly able to stand up against a large force, yet anemones (a suggestion from the next section) are well able to survive and have adapted to their conditions, since they, as many flowers do, use the wind to distribute their seeds. So forget the lyric sentiment. The force of this section is, finally, the declared disproportion, yet relation, of lyric to long poem.[54] A long poem has been marked by its opposite (a lyric).

By his word "inequality," Zukofsky has chosen precisely the semantic term that disturbs lyric "smoothness" with "unevenness and irregularity." "A"-16 is therefore a lyric that undoes itself and asserts itself at the same time, proving, in four words, the counter-law of genre in the long poem. (What's more, in "A"-21, Rudens, Zukofsky produces a section based on yet "another" opposite: a drama seventy pages long. Zukofsky's tiny disjunctive poem and his play within a long poem are both frightening and insouciant.)

What does Zukofsky's lyric gesture mean finally? That "A long *poem* is merely more of a good thing, shall I put it that way?" (LD, 218). His emphasis falls on the word "poem," meaning the wrought thing. Zukofsky claims a long poem is simply a bigger version of a short poem. This is a very drastic adjustment of our understanding, not to say a major shift of our sense of scale. Zukofsky treats the difference between long and short as epiphenomenal – all [good] poems have a more important characteristic; all are through-composed. A long poem, this comes close to saying, if it is a poem (that is, a good poem – this criterion is implied silently) is nothing but an expansion of the same kinds of things one does in a short poem. *If* your utopian goal is through-composed long poems, short works become a model for the practice. That is, a long poem can have the intensity and contradictions of a lyric without the shortness. This formulation has a lot of implications. Proposing that a long poem must be pretty much the same as a short one – but, well, longer – actually seems to be a very subtle dig at the hyper-text "epic," at Pound's or Olson's later long poem model. (Olson's work post-dates much of "*A*" – certainly post-dates its inception in 1928, but could have been one referent of Zukofsky's remark in 1968.) So, with a diction of considerable opacity, Zukofsky will write a long poem as a lyric, by which I mean not a short poem, but a long poem built rhetorically as if it were short: an intense, sonically thick, metaphysically dense, layered, closural, and sometimes even private work: "wrenched" and "distinctive."

There is also a cost to this extreme claim. "*A*" is hard/difficult because, as a through-composed long poem, it is made like a metaphysical lyric – twisting those "red-hot pokers" (modified, bitterly, from Coleridge's quatrain "On Donne's Poetry" which says "Wreathe iron pokers into true-love knots"; see lines 256–7 of "Poem Beginning 'The'").[55] There is hardly a bit of slack in "*A*"; it is a poem that does not relax. The intensity of the lyric, the jeweler's sense of every word as faceted, precious, and multiply determined has given Zukofsky's long poem a diamond-like hardness.

The importance of verbal intensity to Zukofsky is borne out again in a response from the L.S. Dembo interview in 1968.[56] Zukofsky engineers a hermetic-antic escape from Dembo's serious question. "Do you conceive of ["*A*"] as having an overall structure?" (LD, 218). Quite like Bartleby, Zukofsky prefers not to; he turns the question from large to small, and in consequence from structure to word. Dembo is going for the sheer overall scale of the thing, its obviously daunting scope and largeness. Zukofsky answers by insisting (with a nice perversity) on myopia, on the interest to the reader of "the detail" (LD, 218). The fact that Zukofsky turns to the smallest local decision, to verbal intricacy, and to the reader's potential fascination with the part, rather than to the question of scope, structure, prior design, and the whole is a way of insisting that he has written the long poem with the condensation, verbal focus, and pointed choices of a short work. The intensity of the short is built within the extent of the long.

Some people do write their long poems that way. Oppen and Zukofsky both did. Some don't. One could make further distinctions among various modes of the long poem in a functional taxonomy – the encyclopedic hyper-text "epic" of Olson or Williams differentiated from narrative/musical/mythic works (such as H.D.'s *Trilogy* or Alice Notley's *Descent of Alette* or Nathanial Mackey's *Song of the Andoumboulou*), and again from works of seriality (like "Of Being Numerous" or Langston Hughes's "Montage of a Dream Deferred"). Other modes such as odic logbooks of continuance (Robin Blaser's *Image-Nations*), new realist procedurals (Ron Silliman), long poem as essay or conceptual text (Susan Howe) would vary in their degree of "through composition."[57] One sees this contrast in a very careful remark of Alice Notley (in her capacity as author of *Descent of Alette*, a work seriously through-composed, and perhaps in her capacity as the author of *Disobedience*, which has a much looser structure). Notley is commenting on *Iovis* by Anne Waldman. I cite at length: "Parts of the [Waldman] poem may feel thin; I think that is built into the genre, parts of *Maximus*, *Paterson*, and *The Cantos* feel a little thin to me – as well as garrulous, cornpone, flowery, forced, self-indulgent, pretentious, and impenetrable. The form makes flaws possible; possibly poetry should make room for flaws, being a human form. There are other kinds of flaws in other kinds of poetry: stuffiness, coldness, the omission of nearly everything we think about."[58] Notley is indicating that one should not expect "through-composed" long poem work from Waldman, nor from Pound, Williams, and Olson. She uses a humanist/projectivist criterion (as Pound did when, in one of the original Three Cantos, he used the metaphor of a "rag-bag" as a genre indicator) – humans are just like this, sloppy and interesting.

If I may conduct the autobiography (or authobiography) of a practice in public for a moment, the writing of a long poem may proceed by an author's taking up some attitude (in the Philly sense) to lyric, to the short poem. This first occurred for me in relation to gender.[59] My act of beginning *Drafts* (my long poem project) was, I have often enough said, a resistance to the lyric (see my examination of that definition, above) and to the female figure in the lyric. It was, in a sense, a way of starting poetry all over again, differently. Cutting away from normative poetic culture. No longer writing commentary on the existing tradition, but somehow walking away.[60] The word "otherhow" occurred in this context; that word emerged (first in 1985) in *The Pink Guitar* (1990/2006); there are further comments in *Blue Studios* (2006).

The force of that conviction was propulsive; yet it is impossible not to say, coolly, that it might be considered wrongheaded and disobliging. I hardly "got rid" of lyric*ism* in my poem – senses of intensity, contradictions, pan-erotic force – nor did I annul general ideology about gender. I could, however, call attention to general cultural agreements, and I could place lyricism in another context. I did not reduce the force of that ecstatic *akra*, but I applied it to other things, rather than linking it only to one particular love/sexual relationship. (That is the fond joke of the one-off

"Draft 40: One Lyric" in which I do link the poem to specific love and sex – once.) In *Drafts*, I chose to make the erotic more general, more diffuse, more about wonder and Being (ontological erotics one might say, fancily). I put a lyrical tonality and sound in relation to other sounds – rage, political anguish, senses of devastation. And this in the interests of the through-composed as a goal that I value.

Fourth, to continue to discuss the lyric mark in the long poem, one might offer Ron Silliman's analysis of the relation of long poem to lyric. At first this influential explanation appears to hold the two modes apart. In "'As to Violin Music': Time in the Longpoem," Silliman is committed to contrasting the two types of poems. If the short poem is concentrated, the long moves by extent. If the short poem is like all lyrics, constructed in the apparent denial of time, to foreground the urgent sense of absolute presence, the long poem wallows in time, owning up to and owning its own temporalities. Some of its tactics for emphasizing the largeness of time and not its single moment are Williams's thematic and rhetorical "rolling up" by repetition of themes and thematic phrases in new contexts, and the multiple temporalities evoked in citation and gloss. If one might plausibly see some short poems as brilliant, swift, apparently intuitive and expressive *aperçus*, a long poem, unlike those, is "never innocent" – Silliman's words – and is, indeed, "designed against [this temporal] innocence."[61] Against innocence, that is, by being saturated in its own temporality, including failure, "entropy," and struggles of all sorts with one's sense of historical and social time: war, revolution, family history, social location, political confusions, a state funeral – these examples, incidentally, from *"A."*

Ron Silliman argues that the lyric typically wants time to be contained, arrested, held, stopped, summed up, to become "timeless" – which is a-historical. The long poem is precisely opposite. It is inflected not so much by the summing up of a historical era with its lessons for the future, but by an insistent confrontation with time itself, historical, personal, messy, with events and one's responses becoming form. Rejecting the a-historical (even a-political) motivates Silliman's comment – or vow – in his first long poem, *Ketjak* (1974), "A calculated refusal to perform the normal chores of verse," which I take, *inter alia*, to mean the production of timelessness or epiphany, although, to invoke Joyce, there is plenty of *claritas* in Silliman's writing.[62] Instead, time is tracked as activity: both its own ongoingness and the continuing notation of the long poem as an activity in time absorb and represent the force of its time and place. Silliman accomplishes this by a particular sentence-based tactic of writing.

Silliman's work is engaged in scanning the time/space coordinate of *now*, packing as much contingent informative and descriptive observation into one sentence and then another, then sometimes also in gnomic, punning, language observations. In this case, a long poem is not made over on the model of lyric (as in Ashbery and in a different fashion in Zukofsky), but a lyric (as short, freeze-time moment of syntactic intensity and presenting contradictions) is made over into a sentence, whose untranscendent accumulation becomes long poem (often, in Silliman, by a numerological, exponential calculus). Every sentence, although it "stops time," also does time within the ongoing long poem.

So wrestling with a long poem made of discrete additive moments is still wrestling with time and stopping time. And Silliman has done so by inventing a method in which writing equals recording minute by minute, which is an act of "holding things timeless" for the textual length of a sentence. The "now" of recording arrests and negates time's ongoingness and losses. This is why there are often reminders of the concrete material and materiality of the practice in Silliman, pen, hand, notebook, place of writing. The process of joining the sentences affirms and allows time's ongoingness. Yet, by this method, Silliman makes time in this work be only now-time; the long poem *The Alphabet* as well as the works in *The Age of Huts*, despite being more than a thousand pages of text are, in their sentence-based texture, as if simultaneously present. There is a right here, right now, and lots of it. The clock ticks and another sentence or phrase occurs. The work's intelligent optimism rests on this proposition. But some of the optimism occurs precisely because he has exited from the personal lyric into a political sense of "intentionality like mass."[63]

Certainly his "longpoem" is a critique of the romantic lyric. Long poems can never claim to be a unique overflow of feeling, an emotionally authentic entrance into language from sheer impulse, because their extent trips up that instantaneous emotional urgency. A long poem is therefore an argument against *the* lyric because the goal of various modes of lyric condensation is "the denial of time itself." But, as I have shown variously, the long poem in general and Silliman's longpoems in specific put intensity and focus of contradictions into play – therefore put change and the historical into play, and redeploy lyric intensity into each descriptive sentence. But the purpose is different. To accumulate a mass in order to change one's sense of time is to create a revolutionary form. It is in this numerological and political sense that the "longpoem" operates for Silliman.

Such a gesture involving a short unit in a long puts one kind of poetic time inside another. It might be a simple homage, an acknowledgment, or the result of a felt conflict between the temporal modes of short and long poem. It might be a measure of the incommensurable or the uneven (the "inequality," to return to that concept from Zukofsky). Counting, accumulating, negotiating with "length" – poem time and life time – is never far from the ken of those involved in long poems.

This conflict or incommensurability of little and large and its unstable resolution by some of these tactics might be what incites anyone to write a long poem in the first place: a refusal of the putative perfections beyond time in favor of time's messier activities. The endless putting in and taking out of category that this paper has done mimics the endless cultural acts of the long poem itself: creolized, inclusive, errant, omnivorous, palimpsestic, and over-written. Thus the long poem is on principle inadequate within its own excesses and because of them. Its failure or inadequacy is its triumph.

3

More Apparent than Real: The Lyric/Avant-Garde Divide

KERRY DOYLE

All poetry is experimental poetry.
Wallace Stevens

Many now believe there is a difference in kind between so-called conventional lyric poetry, or what Marjorie Perloff calls "straight lyric" (or just plain lyric poetry), and work labeled avant-garde (or experimental). Although no good reader would deny that there are in fact distinctions to be made – say between a poem by Mina Loy, a poem by Wallace Stevens, and a poem by Ezra Pound or, in our current context, between a poem by Steve McCaffery, a poem by Susan Howe, and a poem by P.K. Page – a number of critics have come to see in these differences something other than the existence of multiplicities in writing, in perspective, in engagement. The differences are now presented as binary oppositions at odds with one another, separated from one another by an impassable divide. Likewise, the critical and pedagogical assumption that there are "open" as opposed to "closed" texts has become entrenched in some quarters. If it seems odd that the distinction applies only to modernist, "post-modernist," or contemporary poetry, and not (for example) to medieval poetry, we should probably ask if this divide is not recent, arbitrary, and ideologically motivated.

The case of modernist poetry is of particular interest. As Raymond Williams argues in *Politics of Modernism: Against the New Conformists*, a "selective version" of modernism and the avant-garde, "with convenient slippages between the two loose terms," has obscured the fact that the "positions and practices" of modernism "and even, where [Williams will concentrate], of the avant-garde ... are very much more diverse than their subsequent ideological presentations and that we shall misunderstand and betray a century of remarkable experiments if we go on trying to flatten them to contemporary theoretical and quasi-theoretical positions":[1]

> It is not easy to make simple distinctions between 'Modernism' and the 'avant-garde', especially as many uses of these labels are retrospective. But it can be taken as a working hypothesis that Modernism can be said to begin with ... the alternative, radically innovating, experimental artists and writers – while the avant-garde ... [is] fully oppositional. The old military metaphor of the vanguard, which had been used in politics and in social thought from at latest the 1830s – and which had implied a position within a general human progress – now was directly applicable to these newly militant movements, even when they had renounced the received elements of progressivism. Modernism had proposed a new kind of art for a new kind of social and perceptual world. The avant-garde, aggressive from the beginning, saw itself as the breakthrough to the future ... the militants of a creativity which would revive and liberate humanity. (*PM*, 51)

More specifically, the various avant-garde movements "implicitly but more often explicitly, claimed to be anti-bourgeois," which was not always the case with modernist writers, however experimental (*PM*, 51). The conflation of the terms modernism with avant-garde, and of avant-garde with experimental, limits our appreciation of the diversity Williams writes of. And yet, as I will argue, such a conflation makes it possible to set the sweepingly broad category of avant-garde/experimental/modernist poetry against every other sort of contemporary poetry.

This divide, although not real, is certainly apparent.[2] It is apparent in the constructions of department curricula: in the distinctions drawn between poetry and poetics courses, and again between both of these and creative writing courses. It is apparent in the compilation of anthologies, and in the organization of conferences. A key way the divide has been established is by the argument that conventional lyric poetry works to represent a unified consciousness while avant-garde poetry acknowledges the impossibility of both unified consciousness and of mimetic grounding of a poem in experience. Avant-garde poetry demonstrates what the post-structuralist academy accepts: that the unified, transcendental subject has been revealed as a myth.

Despite the generalization above about a post-structuralist academy, lyric poetry continues to be cited by some for its ability to reveal to us the truth of a poet's vision. In 2000, and from the other side of the divide, Helen Vendler asserts that "the aim of the lyric poem is to show what is going on in the theater of the private mind when you are alone in your room."[3] And similarly, "[w]hen I wrote my first poem at six I thought that a poem was something that scanned and rhymed. It wasn't until I was fifteen … that I saw a poem could tell the truth about one's inner being."[4] Interestingly, it was an (unidentified) Wallace Stevens poem that led Vendler to her great insight. For our purposes here, Vendler and Perloff may serve as metonyms for two apparently opposing ideologies, but ideologies which both rely on a shared concept of the lyric.[5] Both assume that the lyric upholds and represents a notion of truth and subjectivity, confining themselves to what Gérard Genette terms "the classical doctrine of *mimesis*."[6] Vendler is comfortable, to the point of complacency, with this model of lyric; Perloff, in contrast, has found that the same model serves her polemical purposes well. In what follows, by subjecting the mimetic model of lyric to criticism, I hope to call into question the too hastily staked-out boundaries of lyric and avant-garde poetry. Lyric poetry cannot be a synonym for poetry, but nor, I would argue, can non-lyric poetry now stand for what is most important in poetry as a whole, either in the contemporary or modernist milieus.[7]

For Perloff, the significance of avant-garde poetry is that it demonstrates how "poetic language is not a window, to be seen through, a transparent glass pointing to something outside it, but a system of signs with its own semiological 'interconnectedness.'"[8] Perloff does not rigorously apply "avant-garde" as a key term in the early criticism, but in her later studies it becomes, retrospectively, an umbrella term to describe the various modernist, later twentieth-century, and early twenty-first century texts that "work to rupture the lyric paradigm." Among the modernists, Perloff's avant-garde includes the Russian and Italian Futurists, the Surrealists, and those in the "new mode" exemplified for Perloff, and others, by the poetry of Ezra Pound (and later, but differently, by that of John Cage).[9] The divide between the lyric and avant-garde she also positions as the "tension between rival strains of [modernism], the Symbolists or 'High Modernists,' and the 'Other Tradition,'" which embraces a poetics of indeterminacy.[10]

In *Poetic License: Essays on Modernist and Postmodernist Lyric* (1990), Perloff rightly questions the assumptions found in the 1985 anthology of critical essays, *Lyric Poetry*. She notes how the contributors to this volume use the terms "lyric" and "poetry" interchangeably, leaving her (and others) to wonder if there is poetry which is not lyric. Perloff further questions why no consideration is given to how the lyric might have changed over time (*PL*, 17). As if in answer, she suggests "that perhaps the 'poetic' in our own times, is to be found, not in the conventionally isolated lyric poem, so dear to the Romantics and Symbolists, but in texts not immediately recognizable as poetry" (17).

It is with *Radical Artifice: Writing in the Age of Media* (1991), however, that Perloff first makes extended use of the term "avant-garde," mainly in reference to Concrete and Language poetry. But significantly, Perloff sets her understanding of the term in contrast to its established designation as a reference to early twentieth-century movements which strove not only to question but to dismantle the dominant political ideology and practice of capitalism. The theorists of the avant-garde Perloff cites, including Peter Bürger, Hal Foster, Frederic Jameson, and Andreas Huyssen, suggest, in varying ways, that the avant-garde movements (and later "neo-avant-garde" movements which continue in the tradition of, for instance, Dadaist practices), once their works and practices have been absorbed into the dominant culture and found to be legitimate (and thus consumable), no longer can serve to undermine the politics of that culture.[11]

Perloff challenges such claims by insisting that the main quality of avant-garde art is its overt artifice, its "*use* [of] what really happens in the external world as its material" (*RA*, 26), its declaration that the work is a "*made thing* – contrived, constructed, [and] chosen" (*RA*, 28). Perloff denies that radical artifice has ever been recognized by the dominant culture. For this reason, poets "who believe that oppositionality has to do, not only with what a poem says, but with the formal, modal, and generic choices it makes – its use, say, of a non-traditional rhythmic base, a particular vernacular, or an incorporation of cited non-poetic material – these poets continue to be relegated to the margins" (*RA*, 11). Certain kinds of formal practices, like those of the Language poets, count as avant-garde. Such work, Perloff argues in *21st-Century Modernism: The 'New' Poetics*, is the true continuation of the "embryonic phase" and "avant-garde project" of early modernism (*TCM*, 3), for it eschews "the lyric contract" with its "emphasis on sound structure, the personal signature, and the mimetic grounding of experience".[12] Yet, oblivious to avant-garde practices, "most poetry continues to follow the basic assumptions of having a generic, 'sensitive', lyric speaker [who] contemplates a facet of his or her world and makes observations about it, [and who] divulges some hidden emotion or comes to a new understanding" (*TCM*, 161). Perloff's critical position, undeterred by particulars, is anchored in oppositions: the lyric strives to be representational; avant-garde poetry, to be abstract; the lyric is, in Mikhail Bakhtin's terms, monoglossic; avant-garde poetry is heteroglossic. And these oppositions are the artifact of a certain retrospective interpretation and valuation of modernist poetry.

Building on her 1981 devaluation of the lyric in *The Poetics of Indeterminacy*, where Stevens served as exemplar, Perloff elaborates in an essay published four years later upon why Stevens's poetry is paradigmatic of the limits of the modernist lyric. Taking "Notes Toward a Supreme Fiction" as her text, she argues that for Stevens poetry always remains lyric poetry as late Romantic theory (if not always the poetry) had defined it – the poem as short verse utterance (or sequence of such utterances) in which a single speaker expresses in figurative language his subjective vision of truth in a unique insight or epiphany that unites poet and reader.[13]

Perloff suggests, moreover, that the poets of the lyric paradigm avoid "all contact with the language of ordinary prose and therefore with the prose discourses of the novel and of historical writing" (*DOI*, 21). When she makes binaries of poets such as Pound and Stevens, Perloff is not simply describing what she sees as distinct practices; she is claiming that Pound's is the more valuable modernist poetry. Moreover, she claims that the status of the lyric, specifically "whether poetry should be lyric or collage," was the "problem that came to obsess Modernism" (*DOI*, 23). Perloff objects to the conflation of all poetry with lyric poetry, arguing, quite rightly, that not all poetry is in fact lyric. However, instead of expanding the notion of lyric, she argues that the lyric "genre" is a relic of the past, whereas the modern and post-modern poetry of which she approves is another, an avant-garde, "species" (*DI*, 175–6).

For Perloff to argue that what "we mean when we talk of Modernism in poetry" is the practices of its avant-garde writers, is to confine and collapse the varying literary manifestations of an entire era (*DOI*, 21), confirming, in Raymond Williams's terms, how a "late-born ideology of modernism" has imposed its own priorities onto the past. One way this confinement is made possible is by the critical marginalization of early modernist works – only the later groupings or practices of the period are considered truly modernist. So, for instance, Symbolists are set in contrast with Futurists, and the "late-born ideology" aligns itself with the writing and painting that appears to mark "a radical questioning of the processes of representation": "The writers are applauded for their denaturalizing of language, their break with the allegedly prior view that language is either a clear, transparent glass or a mirror, and for making abruptly apparent in the very texture of their narratives the problematic status of the author and his authority … The self-reflexive text assumes the centre of the public and aesthetic stage, and in doing so declaratively repudiates the fixed forms" (*PM*, 33).

Perloff's argumentative moves in *Dance of the Intellect* follow Williams's template all too closely. The modernists are equated or conflated with the avant-garde, the "Poundians" (in Perloff's terms), who "regard Modernism less as a continuation of Romanticism than as a very real rupture with it" (*DOI*, 21). And, ultimately, "the point" of truly avant-garde art "is to bypass Romanticism" (*DOI*, 22) – to leave behind the lyric.

▲●▲

But what is the lyric? DuPlessis contends – and I agree – that "the lyric is a collection of former definitions of the lyric, most of which are obsolete or wrong."[14] Although in what follows I will press Gérard Genette's claim that the lyric is in fact *something*, our received notion of the lyric is nevertheless highly problematic. We confidently suppose that the theoretical object of Aristotle's *Poetics* was "literature"; for clarity, we distinguish drama, epic/narrative, and (lyric) poetry as the three main branches of the Aristotelian tree of literature. But, in fact, the object of the *Poetics* was never literature in a broad modern sense. Its object was the art of imitation in verse.

Moreover, as Genette shows, there were only two branches in the tree of the *Poetics*: that of dramatic verse and that of epic verse. Genette's project, as Robert Scholes explains in his forward to the English translation of *The Architext*, is to "untangle a bit" the "knot of confusions, quid pro quos, and unnoticed substitutions that has lain at the heart of Western poetics for several centuries."[15] That knot is most tangled around the related premises that lyric poetry is a genre, and that it is imitative.

The generic tri-partition of lyric, epic, and dramatic that has been attributed to Plato and Aristotle is, Genette argues, an "error (or rather, a retrospective illusion) deeply rooted in our conscious, or unconscious, literary minds" (TA, 1, 2). He summarizes his analysis as follows. "The first page of the *Poetics* clearly defines poetry as the art of imitation in verse … explicitly excluding imitation in prose … and non-imitative verse – and making no mention at all of non-imitative prose, such as oratory … As for the poems that we would call lyric (for example, those of Sappho or Pindar), neither here nor elsewhere in the *Poetics* does Aristotle mention them; they are plainly outside his field, as they were outside Plato's" (TA, 10). None of the short poem forms that would later be called lyric (such as elegies and odes) imitate, according to Aristotle, human beings in action. Like prayers and speeches, they may express an author's thoughts or feelings, but since thoughts or feelings are not actions; these forms are not mimetic.

Is this tripartite division based, then, on some category other than genre? For Aristotle, it is a work's manner of imitation or mode. Genette contends that when Aristotle considers mode in the *Poetics* – pure narration, mixed narration, dramatic imitation (TA, 61) – he is in fact locating "situations" or "stances" of "enunciating" (TA, 12, 61). Modes, unlike literary genres, are "basic to the pragmatics of language itself … and are therefore extremely persistent across time and cultures."[16] Insofar as Aristotle recognized genres such as dithyramb, epic, tragedy, and comedy, he "allocated" them "among modes" according to whether they fell under "one enunciating stance or another" (TA, 61): namely, enunciation by the poet, enunciation by both the poet and his characters, or enunciation by the poet's characters. Contrary to what later times would suppose, modes of enunciation carry no inherent themes with them. Themes too are persistent, but unlike modes of enunciation they are altered by historical and cultural context.

If Aristotle's exclusions are disappointing, a plausible way to "promote" lyric forms to "poetic dignity" (TA, 28) would be to expand the concept of mimesis to include the representation of states of mind. This is exactly what happened in the late eighteenth century. A versified mode of enunciation that Plato and Aristotle had not even considered a species of imitation rose in cultural prominence to become the "architext" supposed most adequate for representing an individual's thoughts and feelings. Genette surveys Romantic-era criticism of the genres: G.W.F. Hegel, who found the *content* of lyric to be "the individual subject"; Karl Viëtor, who theorized that each genre expressed a "basic attitude," with lyric expressing "feeling"; and Johann Wolfgang von Goethe, who, though he understood epic and drama modally (as "pure narration" and "life-like representation"), defined lyric thematically – as *enthusiastisch aufgeregte*, "a burst of rapture" (*TA*, 62–3).

At this historical moment, two important things happened to the lyric: it was refigured as a genre instead of a mode of enunciation and it was taken to be as representational as epic or drama. As Genette notes, "Friedrich Schlegel, who apparently fires the first shot, retains or rediscovers Platonic division, but he gives it new meaning: in 1797 he claims, roughly speaking ... that the lyric "form" is subjective, the dramatic objective, the epic is subjective-objective" (*TA*, 38). Furthermore, as a genre that imitates the inner "action" of the writer, the lyric in this period is held to have greater literary value than epic or drama. The Romantic attribution of the "theory of the three genres" to the ancients suggests that the genre of lyric – like the genres of epic and drama – is somehow natural. In other words, the theory of the three genres invents what Genette calls "archgenres." These archgenres "always involve a thematic element that eludes purely formal or linguistic description" (*TA*, 64–5). His list of late twentieth-century scholars who accepted the Romantic archgenre of the lyric includes Austin Warren, Northrop Frye, Robert Scholes, and Tzvetan Todorov (the last two both correcting themselves, the first in his introduction to *The Architext*, the second in his *Introduction to Poetics*).

But it is not necessary, Genette argues, to buy into the archgenres in order to accord lyric poetry the literary status it deserves. A more radical appreciation would "break with the dogma of mimesis and proclaim the equal poetic dignity of non-representational utterance" (*TA*, 28). It is what Perloff claims avant-garde poetry does – that is, foreground the fact that the work is a "made thing" (*RA*, 28). This part of her program is in concord with the argument of *L'Architexte*. The second part – which mocks the belief that a poem can be grounded mimetically in experience – is not, since, according to Genette, what we call lyric is a mode of enunciation rather than a mimetic form. When Perloff gets "the lyric contract" in her sights, she is tilting at an archgenre.[17]

▲●▲

The critical (and political) distinction between lyric and avant-garde is handy – and, perhaps, pedagogically irresistible. It is commonly bolstered by the invocation of Mikhail Bakhtin's monoglossia and heteroglossia, concepts which seem to confirm the truth of Perloff's 1985 claim that *Cantos*-like collage poems, in contradistinction to lyric poetry, make contact with "the language of ordinary prose and therefore with the prose discourse of the novel and of historical writing" (*DOI*, 23). Indeed, when Bakhtin wrote the polemic "Discourse in the Novel," he was tempted, as his readers since have been, to insist on a fundamental distinction between the heteroglossia of prose and the monoglossia of poetry, but it should be recalled that the example of monoglossia he provides is the prose of Tolstoy, so the prose=intertextuality rule is not as clear-cut as has been suggested. Perloff, however, embraces the opposition, which Bakhtin himself would come to deny, citing the early Bakhtin in order to contrast the prose quality of collage with the pure and organic quality of lyric, insisting that "though Bakhtin was writing in the thirties and was contrasting the lyric and the novel, we can apply his distinction [between monoglossic and heteroglossic texts] to poetry itself, to the difference between what we might call 'straight lyric' (Dickinson, Crane, Frost, Stevens) … and the 'impure' collage poetry of the Pound tradition" (RC, 61). Bakhtin's early construction of a dichotomy between prose and poetry was motivated by the restrictive historical context he was immersed in, but such a motivation could not be sustained as he developed and clarified his theory of dialogism.

In "Revolving in Crystal: The Supreme Fiction and the Impasse of Modernist Lyric," her critique of Stevens's "Notes Toward a Supreme Fiction," Perloff makes extended use of Bakhtin's initial notion of monoglossia. It is helpful to know what she makes of his formulations from "Discourse and the Novel."[18] She cites the following passages:

> In genres that are poetic in the narrow sense the natural dialogixation of the work is not put to artistic use, the word is sufficient

> unto itself and does not presume alien utterances beyond its own boundaries. Poetic style is by convention suspended from any mutual interaction with alien discourse, any allusion to other discourse.
>
> The language of poetic genres ... often becomes authoritarian, dogmatic, conservative, sealing itself off from the influence of extra literary social dialects. Therefore, such ideas as "special poetic language," a "language of the gods,'" a "priestly language of poetry," and so forth could flourish on poetic soil. It is noteworthy that the poet, should he not accept the given literary language, will sooner resort to the artificial creation of a new language specifically for poetry than he will to the exploitation of actual available social dialects. (RC, 61)

Bakhtin's critique of poetry in the broadest sense "perfectly characterizes what" Perloff views as "problematic" in "Notes Toward a Supreme Fiction" and hence in lyric more generally: "the poet's deep-seated suspicion of the 'impurities of every day life'" (RC, 61). The latter phrase is Bakhtin's way of characterizing everything that the monoglossic shuts out and that the heteroglossic welcomes.

Anti-lyric critics who have found Bakhtin's distinctions useful are in danger of over-emphasizing his notions for their own ends and, as a result, of dismissing the lyric's heteroglossic and/or experimental potential.[19] I think that, when pressed, many who have employed the terms to describe the difference between lyric and avant-garde poetry would concede that all literature is to some degree heteroglossic, however much we might argue about the heteroglossic quality of particular works. But if one wants to insist that the lyric inherently or generically strives for a mimetic presentation of personal truth, a facile distinction between heteroglossia and monoglossia will be convenient. As DuPlessis notes, Bakhtin's generalization "makes poetry a marginalized, inflexible, and unresponsive medium (... in tendentious contrast, of course, to our Bakhtinian hero, the Novel)."[20] And certainly the polemical thread concerning poetry that runs through "Discourse in the Novel" is vulnerable to her criticism, which reminds us how "the modern long poem has often been written in a generative relationship with the social and heteroglossic."[21] Monoglossia, she asserts, cannot successfully describe poems in which "everything is mixed," where there is a "'necessary heterogeneity or hybridity.'" Nevertheless, DuPlessis, like Perloff, does suggest that Bakhtin's critique of poetry *in general* can be better understood as an evaluation of *the lyric*. In other words, there is a "grain of truth in Bakhtin's exaggerations."[22] For polemical reasons the monoglossia vs. polyglossia dichotomy appealed to Bakhtin himself, but since he could not and would not sustain it, even a very careful use of this opposition is highly problematic. The writings of the early Bakhtin will not support the conclusion that lyric poetry is inherently monoglossic.

▲●▲

In her reading of Bakhtin, Julia Kristeva gave us a term now in common (and diluted) use throughout the humanities: intertextuality. According to Kristeva, Bakhtin's "insight" into literary theory was as follows: "any text is constructed as a mosaic of quotations; any text is the absorption and transformation of another. The notion of *intertextuality* replaces that of intersubjectivity and poetic language is read as at least *double*."[23] Like Tzvetan Todorov after her, Kristeva posits that "[n]ot withstanding [the early] Bakhtin … dialogism appears on the level of the Bahktinian denotative word as a principle of every enunciation."[24] Kristeva's nuanced and comprehensive reading of Bakhtin's theory of discourse has been ignored by most critics who draw upon Bakhtin to debunk the lyric. It is perhaps not so surprising that Kristeva's reading of Bakhtin and her somewhat later work on poetic language has not resonated more successfully with critics of the lyric. Like Perloff, though from another social-political context, Kristeva wrote polemics championing the apparent liberty of an avant-garde in opposition to conventional and established ideology and poetic production (as in *Revolution in Poetic Language* [1974]). But, as Tyrus Miller explains in *Singular Examples,* Kristeva's theorizing during the late 1960s and early 1970s does not travel well out of its specific historical and aesthetic context:

> Kristeva's idea of a multidimensional paragrammatic space spanning from poetry across social structures all the way to the totality of social history did not just sketch out a semiotically informed mode of social analysis. It was also a political valorization

> of a particular practice of avant-garde writing, the ambiguously named "revolution in poetic language" being carried out by her comrades-in-pen at *Tel Quel*. By waging war against what they saw as the repressive codes of realism and lyric expressivity, which had petrified the bourgeois subject in language and confirmed the ideological self-image of the bourgeois reader, this avant-garde writing would, they believe, advance the political cause of the revolution.[25]

Kristeva's championing of a certain kind of avant-garde practice now seems to fall into the same contradictions that Bakhtin disentangled himself from in his later work.

Just as concepts from "Discourse in the Novel" can be applied positively to lyric poetry, however, Kristeva's arguments in *Revolution* should not be limited to her own political agenda if they can be found to provide insight into our continued engagement with, and interest in, lyric poetry. Kristeva's theory of poetic language aims to account more fully for how language as "symbolic order" can both limit our conception/reception of a real historical context and free us from limited constructs. Kristeva theorizes that one dimension of language is an arbitrary system, a symbolic order that anchors denotative meaning. Utterance, however, infuses the symbolic with "the semiotic" – which is to say, with pre-linguistic energies, with "rhythms and intonations anterior to the first phonemes, morphemes, lexemes and sentences."[26] The semiotic is not abandoned once a speaker takes on the symbolic order (social language); on the contrary, "these two modalities are inseparable within the signifying process … Because the subject is always both semiotic and symbolic, no signifying system [s]he produces can be either 'exclusively' semiotic or 'exclusively' symbolic, and is instead necessarily marked by an indebtedness to both" (*KR*, 93).

In an early work, "Word, Dialogue, and Novel" (1969), Kristeva credits Bakhtin for his innovative theory of utterance as an intertextual event not confined to prose or the novel. And indeed, it is Bakhtin himself who asks: "[i]s not any writer (even the lyricist) always a 'dramaturge' in the sense that he directs all words to other's voices."[27] He goes still further: the "word is a drama in which three characters participate (it is not a duet, but a trio)" (*SG*, 122). Kristeva helps us understand this trio, explaining that the writer's relation with the word is in itself a doubling. Although the writer must choose the word, every word is also "an intersection of words" where, at the very least, another word can be read. Bakhtin and Kristeva theorize the "field" of the utterance – within which the denotative intersects with the connotative in all its multiplicity, within which the symbolic is infused with the semiotic – as both temporal and spatial. (It is "spatial" in that to take on language is to move out into a social order.)

For the writer, the process of working to render language meaningful and not merely arbitrary is, according to Bakhtin, "[s]elf-objectification … (in the lyric, in the confession, and so forth) as self-alienation and, to a certain degree, a surmounting of the self. By objectifying myself (i.e. by placing myself outside) I gain the opportunity to have an authentic dialogic relation with myself" (SG, 122). As there is a spatial relationship between the author and the word, the author's "self-objectification," there is a similar process of spatialization between the reader and the word. The reader's relationship with the word-text is also always temporal because she cannot replicate the moment of its utterance, nor of the exact experience that underlay its utterance. As the relationship between writer-word and word-reader unfolds in time, it becomes triadic, never merely recapitulating the author's initial self-objectification.

The reader does not just negotiate the writer's doubling of words. She must negotiate, *within and from her time*, her own intertextual understanding of a text. Both poet and reader are engaged with "every latent double in the word."[28] Just as there are not, "nor can there be any pure texts," there are not, nor can there be, any pure writers or pure readers – these may exist in theory, but never in practice, never in utterance (SG, 105). Bakhtin explains:

> language and speech can be identical, since in speech the dialogic boundaries of the utterances are erased. But language and speech communication (as a dialogic exchange of utterances) can never be identical. Two or more sentences can be absolutely identical (when they are superimposed on one another, like two geometrical figures, they coincide); moreover, we must allow that any sentence, even a complex one, in the unlimited speech flow can be repeated an unlimited number of times in completely identical

> form. But as an utterance (or part of an utterance) no one sentence, even if it has only one word, can ever be repeated: it is always a new utterance (even if it is a quotation). (*SG*, 108)

In the final part of this essay, my interpretation of Stevens's "Notes Toward a Supreme Fiction" will suppose that poem to be an utterance in Bakhtin's sense rather than a mid-twentieth century species of the genre known as lyric.

▲●▲

Perloff's judgment that Stevens's poetry lacks "radical artifice" has vacillated over the years.[29] For instance, in her 1998 review of Harold Bloom's *Best of the Best,* she accuses the critic of favoring "a psychology of tropes" and ignoring, in the case of Stevens, crucial "matters of sound, rhythm and syntax" that reveal "the materiality of the poetic language itself" and therefore its artifice.[30] But in 1985, as Perloff is trying to distinguish the poetry of an avant-garde (later labeled "the Other Tradition") from lyric poetry and its conventional representation of personal truths, she focuses not on the materiality of Stevens's language but on the fact that Stevens is a lyric poet "in keeping with the Romantic model" (*DOI*, 21).

In another striking instance, Perloff faults Stevens, and by extension all lyric poets, for failing to engage with "the real action" (RC, 42). Her 1985 reading of "Notes Toward a Supreme Fiction" juxtaposes historical data with Stevens's poem, listing events immediately preceding and surrounding its publication in 1942, and also drawing on his correspondence, to illustrate how little affected the poet seemed by the war. In short, she denigrates the work for its author's "preoccupation with personal and aesthetic truth" (RC, 42). According to Perloff at the time of her writing of this essay, Stevens's lyric sequence is "a kind of anti-meditation, fearful and evasive, whose elaborate and daunting rhetoric is designed to convince both poet and reader that, despite the daily headlines and radio bulletins, the real action takes place in the country of metaphor" (RC, 42).

Perloff reads Stevens's metaphoric sequences as a monoglossic language of "his own" that thrusts the poet's understanding of the "real action," or what really matters to him, upon the reader. For Perloff, Steven's "daunting rhetoric" (RC, 42) and "extravagant metaphoricity" (RC, 61) expound an evasive personal aesthetic, which the inclusion of ordinary prose would dismantle. It is significant that Perloff opposes prose and poetry in a way that is recapitulated by her positioning of avant-garde and lyric and, on a technical level, by the received understanding of the effects of metonymy and metaphor. Unlike the supposedly personal and monoglossic metaphor, metonymy, a hallmark of realist prose, is more social, more heteroglossic, because the contiguity of the metonym is "real" – that is, recognizable as incorporating, and thus apparently reflecting, a social reality. But the argument that metaphor is somehow the poet's very own rendering of the world is false. We recognize a metaphor as such because it is a semantic entity, which is to say the words chosen by the poet cannot be scrubbed free of the social contexts in which s/he has come across them – they cannot excuse themselves from the "real action": "For the poet, language is actually totally saturated with living intonations; it is completely contaminated by rudimentary social evaluations and orientations, and it is precisely with them that the creative process must struggle."[31] The struggle that Bakhtin describes is recapitulated, though never identically replicated, in the struggle by which the reader comes to understand any particular metaphor.

It is understandable why Perloff thinks it imperative to keep historical context, the "real action," as a priority. Stevens's claim that "Reality is a cliché / From which we escape by metaphor / It is only au pays de la métaphore / Qu'on est poète" is served with Perloff's cutting irony: "what was the reality-as-cliché to be escaped in the winter of 1942?"[32] Perloff's analysis reveals a genuine concern that the events of World War II not be ignored in favour of an apolitical, even perhaps an anti-political, aesthetic. Beginning with Hitler's invasion of Poland in September 1939 and ending with the Allied invasion of North Africa in July of 1942, Perloff provides a list of events the import of which she believes was lost on or ignored by Stevens. The Stevens correspondence Perloff cites provides her with another opportunity to blast the poet's aesthetics. Perloff's own history as an Austrian Jew displaced by the Nazi regime provides some insight into both her championing of the avant-gardes and her attack on "Notes Toward a Supreme Fiction." The early twentieth-century avant-garde movements sought to rattle bourgeois hypocrisy as well as to create art that would have tangible and profound effects on our lived reality. Then again, according to Perloff's preferred formulation, avant-garde poetry – a category not limited to those movements of the early twentieth century – has less to do with re-making the social order than with the poet's "formal, modal, and generic choices" (RA, 11) and the extent to which those choices lead readers to recognize how the poem is "a *made thing*" (RA, 28).

Perloff's oppositional reading of "Notes Toward a Supreme Fiction" relies on a political critique of MacCullough, the rather enigmatic figure who appears in canto III of "It Must Be Abstract" and whom other critics have generally taken to be an everyman – not, as Perloff does, "major man."[33] In the canto the speaker asks, "Can we compose a castle-fortress-home, / Even with the help of Viollet-le-Duc, / And set the MacCullough there as major man?" and answers no: "The first idea is an imagined thing" (*WS*, 386). The lines, posed as question and never asserted as possible, play with the notion of Viollet-le-Duc's "restorations" – an "ironic allusion" as Perloff recognizes – in order to assert instead the impossibility of placing "major man" alongside "the first idea" (RC, 57). Although he may be "an expedient" in our desire "to speak the word," the poem itself denies the MacCullough any *a priori* standing in human existence, though he may exist for some in "crystal hypothesis." The "thinker of the first idea" cannot be traced; he is not some sort of linguistic Adam. Even if there once was a "major man" – a possibility the poem denies: "The first idea was not our own. Adam / In Eden was the father of Descartes" – "it does not follow that major man is man [i.e., that "major man" is the or a MacCullough]" (*WS*, 383, 387). Perloff argues, however, that the words "MacCullough" and "major man" are deeply troublesome because the names/characters evoke, in the case of the former, a "Wasp" and "Aryan purity," and in the case of the latter, "the real Major Men … Hitler, Mussolini, and Stalin" (RC, 59).

But Perloff's partial interpretation of "Notes Toward a Supreme Fiction" – she reads nearly the entire piece through the figure of MacCullough – rests on the assumption that the poet should have directly engaged social reality and at the same time prevented the possibility of any slippage between his fictional characters and that reality. She faults Stevens for not naming "real people" as Yeats and Pound do, and for not utilizing what Bakhtin calls the "actual available social dialects" (RC, 59, 61). But one is left to wonder how, in this 1985 demand for a political poetry that would have challenged the likes of Hitler and Mussolini, she could have overlooked the fascist tendencies of Pound (and of Yeats)? Does the collage technique, by incorporating prose (that is, non-literary discourse), successfully destabilize, and thus somehow excuse or undermine, the political meanings of the *Cantos*?

According to Bakhtin, to isolate a finite context, such as the social-political realities of the 1940's, is to ignore both the past and the future which a text is created by and through: "the art work extends its roots into the distant past" and, although the author may be "a captive of his epoch, of his own present, [s]ubsequent times liberate him."[34] Perloff's argument that Stevens ignores the most significant political aspects of his own epoch is in fact a means of anchoring the poem to its first enunciation and, moreover, to the author-function. Bakhtin does insist that it is "impossible to study literature apart from an epoch's entire culture," and thus he takes issue with those practices of Russian Formalism, and Structuralism in general, that ignore the historical context out of which a work of literature comes.[35] He is "against enclosure of the text."[36] But he also warns against giving a decisive priority to the original historical context: "it is … fatal to encapsulate a literary phenomenon in the single epoch of its creation, in its own contemporaneity, so to speak."[37]

Such an understanding as Bakhtin calls for cannot limit the significance or value of a text to the most apparent social realities. The "semantic possibilities" of a text are available to later ages and are, in fact, mutable, changeable, never pinned down by the historical moment, or by the author's desires, or by assumptions about how historical events should be represented. The unity of a text – any text – is an *open* unity. One of the issues with how Bakhtin's theory of utterance and dialogic understanding has been interpreted and applied is the tendency of critics to assume that unless a text provides concrete instances of heteroglossia in its most obvious rendering – examples of the stratification of social languages – then it must be "closed" or monoglossic. Bakhtin – and Kristeva – allow us to understand that a text can be dialogic ("open") even when it does not present us with overt examples of various discourses.

Indeed, for Bakhtin, the more blatant ways of representing dialogic relations are not necessarily the most interesting or the most meaningful: "The narrow understanding of dialogism as argument, polemics, or parody. These are the externally most obvious, but crude, forms of dialogism" (*SG*, 121). He lists, in a delightful asyndeton that disables the hierarchy of the list-form, some of the less obvious manifestations of dialogism: "Confidence in another's word, reverential reception (the authoritative word), apprenticeship, the search for and mandatory nature of deep meaning, *agreement*, its infinite gradations and shadings (but not its logical limitations and not purely referential reservations), the layering of meaning upon meaning, voice upon voice, strengthening through merging (but not identification), the combination of many voices (a corridor of voices) that augments understanding, departure beyond the limits of the understood, and so forth" (SG, 121).

Poetic texts do not need to overtly defy myths of autonomy or of a unified, transcendental ego in order to be dialogic. The ways in which an utterance expresses or solicits agreement is of as much interest to Bakhtin as utterances that announce the impossibility of denotation. In this rich theoretical matrix, lyric poetry can be as significant to our understanding of both the real world and of language as any work named avant-garde.

Before applying Bakhtinian theory to Stevens's lyric sequence, a return to Genette will help clarify how "Notes Toward a Supreme Fiction" and the lyric in general can be understood as dialogic, and thus as a means of eliciting "self-awareness" and "self-objectification" without recourse to upholding an ideology that avows the lyric speaker's "individuality" and "truth" – or, for that matter, the reader's individuality or truth. Genette's work in *The Architext*, which argues that the lyric should be understood as a non-mimetic mode of utterance, as holding a pragmatic instead of a generic position, is only one instance of his foray into theories of mimesis. In his short essay "Valéry and the Poetics of Language," and his book length study *Mimologics*, published in French in 1978 (but not translated into English until 1994), he considers how poetry can "play" with our knowledge of the arbitrary nature of language, answering our desire to find meaning in that which does not inherently mean. In both works, Genette deploys Plato's figures Cratylus, who argued for the "fitness of signs," or mimetic motivation, and Hermogenes, who upheld what Saussure would come to insist upon, the arbitrariness of language, in order to explain the two "opposing – but not contradictory" concepts of language.[38] These concepts are not "contradictory" because of the phenomenon Genette explores – that language can *seem* to be rendered mimetic when we know it is not.[39] He argues that although we renounce, like Hermogenes, "all deductions of the analogical relation," we still "desire," poets and readers, to make language work as "an analogue of the real."[40] "Mimology" is a term Genette coins to designate "a certain turn of thought or of imagination which assumes, rightly or wrongly, a relation of reflective analogy (imitation) between 'word' and 'thing' that *motivates*, or justifies, the existence and the choice of the former ... the delightful reverie this relation evokes [he calls] *mimologic*; and the linguistic fact in which this relation operates or is surmised to operate, and by metonymic extension the discourse presupposing this relation and the doctrine invested in it, *mimologism*" (*MM*, 5).

This "certain turn of thought," this "desire," points again to how we submit to the denotative stasis of the symbolic order/language while refusing such submission, creating through desire and imagination the dialogism of the word. "Notes Toward a Supreme Fiction" exemplifies such desire, announcing on the one hand the impossibility that writing can represent social reality as it appears for an individual subject, and on the other, the power of imagination and of poetry to make us, "for a moment," believe in "a pure power ... That gives a candid kind to everything," and to bring us to "late plural candor," where candour recalls an older meaning (generosity) (*WS*, 382).

Genette enumerates the many times Valéry affirmed both language's arbitrariness and his awareness that poetry can instigate the "illusion" of a meaningful relationship between the phonetic and the semantic. That it is only an illusion is the very thing which motivates the poet to struggle with language: "[t]he non-mimetic character of language is," Genette suggests, "the opportunity and the condition for poetry to exist. Poetry exists only to 'remunerate,' in other words, to repair and compensate for the 'defect of languages.' If language were perfect, poetry would have no reason for being, since it would have nothing to repair. Language itself would be a poem and poetry would be everywhere, which obviously means that it would be nowhere."[41] And the reader who, in turn, takes part in the illusion, who allows for a suspension of disbelief, becomes "the Cratylian thaumaturge."[42] This is not to argue that the reader embraces the poem as an example of immutable truth, but that "[w]e feel a fleeting surprise, generally followed or accompanied by a sort of acquiescence, or semi-acquiescence, or marginal protest, which signals just as surely the entry into the game and the effective operation of the trap ... An unexpected but happy marriage, every successful mimologism is an authentic creation, or both an invention and a discovery: an active disavowal and an immanent refutation of the insipid – and impotent – aesthetic of resemblance" (*MM*, 335). Stevens's aphorism in *Adagia* – "All poetry is experimental poetry" – suggests the process that Kristeva, Bakhtin, and Genette each hypothesize.[43] The poet's struggle to make meaningful what is arbitrary, the process by which s/he works to infuse the symbolic with meaning beyond the symbolic, is experimentation. The denotative is made the connotative: "As reason destroys, the poet must create."[44]

For Stevens (and other modernists), experimentation of this sort went hand in hand with an aggressive striving "against conventional reading practices."[45] The difficulty of Stevens's "extravagant metaphoricity" (RC, 61) and his complex use of "conventional" techniques such as blank verse, strophic forms and rhyme challenge readers to wrestle with language, to attempt the "self-objectification" with which Bakhtin suggests the writer must engage. "One might say," Charles Altieri proposes, "that the ultimate meaning of a Stevens poem is the mode of self-awareness that the readers take on as they flesh out the words and rhythms."[46] "Notes Toward a Supreme Fiction," that is, by no means simply propounds its meaning. The poem offers not a single, monoglossic vision of truth, but instead approximates the movement between the desire of the individual subject to make meaning of her experience of reality through language and her knowledge of the limits placed upon any such meaning-making by the arbitrary and social nature of language. It is in the space between these positions, or more specifically, in the movement of joining, if only momentarily, these positions, that a reader can experience both language and reality as meaningful.

"Notes Toward a Supreme Fiction" is just such a conjunction, just such dialogism. The apparently static structure – Helen Vendler describes it as a "massively solid structure, the most harmonious expression" with its "three broad, but stern, headings, which give the poem its extremely satisfactory triadic plan, so much firmer than the structure of its predecessors" – in fact enables a dialectical movement between the visual and the aural.[47] Iambic pentameter, which dominates, creates a rhythmic quality in this poem that bodies forth the "ennui" provoked by the (alluded-to) real. The human and the natural, the "apartments" and the "stale moonlight," which through repetition become stagnant, meaningless, are set to a steady and pleasing musicality that transforms but does not displace the mundane and the repetitive.

That this long poem is a sequence of lyrics is another means by which the poet creates dialectical properties. The movement through the three sections does not have a strictly linear, progressive quality; the sequence resists sequential understanding, and this resistance undermines closure or unity. The solidity of the structure is an illusion. Even its title emphasizes "the broken, partial nature of the poem, the way it is a piece of something larger, or is only an indirect and incomplete movement toward its object, something preliminary and unfinished."[48] The tercets provide a further "impression of visual orderliness on the printed page. They suggest stability, regularity, predictability" yet, as Beverly Maeder insists, "Their spatial regularity places pressure on the syntactic linearity of the poem's language."[49] The visual cues of the poem lead to expectations of static precision, as does, in a cursory reading, the metrical uniformity. Such gestures to order come into collision with the many moments in "Notes Toward a Supreme Fiction" that defy easy, or transparent, denotative paraphrase. The apparent order of the three sections is another example of how structural choices are in tension with the effect of the poem's unfolding. The concept of Kristevian intertextuality enables an understanding of how "conventional" poetic devices, such as meter and structure, can indeed be worked by the poet in ways that allow us to partake in the struggle of being *in* language. Kristeva laments that intertextuality "has often been understood in the banal sense of 'study of sources'" when in fact, "*intertextuality* denotes [a] transposition of one (or several) sign-system(s) into another" (KR, 111). A sign system, such as music, can be transfused into another system, such as language, in order to achieve new registers of experience (KR, 93). In Kristevian terms, the rhythm is what guarantees that the words will be more or other than the symbolic/denotative allows.

Section III of "It Must Be Abstract" epitomizes Stevens's defense and championing of poetry. In a world that has lost or let go of the pre-Cartesian certainties, that has come to "the inevitable exhaustion of religious myth" (OEW, 178), Stevens asserts poetry's peculiar power to evoke life/reality as-if-new, to provide a means that "satisfies" beyond convention or repetition our desire to believe in something:

> The poem refreshes life so that we share,
> For a moment, the first idea ... It satisfies

Belief in an immaculate beginning

And sends us, winged by an unconscious will,
To an immaculate end. We move between these points:
From that ever-early candor to its late plural

And the candor of them is the strong exhilaration
Of what we feel from what we think, of thought
Beating in the heart, as if blood newly came,

An elixir, an excitation, a pure power.
The poem, through candor, brings back a power again
That gives a candid kind to everything.

We say: At night an Arabian in my room,
With his damned hoobla-hoobla-hoobla-how,
Inscribes a primitive astronomy

Across the unscrawled fores the future casts
And throws his stars around the floor. By day
The wood-dove used to chant his hoobla-hoo

And still the grossest iridescence of ocean
Howls hoo and rises and howls hoo and falls.
Life's nonsense pierces us with strange relation
(*WS*, 382–3).

Stevens casts natural repetition, the sound of the wood-dove, of the oceans' tidal movements, as both monotonously repetitive and meaningfully differentiated. Language has the same quality. Following "the first idea," words catch at difference, if only as illusion, and then repeat. In our desire to make meaning, we come out from under linguistic convention. In Kristeva's terms, we infuse our words with semiotic energies, those "rhythms and intonations anterior to" the order of language: an exhilaration "of thought / Beating in the heart, as if blood newly came." Unexpectedly, the ocean that repeatedly "Howls hoo" – in spondees – introduces rhythmic variation, whereas the Arabian, with "his damned hoobla-hoobla-hoobla-how" (*ws*, 383), repeats himself in unchanging iambic feet: "And throws his stars around the floor." Semantically, "Life's nonsense" is typified by the "primitive" attempt to find meaning – religion, supernatural intervention – but rhythmically, the "strange relation" that we experience, however fortuitously, "pierces us."

Another instance of sound repetition, this time in the section vi of "It Must Change," further plays with the monotony of nonsenses (un-meanings) and our need to find meaning within these. The call of the sparrow and the wren are juxtaposed but, through repetition, the reader must acknowledge that both bird calls are "A single text, granite monotony" (*ws*, 394). At first the "ké-ké" of the wren appears nonsensical, banal, in relation to the "bethou" of the sparrow which is read/heard as meaningful for its "strange relation" to be thou. Vendler's insistence, antithetical to Perloff's, that Stevens is in fact engaged with historical reality, does in her own way by-pass how "Notes Toward a Supreme Fiction" is working to articulate a different, if less empirically recognizable, phenomenon. Vendler does admit, for instance, that the bird calls are, through repetition, revealed as tedious, but that the "true centre of revulsion in the canto" is not the monotony of the bird calls, but "the anger at the inevitable exhaustion of religious myth. Though the celestial and ecclesiastical are theoretically used as metaphorical vehicles to illustrate the tedium of the natural, actually *they* are the true subject of the poem" (*OEW*, 178). I would suggest the repetition reveals less the anger of the speaker at such an exhaustion, and more a frustration that the myth is still "inscribed" – that the sounds of nature are not recognized as sounds "like any other" (*ws*, 394). The sparrow's "bethou" becomes as nonsensical as the robin's "ké-ké" and what is revealed is not that bethou "is all the more delusive just because it seems so heavenly at first" (*OEW*, 178), but that if it seemed heavenly it did so due to a human desire to project meaning onto and beyond the actual. Stevens's further desire – and theme – is that we recognize our "power" to imbue both the physical world and language with signification and that we not project this power onto what is other; and thus, in effect, that we relinquish such power.

It is we who insist on the meaningfulness of meaningless sound, but it is also we who derive pleasure and purpose from such insistence, however false or illusionary. Human sounds can mimic natural sounds; the onomatopoetic repetition of these – ké-ké ké-ké – throws into relief the falsity of such efforts as well as (and at the same time) the desire that such efforts not be in vain. For Genette, onomatopoeia is "the bone to gnaw on which the [language] system tosses to mimetic desire," a desire which exists despite "the practical *impossibility* of a mimetic language ... and [humanity] being forever doomed to the 'betrayal' of the real which founds every natural language" (*MM*, 332, 333). Whereas Vendler reads "Notes Toward a Supreme Fiction" as a poem grappling with the loss of myths and the death of God, Perloff urges us to turn away from this unsatisfactory poem in order to attend to others that better foreground "radical artifice." Both fail to recognize how remarkably "Notes Toward a Supreme Fiction" gives form to mimetic desire – making, as it were, that desire visible. Indeed, through its dialogic relations as well as its thematic preoccupations, Stevens's great poem embodies and enacts our desire, a desire made irresistible, perhaps, because "we live in a place / That is not our own and, much more, not ourselves / And hard it is in spite of blazoned days" (*WS*, 383).

4

Hannah Weiner's Book in Air: *Clairvoyant Journal* and the Clair-Style Poems

JENNIFER RUSSO

In the East Village of New York City, in August 1972, the experimental poet Hannah Weiner began seeing words – hallucinations appearing on surfaces around her, including her own forehead, which she could "read" from within. She believed she was clairvoyantly receiving directions and commentary from unseen guiding spirits. She had been seeing "images and energy fields" for over a year, and she had been writing about what she saw, carefully recording it all, certain that she was the addressee.[1] When she sees the first word Weiner is thrilled – despite the fact that the word is "wrong." She believes that if the "forces," as she calls them, speak to her through words, the messages will be clearer to her, will help her.[2] By recording her struggle to decipher the instructions for healing, enlightenment, and literary success she's sure are locked in the words she sees, Weiner creates a poetics, which she calls "clair-style," that gives her a way to document her experience as she struggles to regain control of her life. Weiner discovers, however, that reclaiming control requires giving in to the words and allowing them to dictate not just her poetry, but her life. Though her personal agency is diluted, Weiner trades authority for what she wants more: to create important new poetry that leads her and her readers to healing and enlightenment.

Weiner was born in 1928 in Providence, Rhode Island, to a middle-class family, and attended Radcliffe College, graduating with a BA in English

Literature in 1950. As a longtime resident of the East Village, Weiner was an active participant in the experimental art scene so vibrant there in the 1960s and 1970s. In a one-page, third-person autobiographical piece published in 1994, Weiner describes her adult life before she began writing: "she … worked for three publishing houses got fired from all of them … she then turned to retailing and was an assistant buyer for fat ladies dresses in bloomingdales basement she married a psychiatrist freudian and divorced him four years later then she exaggerated but not lied herself into a job designing lingerie and turned down her second request for marriage."[3] Weiner recounts as well her beginnings in the New York poetry scene: "by this time she was making the rounds of galleries and parties in the early sixties and began to write poetry in 1963" (ST, 69).

Weiner's successful career as a lingerie designer for Maidenform led to some of her first connections to the world of performance art. Ron Silliman, in a report on the "70th birthday memorial celebration of Hannah Weiner" hosted in 1998 by St Mark's Poetry Project – a space with which Weiner had long been connected – recounts a humorous story told by the performance artist Carolee Schneeman: "Carolee described meeting Hannah as the result of a planned performance piece in which, at a very late moment before the event, the sponsors indicated that the performers could not, in fact, appear nude, so that she went to Maidenform to ask about 'experimental underwear' and the folks at Maidenform said 'you must meet Hannah Weiner.'"[4] Weiner was laid off in the late 70s, supporting herself with disability checks and, on occasion, money from her parents, but by then she had already devoted her life to writing poetry.

The 60s and 70s were a time in New York when poor artists, Weiner among them, could still afford to live in the Lower East Side and East Village in lofts in various states of decrepitude. She explored drugs and Eastern philosophy and wrote openly about her sex life. A little older than many involved in the counter-culture of New York City, Weiner was known and liked for her kindness and generosity towards younger poets. In 1969 she co-organized, with *Village Voice* art critic John Perreault, the Poetry Fashion Show, which featured garments designed by Claes Oldenburg and Andy Warhol, among others. This event, she recalls, was "very well reviewed because the art critic of the village voice was one of her partners" (ST, 69). In one of her first explanations of her art – in a flier for a performance piece entitled "Hannah Weiner at her Job" – she writes, "My life is my art. I am object, a product of the process of self-awareness."[5]

Weiner was first a student of New York School poetry, and took a class with Kenneth Koch at the New School. By the later 1960s she had established herself as an East Village poet and performer, interested in part in recording altered states of consciousness. In the 1970s, after participating in Bernadette Mayer's workshops at the Poetry Project, she became associated with Language Poetry.[6] These workshops, and Mayer's work in general, veered away from New York School poetry and "offered a set of new literary and evaluative standards that moved toward a more overtly theoretical poetics of multiple referentiality and syntactical rupture that was generally suspicious of the poem as an emotive or expressivist composition."[7] This reimagining of poetry was compelling to Weiner, who had "found she couldnt write new york school poetry in fact she couldnt write her own words at all" (ST, 69).

Her claim that she was unable to "write her own words" is a bit of an exaggeration, as in her first book of poetry, *The Magritte Poems*, she does just that. What she seems to be admitting is dissatisfaction with the words she could write, and this dissatisfaction leads her to look elsewhere for mediating devices through which she could construct poems. She became increasingly interested in the use of codes and symbols, particularly those that lend themselves to the creation of visual poetry or performance art. Weiner explains that "happily she discovered the international code of signals and found she could write about almost anything by using the code books" (ST, 69). Her 1968 book *Code Poems* is the result of Weiner's use of these standard nautical signs: "performance pieces using two figures and flags and … found material based on the International Code of Signals for Ships at Sea" (*OH*, 122). Visual representations of semaphore flags correspond to the letters of the alphabet, and visual representations of Morse code translate the flag combinations. Weiner lists the letter-code combinations, and then their full meaning, arranging these standard messages (such as "LWC Follow me" or "YZ Are you in want of water?") into witty, suggestive poems, which then "became rather wild performances" in Central Park (ST, 69). In the second edition of *Technicians of the Sacred*, Jerome Rothenberg's anthology of ethnopoetics, in the "Addenda" of the note on "The Lovers," a visual text from the Ekoi, there is an excerpt from *Code*

Poems. It is an image from the book: a sequence of flags each with a geometric pattern in white on black (an inversion of the color scheme of the nautical code). The excerpt is followed by this explanation: "In addition to the flag forms of the International Signal Code, Weiner's performances utilized semaphore (light signals) & morse code."[8]

Rothenberg connects Weiner's work to the sacred traditions of shaman or seer found in, what he calls, with a careful definition, "primitive" cultures. Weiner's work is also included in the second volume of the influential anthology *Poems for the Millennium* (1998), edited by Jerome Rothenberg and Pierre Joris, in which the editors relate her experiences to those of "many traditional poet-mystics."[9] In the 1984 preface to *Technicians of the Sacred*, Rothenberg writes about the late 1960s, when the book was first published: "Our ideas of poetry – including, significantly, our idea of the poet – began to look back *consciously* to the early & late shamans of those other worlds: not as a title to be seized but as a model for the shaping of meanings & intensities through language. As the reflection of our yearning creates a meaningful ritual life – a life lived at the level of poetry – that looking-back related to the emergence of a new poetry & art rooted in performance & the oldest, most universal of human traditions."[10]

Weiner, too, was "looking back" to ancient traditions of performance – but also, and more basically, she was troubled by health problems including persistent knee and digestive pain. Like many of her contemporaries, she sought both physical and psychic healing through non-traditional, non-Western means. She practiced yoga, visited integrative doctors and chiropractors, and experimented with eliminating certain foods from her diet.

Weiner's psychological state affected her life profoundly. When reminiscing about her early days in the art world, once again in third-person, she explains, "all this glory ended in 1970 when she became extremely psychic and hiding out in a cheap apartment wrote about nothing else in almost 100 notebooks" (ST, 69). Weiner's poetry documents the hallucinatory experiences that permeate her life – in medical terms, "psychotic episodes indicative of schizophrenia" – which Weiner unwaveringly believes to be clairvoyantly received messages.[11] Her hallucinations dominated her life and influenced her behavior. But Weiner, according to her longtime friend the poet Charles Bernstein, in a tribute published in the Poetry

Project *Newsletter* soon after her death in 1997, and reprinted in *Jacket* in 2000, "did not accept any characterization of herself as mentally ill."[12]

In 1974, Weiner responded to a questionnaire sent her by Radcliffe College. (Her reply was found by scholar Kaplan Harris in the alumni office archives and published in the booklet for a November 2007 event at the Poetry Project celebrating the publication of a new collection of Weiner's unpublished and out-of-print work, *Hannah Weiner's Open House.*) One question was "What experiments in your life have had a major effect on the choices you have made? List below briefly."[13] Weiner wrote, "TAKING ACID, becoming a 39 yr old hippie." In her other responses she refers to her "psychic experiences." Critic Thom Donavan's report on the 2007 event explores the way in which Weiner's dearest friends talk about the delicate matter of her mental state. He concludes that it is impossible to ascribe Weiner's visions to any single or simple cause:

> The transformation that occurred in Weiner was no doubt influenced by LSD, but also a response to the vital literary and visual arts communities flourishing Downtown in the 1960s and 1970s. Insofar as Weiner did "TOO MUCH ACID" (Weiner's own words from *Clairvoyant Journal*) she was, in her own way, a victim of the climate of radical experimentation during the psychedelic era. Inasmuch as Weiner was a gifted, sensitive and educated person, she brought to her LSD trips insights about "the Word" as visible fact among a much wider conversation, a continuum of mainstream and marginal culture workers and artists, what poet Robert Duncan called "a symposium of the whole."[14]

Whether it's called illness or clairvoyance, Weiner's poetics is a product of her unique experience. Her work strives toward a direct, honest translation of an unstable consciousness continually contested and interrupted by "the voices."

Marked by humour as much as by endless interruptions, "clair-style" is a page-oriented, visual technique. Weiner is ever mindful of how the work will look on the page, and particular pages can be read as discrete visual poems. The journal entries gathered in *Clairvoyant Journal* are often no longer than a single page and, at times, end with commentary that serves to reinforce Weiner's, and the forces', emphasis on the page as a poetic unit.[15] She writes, "CUT THIS PAGE SHORT" (*CJ*, 4), "SORRY ABOUT THIS PAGE STUPID" (*CJ*, 5), "I DONST FINISH THIS PAGE" (*CJ*, 36), "THIS IS A GO PAGE" (*CJ*, 42), and, in perhaps the most telling of these end comments, "IT'S A TRAGEDY YOU DIDN'T FINISH ME says the bottom of the page YOU DON'T LIKE THE BOTTOM OF THIS PAGE" (*CJ*, 22). While Gertrude Stein famously opined "A Sentence is not emotional a paragraph is," Weiner's emotional canvas is typically the page.[16] Charles Olson's idea of projective verse also seems to have influenced Weiner's poetic practice, and her poetry literalizes Olson's "FORM IS NEVER MORE THAN AN EXTENSION OF CONTENT."[17] The composition by field that he advances parallels Weiner's methods: "From the moment [a poet] ventures into FIELD COMPOSITION – puts himself in the open – he can go by no track other than the one the poem under hand declares, for itself … [H]e has to … be, instant by instant, aware of some several forces just now beginning to be examined" (*PCO*, 240). Obedience – to the body and breath for Olson, to the forces for Weiner – is essential in order to create and to stay on a natural path.

Hard to read, and harder to classify, Weiner's work is genre-busting. She opens her 1986 essay, "Mostly About the Sentence," by complaining, "Before the Code Poems please I was just short page an ordinary writer no instructions and one book was published" (MS, 122). Weiner doesn't want to be an "ordinary writer," and so, when the words appear and she becomes "my clairvoyant writer myself" she develops a methodology or code for recording them as well (MS, 122). Weiner's understanding of her clairvoyance is simple: she sees words and images that she knows to be messages addressed to her for her benefit. She has been chosen, by the forces, to receive their wisdom because she has worked hard to open herself to the spiritual world and because she needs its guidance. There is a symbiotic tinge to her poetic autobiography. She is writing that which insists on writing itself and on documenting this writing; she is subject and author, reader and writer. Weiner explains that through her new form, her clair-style, she is "trying to show the mind" (MS, 129). This is a task rooted not in completion, which is impossible, but in the attempt, the process. Or, as Olson remarks, "all the thots that men are capable of can be entered on the back of a postage stamp. So, is it not the PLAY of a mind we are after, is not that that shows whether a mind is there at all?" (*PCO*, 243). Weiner's poetry reveals the play of a mind trying to read and write and interpret the words she sees.

Weiner's clairvoyance has obvious precedents in the work of other poets who claimed to be visionaries, such as Blake and Coleridge, or even H.D., who professed to seeing hieroglyphs appear before her when visiting Egypt. But Weiner's method for dealing with her visions, her insistence on recording, has a more significant connection to the work of the poet Jack Spicer. Spicer and Weiner use a similar vocabulary to talk about their poetic processes and are also part of the same poetic lineage, associating with overlapping circles of poets. Additionally, Weiner attended the important 1965 Berkeley Poetry Conference where Spicer gave one of his famous lectures. Spicer made the claim that the poet's role is to take "dictation" and that "essentially [the poet is] something which is being transmitted into."[18] In a lecture given in Vancouver in 1965 he explained: "there is an Outside to the poet. Now what the Outside is like is described differently by different poets. And some of them believe that there's a welling up of the subconscious or of the racial memory or the this or the that, and they try to put it inside the poet. Others take it from the Outside. Olson's idea of energy and projective verse is something that comes from the Outside" (*JB*, 5). Weiner too insists that the words she sees are other, or "Outside." Both Weiner and Spicer claim to be taking dictation (Spicer's source is "Martians," which he admits is a term he uses "just to be funny," and is actually interchangeable with any unknowable force [*JB*, 24]), but Weiner cares very much about the source, because she is looking for answers as much as for poetry in the words. Spicer speaks of "outer space" and "Martians" as a way to undercut "serious" critical vocabulary and return poetry to the realm of popular culture, while Weiner is more invested in merging the popular with the spiritual in poetry.

The early clair-style works of Weiner are autobiographical long poems that successfully capture her experience with the words *because* she yields to the words, believes in them, allowing for continuous interruptions of her life, and thereby of the texts she creates to document her life. *Pictures and Early Words*, *Big Words*, and, her best known work, *Clairvoyant Journal*, are all examples of a sort of late twentieth-century quest narrative. In *Clairvoyant Journal*, Weiner explains that she is on a mission to understand the source, and also the content, of the words:

> All these words occur whether I write or not, in my ordinary conscious state, not in a trance, and sometimes in sleep GET UPS appears on my forehead to wake me in time. FOR WHAT. Anything.
>
> I am trying to understand through my continued writing which of these WORDS I see are 1) my own ordinary conscious thought; 2) from my developed superconscious mind which has precognitive, clairvoyant powers; 3) telepathic connections with living people; 4) BIG QUESTION communications from non-living forces. (*OH*, 63)

Weiner is intent on figuring things out, on making sense of her experiences, and it is through her poetry, on the page, that she attempts to do so.

Her quest, however, is not future directed; it focuses on the present as an absolute. This is why clair-style is bound to a diaristic form – it is a present tense, real-time reckoning. Or, as she explains, "Many things happen at once, peculiar to journal form, to force interruptions" (*OH*, 129). Weiner is speaking literally: as she writes about the words she sees, new words appear, making it difficult to record them all. When words appear as she types her notebooks into manuscripts, these words, too, are typed into the text. Far from a poetics of concentration or precision, hers is one of inclusion, blind and without judgment. Nothing is left out, nothing is deemed unworthy of documentation. The words expose Weiner's private life to the reader ("*you slept with Rhys no orgasm*" [*CJ*, 27]). They are endlessly giving unasked-for relationship advice regarding her multiple lovers. But if Weiner listens to the commands and transcribes the voices, she also documents a life outside of the mind. Clair-style is the means through which she can do both. It marks an erasure of all boundaries between the inside life and the outside life and between public and private. Clair-style is her way of getting it all in.

Weiner's quest goes beyond the fact of the words, and one aspect of her experience of clairvoyance about which Weiner remains certain through all the early notebooks is that there is a reason for the words, and the signs before them. She's always certain that the "WORDS have political, ecological awareness, concern for others as well as myself, always suggesting a course that is to the most benefit of all concerned, to increase physical, psychological and mental well being, and reduce suffering[.]"[19] The painful, overwhelming nature of her encounter with this reality, whatever its source, has not deflated her expectation of enlightenment or a psychic boon. She remains convinced that the words are there to heal her even as they hurt her, and even as she admits her dissatisfaction with the quality of advice coming from the voices that insist on offering it. In *Pictures and Early Words*, written in 1972, she complains, "I'm still not getting what I ask for. Which is practical advice   All I'm getting is the no's."[20] The voices construct a prison of refusals, tethering her to her apartment. She tells the "unfriendly spirits" that she is "not going to listen" (PE, 23). But she can't ignore that which insists on being seen, that which tantalizes with the promise of transcendence. She yields because she sees herself as a student of the voices and of the universe they speak. The appearance of the first word is truly a defining moment in her life: she is instantly transformed from a poet to a mystic, a seer. And for Weiner this process is both serious and a joke: When she asks the voices, "When am I going to get to higher mind?" she reports that her "Navel says NOT YET NOT THIS BOOK" (PE, 34).

It is in the sprawling, stuttering, messy, never-published, 200-page manuscript *Big Words*, written in 1973, that her project begins to develop, and clair-style stumbles into being. The text begins, as does *Clairvoyant Journal*, at a yoga retreat; Weiner is convinced that yoga and meditation can help ease her physical ailments (digestive problems, sciatica, a sore hip and knee), and teach her how to read and decode "the words" (by this time omnipresent). The voices are a constant interference, but she wants to feel better and be better.

Big Words is written largely in the third person. On the face of it, her role is like that of a dispassionate scribe. However this text, like most of Weiner's others, offers a first-person explanation, on a page of its own, before the title page, before the book "really" starts. As usual, this information seems to have been added after the manuscript was written. It opens with the elucidation shown in figure 4.1.

Weiner has opened a conversation with the voices: a dictate is issued and Weiner complies, sort of.

Her "explanation" is more of a map key than a meaningful exploration of herself or the experiences she documents within the text. Rather than "explain herself" she explains the methodology of her writing, and thus draws a line between self and writing only to erase it almost immediately. But before she launches into the lengthiest textual explanation in any of

EXPLAIN YOURSELF

I SEE

words, IN CAPITAL LETTERS, on the typewriter page, on my forehead
(very large clear ones) on other people's foreheads, in the air,
on furniture, everywhere, in different sizes. I type them
in capital letters, or "put them in parentheses". NEGATIVE.
Certain phrases or positions of words are to be read in the negative
(just heard a voice say 'primitive' -THIRD EAR- astral hearing).
Words that R and @ these phrases are negative. ENOUGH. This word
E
means the A REVERSE as do other indefinite words such as now, soon, too
D
KNOWLEDGE. Some of these words convey information from
D
O psychic forces, some of it is accurate NOT ALL OF IT,
W
N and some words are OTHER PEOPLE'S thoughts.
kitty
The words between the lines are words I see and type in.

4.1 Hannah Weiner, *Clairvoyant Journal* (New York, NY: Angel Hair Books, 1974), 1. Image used by permission of Charles Bernstein for Hannah Weiner in trust.

the early notebooks, she pauses, narrows the reader's attention to two words, the two words that are the entire reason Weiner is writing *Big Words* and creating clair-style: "I SEE." Weiner is well aware that the cipher is complex and confusing, both to her, and thus, necessarily, to the reader. In this introductory note she is scientific about the genesis of the voices and words: they are outside, they are other. By disowning the words, she validates their message, attesting to their existence independent of herself; rather than just being the product of a disoriented mind, they become meaningful. However, since the phrase "I SEE" is itself in capital letters, according to the code just spelled out, the "I" is not Weiner. That is, the text begins with Weiner breaking the premise of the code, destabilizing as she defines, which seems to be a part of the game Weiner is playing. Perhaps the exact source of the words and whether they're to be read as instructions or as instructions to do the opposite – signified by "negative" and "reverse" in Weiner's early dealing with the voices – is less important to the reader, and to the reader's enjoyment or at least experience of the text, than to Weiner, who is convinced her health and happiness depend on getting it right. Weiner offers this key to her reader but also as a reminder to herself: if she can master the code, she can master the voices and regain control over her life.

Her sustained use of the third person – which begins with this manuscript – serves to distance Weiner from the confusion of her life and allows her to become an object of self-scrutiny. She types "for objective I suppose I should write in the 3rd person."[21] This ungrammatical resolution leaves the word "objective" open to being read as either an adjective or a noun. Yes, she wants to find a way to see her unique situation from the outside, objectively, but she is always writing with an object in mind: healing, clarity, and literary production. Her use of the third person is also a mandate from the voices, who near the top of the second page of the text, precede the sentence "I didn't want to walk, hip tired," with "SHE" and follow it with "3RD PERSON." This corrective insistence is emblematic of the overriding influence the forces have on her writing. She is grateful for the voices' corrective means of leading her to enlightenment; their insistent guidance is a gift. She claims, "she can't use I it's a game she doesn't know the rules SURPRISE she is supposed to be objective" (BW, 98). She reveals her continued confusion: "The words all in capitals, or all in small letters are written by them. They have the easy ones. She (I) uses Caps and smalls. The question is should we use she or I when referring to the SECRETARY" (BW, 164). According to this construct, Weiner's value as a poet is that she can transcribe the ephemeral and take dictation from the ether. The emphasis on the disowning of self for the sake of the product – the text – is echoed at another moment: "She, I, I am I again, wonder who writes the best record. who has the best records, plays? What does record refer to? WRITING" (BW, 27).

Although she may appear to be at the whim of the voices, and may "feel like a puppet to something someone" (BW, 147), there is a preternatural awareness in the writing about the possibilities that her often miserable experiences hold for literature. She is constructing something new, and not in order to fetishize "the new," but because the situation, the words, demand it. "DISTURB LANGUAGE" (BW, 172), the words say, and she and they together, do. She knows the book has created a new way of writing the life of the mind, and she writes, "Is thereanother book on open thought, another bookin air" (BW, 109).[22] It's fascinating to see Weiner construe this as a book "on" a specific topic. It seems more like a book that represents the experience of "open thought" – as she's calling it here for the first time – than one that contains an analysis of such. But of course, as usual, Weiner is quick to retract that scientific seriousness with the description of the text as a "bookin air." The book is perhaps best described by the words themselves as a text that answers the call to "KEEP POETRY ALIVE" (BW, 42). The poetry here is alive because the words it comprises have agency, are themselves, to Weiner, alive, and Weiner's job is to get them onto the page. Even before she writes it, the book exists. It is a strange collaboration between the writer and the words, which, according to her, she is not writing but that are otherwise willed into being by unknown forces. This confederation of voices *is* clair-style.

Clairvoyant Journal, published by Anne Waldman and Lewis Warsh's Angel Hair Books in 1978, is Weiner's masterpiece. Chronicling approximately four months in 1974, this long poem is the clair-style culmination of Weiner's ritualizing and systematizing of experience. Twenty years later, in "Silent Teacher," she describes *Clairvoyant Journal* as "a three voice / performance poetry book about learning explaining instructions / and the counter voice."[23] The only of her journals to actually be titled as such, it is both record of, and instructions for the performance of, a fraught but enlivening experience of "open thought."

The specificity with which she records is vital to the development of her autobiography as a record not of her past, but her present. Weiner is audience to the avant-garde New York art scene just as she is audience to the words. And, by interweaving the two terrains in her *Journal*, she creates an equivalency. They are all to be consumed and incorporated into her own project. Every aspect of her life is written and everything she sees or hears belongs to her. Thus in this first section of the first page alone, we are told of two performances, one by Phillip Glass and one by "Joe"; three performance spaces, La Mama, Tin Palace, and Sobosseks; and a popular publishing company, Doubleday. The pages of *Clairvoyant Journal* are also filled with names, as Weiner seems desperate to name everyone she meets everywhere she goes. Her experimental artist friends – including Bernadette Mayer, Rhys Chatham, Phil Niblock, and Charlemagne Palestine – she generally acknowledges by first name. Literary celebrities (such as Anaïs Nin) merit mention as well. Weiner lets her reader know that the hermitage period recorded in the earlier journals is over and rather than allowing her life to be stymied by the existence of the words, they have become a part of her life. And by capturing her experience of the time on the page, she captures the time.

With *Clairvoyant Journal,* the project of looking for coded messages in the words she sees shifts, and instead, Weiner makes her own code. It opens with this key:

> I SEE words on my forehead IN THE AIR
> On other people   on the typewriter   on the
> Page   These appear in the text in CAPITALS
>   Or *italics*   (*CJ*, 1)

Later, in the essay "Mostly about the Sentence," she would elaborate on her method:

> I bought a new electric typewriter in January 74 and said quite clearly, perhaps aloud, to the words (I talked to them as if they were separate from me, as indeed the part of my mind they came from is not known to me) I have this new typewriter and can only type lower case, capitals or underlines (somehow I forgot, ignored or couldn't cope with in the speed I was seeing things, a fourth voice, underlined capitals) so you will have to settle yourself into three different prints. Thereafter I typed the large printed words I saw in CAPITALS, the words that appeared on the typewriter or the paper I was typing on in underlines (italics) and wrote the part of the journal that was unseen, my own words, in regular upper and lower case.
>
> It turned out that the regular upper and lower case words described what I was doing, the CAPITALS gave me orders, and the underlines or italics made comments. This is not 100% true, but mostly so. (*OH*, 127)

The lowercase, non-italicized voice of Weiner in *Clairvoyant Journal* is nearly drowned out in the cacophony of instructions, comments on the text, random interruptions, and obscure personal and literary references. A reader will discern hostility in the voices towards Weiner and her text, and a reciprocal hostility on Weiner's part. In addition to transcribing the words she sees, where she sees them, and what they look like, she also includes her direct reply to these words, and a diary-like recounting of her everyday life.

Visually, clair-style is striking. The text resists the confines of typical typographic layout, and words creep up on each other, at times overlaid. Some words take on shapes or are written backwards. Other words are much larger than the rest, giving a sense of insistence, as if yelling at Weiner, demanding she heed their commands. Words fill the page, running, at times, vertically, diagonally, or even in a circle, all the while intersecting with the horizontal text. The linear text that unfolds in time is blasted to bits. With her typewriter, Weiner records a composition by committee, one page at a time.

Olson had characterized the typewriter as "the personal and instantaneous recorder of the poet's work," allowing the poet to compose "as though verse was to have the reading its writing involved, as though not the eye but the ear was to be its measurer, as though the intervals of its composition could be so carefully put down as to be precisely the intervals of its registration" (PCO, 246). To a comparable degree, the typewriter mediates Weiner's poetics:

> It is the advantage of the typewriter that, due to its rigidity and its space precisions, it can, for a poet, indicate exactly the breath, the pauses, the suspensions even of syllables, the juxtapositions even of parts of phrases, which he intends … For the first time he can, without the convention of rime and meter, record the listening he has done to his own speech and by that one act indicate how he would want any reader, silently or otherwise, to voice his work. (PCO, 245)

Weiner and Olson see the typewriter as a means to enhance communication through written language. With the use of this machine, the poet, not the printer or editor, is in control. Olson wants the typewriter to transcribe the poet's breath with a new nuance, but Weiner uses it to record something already external to herself. The words, while partially compliant to Weiner's recording them via typewriter, require that she break the very "rigidity" and "precisions" Olson relies on as meaningful to the reader, creating unexpected shapes and irregularities that themselves are expressive, and more importantly to the forces, accurately replicate what she sees.

In her dutiful recording of all the words that the forces show to her, Weiner proves her dedication to the project. Since every aspect of her life is invaded by the words, the content of the text really cannot be unlocked from its form. As her text is interrupted, so too is her life, and readers are witness to her writing of this trouble. The forces feel free to interrupt Weiner's daily life – "There's so much interference while I wash dishes" (CJ, 5) – but to them nothing is uninterruptable – "interference when we were about to fuck" (CJ, 31). The forces, though determined to help Weiner get it right, don't stop their interruptions even when she does as they ask: "How can I describe anything when all these interruptions keep *arriving* and then tell me I dont describe it well" (CJ, 6). The words don't just appear; they "arrive," which implies both an origin – unknown – and a destination – Weiner's field of view. These interruptions work their way into the text, defining it, but also prevent its completion.

Although the group writing of *Clairvoyant Journal* is continually foregrounded by the font system of capitals and italics, the text reveals much about Weiner's writing as a project guided by individual purpose. She writes pointedly about words in general, as opposed to the words she sees: "*eliminate the message* GOOD WORK *talk about* word as message, information story ... word as order *just* command unit of speech Word as instruction" (CJ, 2). She wants to reduce words to an indivisible, elemental state. And yet her goal seems more complicated than just that. The voices are telling her to strip language of its meaning ("*eliminate the message*"), but "the word" remains somehow pure, and most importantly, expressive. In order to convey or collect her ideas about the words she must "*talk about*" it. And yet she seems to be suggesting that *because* words contain messages they are simply ("*just*") instructions or commands, or orders that instill order. The voices are there to help with this very struggle to explain words through words.

Weiner works to free her readers from the tyranny of authority in order to open their minds to truth, just as she, by relinquishing her own authority, becomes an author of texts charged with metaphysical authority. She has not abandoned her earlier goal of being "full of energy and wide awake" and of gaining access to a "higher mind."[24] She wants to effect these enlightened states in her readers, and has a plan for doing so. Only a broken text, built up out of the incomplete and interrupted sentence, can penetrate the reader's consciousness.[25] Weiner creates works that are not about writing but "clear" communication, or as she proclaims in her book *Spoke*, written in 1981, "its not writing time show the mind."[26] Weiner's rationale for the erasure of the ego is directly tied to her insistence on her own clairvoyance, which itself directs her form and content. Her mission requires the production of texts that trace and testify to her self-erasure, recorded everywhere in her books.

As Weiner writes about her life, she creates a text that also lives: "*realize write something you are documenting it*" (CJ, 30). More than simply documenting, her consciousness of doing so makes the words, and her experience of seeing the words, real, material, and "*realize*" becomes multiple. Heeding the instructions means she's not passive, she's subject, and when she tells us that the words tell her "DONT TALK YOU SEE WORDS" (CJ, 3), she accepts her role. Weiner is important to the text because only she is capable of seeing the words and, therefore, of writing them. The forces won't let her forget that her active role in the production of the text requires a passivity on her part. Weiner's "talking" would merely be a waste of misdirected energy – her job is to see clearly, clairvoyantly. Seeing is doing; she is stenographer for a world that for others is outside of consciousness.

Weiner's disappearing act is supposed to allow for a direct relation between the words she sees and the words on the page. But it is an illusory disappearance, just as the transparency of language – the invisibility of the cultural apparatuses that lend words meanings – is an illusion. This parallel is productive poetically: the clunky ineffective beauty of language is projected onto Weiner's body and her texts. If she got it right and with perfect unobtrusiveness, leaving no trace of herself, followed the instructions and documented the words, there would be no text, because the heart of *Clairvoyant Journal* is the documenting of the impossibility of scribal invisibility. Weiner claims to be following orders issued by forces that are themselves fixated on their successful transcription; the words want her to get it right and quote them correctly without revealing too much of herself. She's reprimanded by voices who insist she "*just retype this original page*" (CJ, 5) and "*write much simpler*" (CJ, 16) and "CLOSE THIS SPACE" (CJ, 27), and following these orders amounts to the diminution of Weiner's authority, her authorship.

This text is not to be crafted, but written by rote. And, as the recording of consciousness is the recording of time (as experienced), there is an urgent need for Weiner to "MAKE IT CORRECT TOO MANY STOPS THE ENERGY INCREASES" (*CJ*, 17). She needs to get it right the first time, as the words are translated from air to page, and she is warned, "DONT MAKE ANY MORE CORRECTIONS" (*CJ*, 28) and "*dont edit it spoils the sequence*" (*CJ*, 31). Weiner, and the reader, cannot forget that the *Journal* is a product of dictation. Editing disturbs the immediacy of the communiqué and risks mistranslating the message. It's dangerous: "You pick up the Oct ms hear Jim's voice BE CAREFUL a shout you put it back, SLEEPY lie down, take Oct in the bedroom, DON EDIT [...] Comments as you read Oct you dont dare edit it" (*CJ*, 34). Weiner is the reader of the original words, and when she reads the manuscripts in which she recorded these words, she sees more words, and documents them as she documents her reading of the manuscript.

Her major flaw as a scribe is her voice – her style, her wit, her humour – which is everywhere, and which, when too muffled for too long, complains, "it's doing all the writing," only to be answered, "YOU SHOULD COMMENT" (*CJ*, 22). The voices offer her a diluted version of agency – she's reduced to a commenter in her own book: "Jesus Christ all these words are underlinings" is followed by the all caps, "UNDELINE YOUR OWN THATS THE ANSWER." To which Weiner responds, "no more words" (*CJ*, 19). Again, the voices give her permission to write, but underlining her own words would mean assigning them to the spirits, so even her words would belong to them. She recognizes that there is only one way for her to really write her own book and that is if there were "no more words," which would of course make the very writing of such a book impossible. This issue of ownership is complicated by the sentence "THIS IS MY POEM" (*CJ*, 56), in all capital letters, which has the rare privilege of being alone on a line, interference free. Weiner wonders, "who is I, you, me *the pronouns*" (*CJ*, 42).

For Weiner, the production of the text – and the experience it records – is all still leading somewhere, and although she is committed to scribing, she can't give up her need to read the words as well, ever searching for latent meaning, as the passage reproduced in figure 4.2 demonstrates.

She tries to please the voices by following their confusing "orders," and in return she gets "clues" to the secrets of the metaphysical world, to healing. Perhaps most keenly for her, she reads – and transcribes – the words

and *wear dungarees* *oh h a n n a h* these words appear BIG RHYS OPERA that's Mike
not alright June everything is a clue or an order or writing *not so take a walk*
Bernadette where's the *clues* The underlines and caps I see HEAL ME
oversensitive
You I hear this but usually *ugly see Joan* stomach problem YOU'LL HIT ME sure
NEGATIVE was glad to find *not in the winter be grateful* that was an ESP
term your name SO WHAT has been appearing around here a lot so it's in this
book JUNIOR some publisher is looking at it now *big question stop typing* BIG

4.2 Hannah Weiner, *Clairvoyant Journal* (New York, NY: Angel Hair Books, 1974), 29. Image used by permission of Charles Bernstein for Hannah Weiner in trust.

as writing. For instance, she informs the reader, "SO WHAT has been appearing around here a lot so it's in this book." The formula is that simple for the writing, while she continually has cause to lament that the clues and orders are too obtuse and opaque to be truly useful. And yet, Weiner trusts the words more than ever, and can now unwaveringly state, "The underlines and caps I see HEAL ME." What could have once been read as a plea is presented as fact.

She's healed when she "*let it happens read it write*":

was in the hotel for Sunday services *see the hospital* *he tried twice*
Bowery
Phil Niblock TELL YOU WHY *phone off the hook* *penis deficiency* *petty*
let it ring
novel *one more week* *let it happens read it write* *get instructions* *Charlestein*
written
degraded him also *Charlatan* *who* *see the little* BIG WHO IN *your money*

4.3 Hannah Weiner, *Clairvoyant Journal* (New York, NY: Angel Hair Books, 1974), 16. Image used by permission of Charles Bernstein for Hannah Weiner in trust.

The "let it happens" and the "get instructions" once again speak to the authorial emptying at the core of her project: Weiner's work is to do what she's told. The punning on "read it right" and "read it write" displays a typically dense moment of layered meanings in Weiner's vocabulary; getting it right, mastering the code, is a matter of conflating reading and writing. Her self-abasement is the invalidating of the unitary self as a literary source, but it's also premised on the self as a vessel or scribe-self that rather than being abased is elevated.

If she empties herself for the words, they will fill her with something better, thus the promise that she "CAN TRANSCEND THIS STUPID bad girl REALITY":

> BIG EMOTIONS BIG FOOL you're an important WOW someone THING is
> trying give up SLEEP SYMPATHY HE APPROVES happiness you have
> enough money in purse PROVI dence YOU CAN TRANSCEND THIS STUPID
> bad girl REALITY WALK TWO DAYS DONT LEAVE TELL THE VERY

4.4 Hannah Weiner, *Clairvoyant Journal* (New York, NY: Angel Hair Books, 1974), 48. Image used by permission of Charles Bernstein for Hannah Weiner in trust.

The lowercase words in this excerpt, "you're an important someone is trying give up happiness," combined with the sequential appearance of "BIG EMOTIONS BIG FOOL," reveal the evolution of Weiner's poetics. Being "important" requires sloughing off all human emotions, which are not productive, but the purview of a "big fool." For Weiner, transcendence requires absolute submission of herself to the experience of seeing words, and allowing "normal," ego-driven, emotional life to be ruled by her own reception and transcription of them.

The same thing that she believes gives her power – access to the words – also amounts to an endless process of transcending the self but only by relinquishing the self. This idea is rooted in the Yogic philosophy that was so important to Weiner, but, again, echoes Spicer's dictum: "try to keep as much of yourself as possible out of the poem" (*JB*, 8). The stacking of "*crazy girl*" on top of "WRITE YOU HAVE SIMPLE ORDERS" (*CJ*, 57) crystallizes the problem for Weiner. There is discord between the world of the words and the world of the self. She's being told that she has "SIMPLE ORDERS," but these directives either are making her a "*crazy girl*" or exist because she already is one. The same voices that insist on her special abilities also must convince her of her lack of any specialness, so she'll freely abandon herself to the words and serve them. She's tantalized: "IT COULD WRITE YOU COULD BE DISTINGUISHED HAPPY WRITE POEMS" (*CJ*, 56). If she lets "IT" write, the "YOU" can take the credit and find literary success.

Eventually, the voices are satisfied with her technique and so compliments directed at the text are incorporated into the text. She records,

"HANNAH THIS IS THE BEST PAGE HANNAH THIS IS MAY" (*CJ*, 30). By the end, both the words and Weiner realize that together they've succeeded poetically: "you read April MAKE NOTES it's pretty funny you think you're a genius WE ALL ARE" (*CJ*, 35).

While in some ways it appears that aesthetic or poetic goals have overshadowed Weiner's spiritual quest, in reality, the successful development of clair-style, her accomplishment as a writer in finding a way to document her life and experience, allows her to accept her situation, which is reflected in the words she sees. Weiner's spiritual quest evolves in tandem with her poetics. The very first words in the book are "GO FOR A SAMADHI / *feel different.*"[27] Weiner links a practical, immanent goal to a transcendental one: she wants her spiritual work to reap real results. By the end of the *Journal*, Weiner receives the message, "YOU COME HOME YOUR OBEDIENCE TRIAL ARE OV.R. no TRIALS YOU ARE AN OBEDIENT GIRL" (*CJ*, 44).

For Weiner, the book is a literary, and therefore, in her own construct, spiritual, success: "YOU REACH SAMADHI YOU HAVE A BIG ANNOUNCEMENT YOU *hear* ONE FEEL DIFFERENT CONSCIOUS TELE-phone. That's a *think about it*" (*CJ*, 50). The goal stated at the start of the book is reached. She feels different because she has (apparently) achieved enlightenment. "SAMADHI" and "ANNOUNCEMENT" are connected and bracketed by " YOU," Weiner. For her, this new state of consciousness is coextensive with its "BIG ANNOUNCEMENT," which is to say, its writing. The very last word in *Clairvoyant Journal* is "COMPLETE," and indeed Weiner has not just finished but successfully completed her project of developing a poetics to convey the unsettled terms of authorship that rule the book and her life.[28] In a move that somehow eerily and awkwardly captures the experience of reading *Clairvoyant Journal*, Weiner writes, "POETRY: YOU CAN REACH A HIGHER LEVEL OF INSANITY" (*CJ*, 47). Just on top of the word "REACH," overlapping but barely, in Weiner's own non-italicized, lower-case font, is the word "joke."

Weiner laces *Clairvoyant Journal* with a disarming humour that softens the sadness and horror of her loss of control over her life and normalizes the "INSANITY" of the situation. If she can laugh at her reality, she can control it. If she laughs when the words mock her, she's in on the joke. And so is the reader. Weiner's jokes or plays on words are often linked to the making of the text and to the process of her experiences: "*take her out* COMMENT of the book or to dinner?" (*CJ*, 2). These moments can be shocking to the reader as they often materialize in the midst of what is purported to be a document of a traumatic experience. Her earlier works skirt around humour and the ridiculous in ways that foreshadow her future reliance on both; in *The Fast* she writes, "I began to laugh at my melodrama and the embarrassing spectacle I was making of myself."[29] Later, when reflecting on some of the more playful rituals she created during the three-week period described in *The Fast* (including covering herself in blueberry syrup and decorating her arm in fennel seeds), she writes, "I was never totally serious about doing these things – they seemed amusing ways to entertain myself."[30] And so, when Weiner, in *Clairvoyant Journal*, records a conversation with Rhys Chatham – "Told him how … the forces showed me all my failings with words in order to overcome he said it was *hemorroids* no purification by fire" (CJ, 4) – there's a joke (at her own expense, as is typical) in the middle of something that Weiner seems to want us to believe is dead serious. A spiritual conversation between lovers does double duty as potty humour because Weiner complies and lets the voices interrupt her text.

This issue of seriousness is as complicated as it is important. It's difficult for a reader to accept that Weiner's writing isn't at core genuine. If she was writing merely to entertain herself rather than to reach the objectives to which she's committed, it would be an affront to the reader. While *Clairvoyant Journal* itself may be a piece that can be staged, the Weiner we see in the book cannot, must not, be simply putting it on for her readers. The time during which she was writing the early journals appears to have been more troubling for Weiner than when she was writing *Clairvoyant Journal*. Weiner would have been manipulating the reader if her straightforward documentation in the early journals was not really that, but a game or a ruse. However, by the time she's writing *Clairvoyant Journal*, clair-style is full realized, and she's following the rules that she recognizes as defining clair-style. It's a codified poetics, regardless of its source or muse or etiology. The words that Weiner tells the reader are directing the creation of the text as such, become, in fact, the words of the text.

Despite her role as the butt of the voices' jokes, Weiner is desperate to maintain a levity of her own. At a yoga retreat (the visit to which she documents at the end of *Clairvoyant Journal*), she is having a difficult time gaining access to the ashram's typewriter. She agrees to do the work of transcribing the speeches of the yogi Satchidananda – Weiner's guru at the time – from tape to type in order to be allowed to use the machine for her own transcription project. She's disappointed when the words won't amuse on cue: "You have a typewriter and *complain* CLEAN THOUG cravings for typewriters CUT IT SHORT when you couldn't type Sun Mon ADDICT IT'S COOL in the typing room so why won't they be funny" (*CJ*, 54)

Perhaps the most distinguishable sign that Weiner's work while serious isn't overly earnest is the cover of *Clairvoyant Journal*. The photograph on the cover of the book is of a smiling Weiner with "I SEE WORDS" written on her forehead in what looks to be black marker. If not a joke, the depiction of Weiner with words visible on her forehead is clearly an exaggeration of what Weiner claims to be true. The photograph participates in the blurring between inside and outside, reality and delusion, present everywhere in Weiner's work, and displays how these problems can be tempered by humour. This single image embodies much of the complexities of identity, authorship, and consciousness that Weiner manipulates in her work. She's literally marked by the words, but she's still laughing; and by making the words she sees visible in the place where she often sees them, she wryly stages her claim.

The levity of the work is unmistakable when it is performed, as it has been a number of times in different versions and in different manners. It is only in the multi-voice performances of pieces of *Clairvoyant Journal* that the work is fully actualized for the reader/audience. The three-person performances by Weiner and her collaborators are gleeful. The performers' embodying of these words has another effect, which, partially, accounts for the light-heartedness of the performances: the words lose their initial associations with what Weiner believes to be their metaphysical sources, the forces that harassed her into creating the text.

In a 1978 studio recording of the March section, Weiner starts at the beginning of the text, offering her typical introductory explanation of the textual code, but adding the readers' names, explaining that Sharon Mattlin reads the capital letters and Margaret De Coursey reads the underlines.[31] "I read mine," she continues. And, with an "I begins," the reading of the text commences. Midway through the second page Weiner ad-libs an "I see words" after the words "*code poem*," which are italicized in the text, are read. For the first few minutes, Weiner seems hardly able to follow her own text, forgetting to stop when the text is no longer the lower-case, non-italicized font that is hers. "I get confused," she extemporizes.

Weiner incorporates the names of her collaborators, "Peggy" and "Sharon": sometimes tying the name to a phrase in the text and other times just randomly voicing it. She also mentions the name "Charlie," referring to Charlie Morrow, who is presumably nearby doing the work of recording the performance. The people in the room are becoming part of the reading. Towards the end, Weiner adds, "Mention your friends. It doesn't seem fair not to." A restive practice makes an unstable text. Everything and everyone Weiner rubs against sticks to the text. She's compelled to turn it all into content, into the *Journal*. She feels free to improvise, obligated perhaps. To add yet another layer of disjointed and confused authority, she also instructs Mattlin and De Coursey to "read faster," and laughs. Weiner, receiver of endless instructions, is the one making demands here.

Clairvoyant Journal needs an audience, and becomes most animated when performed for other people. Charlie Morrow also recorded a reading by Rochelle Kraut, Sharon Mattlin, and Weiner of the May section of the *Journal*, performed at St Mark's Poetry Project in New York City in 1978.[32] Weiner issues a directive to herself to "introduce your readers," which she immediately heeds: "That's Sharon reading the capitals." Then a few lines later, "introduce Shelley as she reads the underlines. They're the little words that appear, you know, in little places like my forehead and things." The audience's response is laughter. Weiner, still with laughter in her voice says, "You're interrupting my reading" to either the readers or the audience. As in the studio recording, she repeatedly interjects the readers' names into the performance. She also explains just a few minutes in, "This is last year's script" and a minute or so later states, "this is a journal." And she's not the only one free to ad-lib. Mattlin acknowledges a mistake – "oops, I skipped a line" – adding to an already chaotic performance. Things seem to fall apart a bit as the readers scramble to keep their spots and are forced by the text to read over each other. The reaction from the readers and the crowd is the same: pleasure. Weiner is incorporating demands here too, including "skip a line." "They read together," Weiner announces just after Mattlin and Kraut do, but then says, "no more comments." In its performance, the real-time text-making of the written *Journal* becomes even more present tense than before. It's a text that is being amended, rewritten, as it's read. "Make Shelley make more comments," Weiner says, and Shelley responds, "ha ha," making Weiner chuckle. During a personal section about her troubled relationship with Rhys Chatham she seems surprised that "nobody laughs," which makes some laugh. A section about Weiner eating donuts out of the garbage seems to amuse the crowd and they laugh even as Mattlin reads the "DON'T LAUGH" that is repeated in the text.

The only people who are aware of the degree to which things are being interpolated during the performance are Weiner and her readers. And so when Weiner says, "skip the rest of the page," and the readers do, the listener has no way of knowing if they're missing out on something or if this direction originated with the voices. The performers take Weiner's position, and not because they are reading her *Journal*, but because they are now subject to the voices and the subject of the voices and they, too, are overwhelmed by the words. Weiner's "read fast," which becomes part of the aural text, is directed at them.

The very last page of the manuscript version of *Clairvoyant Journal*, dated "Nov 2 1977" contains Weiner's reflection on the performance of the *Journal*, written at a time when she was no longer seeing words regularly. The entry begins, "TONIGHT WAS A REHEARSAL Lots of people laughed Is that good question mark." It seems strange that Weiner, who has used humour so purposefully and deftly in *Clairvoyant Journal* would wonder how to read the laughter of the audience. Especially since, later on the same page she writes, "I loved the reading tonight both sharon and shelly were insanely good and laughed and poked and skipped nots too much and it charlie worked real hard boy was that a FREE gift." The laughter of the readers is a benefit to the performance, an essential part of it, Weiner seems to imply. But, perhaps her insecurity about the audience's laughter is rooted in her own insecurities about the text and what the people she knows are thinking of her and her claim to have special access to higher knowledge. *Clairvoyant Journal* rivals confessional poetry in its nakedness, and Weiner embraces this nakedness. When she says she is clairvoyant, she wants to be believed.

While Weiner's diagnosis as mentally ill is less easy to pin down than the opinions of others as to what caused the illness or Weiner's rejection of said diagnosis – there is no authoritative biography in existence – here, on this very last page of the manuscript of the *Journal*, Weiner writes, "because im insane i get social security i can write and complain til IS DIE." This moves beyond the casual references to being "crazy" peppering her books because here she refers to the reality of this claim, an official confirmation of her mental status, however ironically she may view it. She may not think she is mentally ill, but the state does, which provides her with the money to fund her life as a writer.

The related question of whether Weiner was genuinely clairvoyant is hard to avoid. In her review of *Hannah Weiner's Open House*, critic Maria Damon writes of the photo of a young Weiner that is on the book's cover, "She doesn't look as if she would end up schizophrenic, alone, reclusive, delusional/clairvoyant, loved by her sorely tested literary friends and supporters but ultimately beyond their reach, which she did."[33] Damon's use of "delusional/clairvoyant" reflects the reader's apprehension about Weiner's insistence on the external origin of the words. Even without hearing the lighthearted recordings of the performance of *Clairvoyant Journal*, the book as an object provokes uncertainty. The striking cover of the book is matched by the statement on the back cover by Jackson Mac Low:

> Hannah Weiner is the only clairvoyant I know, or that I've ever known, as far as I know. She is also the only person on record – or so she believes as a result of her extensive investigations into both medical & parapsychic literature – to have experienced the particular phenomenon this journal represents, that of being "spoken to" by several persons, most of them seemingly external to herself, by means of printed words in various colors & sizes that appear both on other persons & objects & on her own forehead (in such a way that she can perceive them from within). Hers, however, might have been but a "remarkable case," were it not for the fact that she is an artist. Her achievement – & it is a considerable one – lies in her having developed a literary form through which to convey her remarkable experience.

In many ways this statement encapsulates the problem of Weiner's poetics. Mac Low's qualifying of his statement, through the use of quotation marks, and the phrase "seemingly external to herself," calls into question the reality of her claim to be clairvoyant. Likewise, after Weiner's death, Bernstein writes, "I found her insistence on her clairvoyance to be a welcome relief from the heavy-handed rhetoric of poet as prophet that she so utterly rejected."[34] An "insistence on clairvoyance" is not the same thing as clairvoyance.

In her review of *Clairvoyant Journal*, published in the May–June 1979 issue of the *Poetry Project Newsletter*, Sharon Mattlin, one of the performers of the *Journal*, reinforces the idea that Weiner's clairvoyance was always a contested fact or an open question:

> "Is she really clairvoyant," is a question frequently asked of me in reference to Hannah Weiner. "Does she really see words?" is another.
>
> Hannah's journal, while "clairvoyant" in the dictionary sense of "having the power of seeing objects or actions beyond the normal range of vision," has the more significant power to reveal the workings of our own minds to us. She has an exceptional ability to transcribe the language of the mind talking to itself. She traces the self-denigration we all suffer, "stupid girl," as well as the self-congratulation, "this is terrific old girl"; the maternal aspect that has us advise ourselves to "GO OUT, GET A HARD ROLL," and the obsessive quality of a crush that might express itself in recurring admonitions to "call Rhys."
>
> This writing is spiritual, not so much in its references to retreats, Satchidananda, or Rimpoche, but more in the way it practices the Buddhist dictum to "watch your thoughts." Though meditation is, for me, a spectator sport only, I recognize *Clairvoyant Journal* as a form of meditation-in-action, or meditation-in-art.
>
> The answer to question number 2 is also yes. I'm convinced that she really does "see", in some sort of visual and/or audio hallucination, the words she writes. But, as with Castaneda's supposedly anthropological investigations, I don't think it really matters whether this is truth or fiction. The value lies in the literary achievement.[35]

Mattlin's laudatory review, like Mac Low's statement and the obituary written by Bernstein (cited above), complicates more than clarifies. When Mattlin claims that the "power" of Weiner's work resides in its "transcrib[ing] the language of the mind talking to itself," she in effect erases the singularity of Weiner's experiences. The assertion that Weiner makes so neatly – "I see words" – is hard to buy, and Mattlin testifies to her belief in its veracity only to immediately state that the truthfulness of the statement is irrelevant. Although she insists she's "convinced," she uses the literal definition of clairvoyance to undercut Weiner's own beliefs and the claims. The one thing that everyone agrees on is that the book is funny, however uncomfortable it may be to laugh.

Weiner herself never doubted her clairvoyance. The words were always a gift. They made her, and in turn her writing, special, "novel." Her desire to write new, exciting, innovative poetry was not odd; in fact, it was what connected her to the larger experimental poetry scene in New York and elsewhere. But clair-style did set Weiner apart. In the *Journal* entry dated "Jan 77 p3" – in the manuscript version – when the words had largely disappeared, Weiner wrote, "Oh how I miss them." They made life hard, but writing easy. About the quieting of the words and voices that had hectored her into typing her book in air, she added, "I notice lately I have been able to complete sentence. I ALSO. Don be ashamed. But I am. Everyone can complete sentences ANYONE and it was so much fun being interrupted like way back in 74 PICKLES but that doesn't happen anymore. I dont even eat pickles anymore."[36]

5

The Lyric Turn: A Poetics of Falling

ERÍN MOURE

> Todos os discursos, qualquer que fosse o seu estatuto,
> a sua forma, o seu valor, e qualquer que fosse o tratamento
> que se lhes desse, desenrolar-se-iam no anonimato do murmúrio.
> Michel Foucault, *Ditos e Escritos III*[1]

O cadoiro is, literally, *the place where falling is made*. In Galician, *cadoiro* is one word for waterfall. *Cataract*, perhaps. Thus, *the fall*. This to me is the place of poetry. For whoever writes poetry must be prepared, ever, to fall down.

And in 2004 I did fall. Having already fallen into Galician and then Portuguese, I had barely stood up again when I fell – or leapt – into one of the founts of lyric in Western Europe, the troubadour poetry of the medieval Galician-Portuguese songbooks, the *cancioneiros*. These songbooks hold what remains to us of the two hundred years of medieval Iberian poetry, all written in Galician-Portuguese, predecessor of both modern Portuguese and modern Galician. Influenced by Provençal verse of courtly love, the Iberian peninsular *cantigas* also bent and amplified that lineage, incorporating indigenous elements, such as evocations of the sea, or the tradition of women's song.

The troubadour verse speaks to us in the first-person singular, in a breach with the epic narrative mode and with ecclesiastical modes of praise. Gregorian chant and Arab love poetry preceded and infiltrated it, just as Provençal poetry was concurrent with it. Richard Zenith, attentive translator of these Iberian *cantigas* into English,[2] in his *An Unsung Literature* wrote: "The troubadour poetry that began in Provence and spread in all directions – northern France, Germany, Italy and Iberia – was one of the first expressions of the unrelenting individuality that was to shake the Church's foundations via heterodox reform movements and eventually lead to the Renaissance."[3] In this verse, the speaker's own subjectivity, own feelings, are the poetic "substance," yet these are quite consciously *constructed* by the poet, never "unmediated," always social, intended, and profane: directed toward another human, not to God. This human "turn" is at the very root of lyric, and the act of turning is a movement of incredible fragility and febrility – a turning away from God's love and its purported sufficiency toward a secular love that never purports sufficiency.

Three Iberian songbooks have come down to us. Together (for they are not entirely coincident), they hold three main types of poems: *de amor, de amigo, de escarnio e maldizer.* Courtly love; feminine longing for the absent lover; scorn and slander: such ripples in language. After years of dreaming "Erín, go to Lisbon to read the books," I went to live in Lisbon in early 2004 to read these *cancioneiros.*

It was as if the geeky Lee Meriwether had let go of her clipboard and entered The Time Tunnel.[4] Reading is already ever a wandering and in Lisboa, Olispoa, port of Odysseus, I entered the *cancioneiros.* The "fingerprints" of these books – their inscription, their orthography, their graphemes – took hold of me. How I loved the movements and jointings of the lines and letters that lay bare the cadence of voices and the attention/inattention of the copying hand. In the *cantigas de amigo* of the *Cancioneiro da Biblioteca Nacional,* and in the *cantigas de amor* of the *Cancioneiro de Ajuda,* I fell into such tapestries of word and sound, the "wallpaper"-repetitive sonorities of, yes, an unrequited love. Oh *cancioneiros,* oh ports of portu-cale, with the lilt of Celtic marking the vernacular of vanished Rome. *Camiñarmos polas palabras …*

▲●▲

The most extensive of these three songbooks, the *Cancioneiro da Biblioteca Nacional,* holds over sixteen hundred *cantigas* of all types. It was copied, or created, in the sixteenth century, three hundred and fifty years after the *cantigas* were first written and, curiously, not in Portugal or Galicia but in Italy, from an earlier copy or perhaps two copies on scrolls that were likely disintegrating at the time of transcription and which may have been contemporary with the troubadours. At the time of this copying, the first grammars of Portuguese were only just appearing; the written language was not yet as settled as our English is now.[5] As such, the script of the *cancioneiro* follows the pace and expression of the troubadours' voices. In these songbooks, poetry works against itself as mythic quantity, as transcendence, as voice; here, writing itself scratches the lyric.

By closely studying the poems in a lithographed reproduction of a photographic facsimile of the sixteenth-century manuscript (the "original" was too fragile), itself copied from an "original" and vanished apograph, and studying later transcriptions as well – critical/diplomatic but also modern anthologized versions, I hoped to respond with my own corporeal presence to questions that burned, and burn, for me:

What is a work of art?
What is an archive?
What does it mean to "trobar" today?

▲●▲

Reading the songbooks, I was very aware of reading a copy of a copy of a copy. With Derrida's *Mal d'archive* and Foucault's *Archéologie du savoir* echoing in me, I let the poems' so-called secondary effects absorb me – the many aspects of the poems eliminated by modernizing transcribers who diverge and alter them in their effort to make "content," "regularities of form," and the "author's intent" appear. I began to recognize that the idea of an "original" poem is ever-elusive; the original exceeds our grasp *always*.

I looked to discern, in my own way, the first copyist's (who was of course never first at all) markings, looked for the surfaces the copyists might have seen and then reproduced, and I examined how they made the forms before my eyes. The original script – simple, smudged, and worn – is beautiful; in it, the words' physical presence is a veritable record of breath and rhythms of speech, of accent. In this script, and in its forms on the page, I looked at what propelled lyric, what made it *palpable*. What could not be standardized, so was later dropped. What was called an error.

The poems awed me with the liquidity of their repetitive sonority, the levels of non-meaning, of plaint, of vibratory extension. This sonority breaks against the reader's own *langue de fond* as surprise and murmur, in that traverse or cut that a person schooled in one language experiences in reading another.

The *cantigas* opened other lyric doors to me, too. I discovered the medieval synchronic sense of time, a space where the solace of the Fichtean curve (with its rising action, conflict, climax, denouement) does not operate. As Portuguese scholar Stephen Reckert says: "we see here the typical medieval disregard for chronological sequence, often substituted by a vision of events that was simultaneous and pictorial."[6] Narrative advances differently. The aspect of salvation and new life, introduced later into lyric by Dante in his *Vita Nuova*, is not yet present, and without the prospect of salvation – the resacralization of the profane – linearity does not function in the same overarching way.

▲●▲

The *cantigas de amor* especially and perversely drew me. They are the poems most influenced by Provençal verse, that is, by the conventions of courtly love, and express a kind of sexless longing where bodies never touched and names were never named: a sexual tension and withholding. These *cantigas* are so repetitive, so predictable, yet within a few set phrases and conceits, schemes of very regular rhyme and metre, they induce such *saudade*, longing, *soidade*, loneliness. Their sonority is their beauty; their repetition is their glamour. They embrace banality on banality's terrain and then exit it on some other field entirely. What emerges is an expression of great peace and longing and breath and orphic variability. Variability, yes, for mastery was often shown by deviations, by a simple twist, a break, by a line that didn't rhyme. These disruptions of expectation, these disjoints, marked delight, excellence.

The *cantigas de amigo* are much closer to what we today recognize as lyric – on the surface. Beneath it, there's a sexual mixage and gender usurpation that highlights the constructedness of the voice – for men write in the voices of women, borrowing from a long-standing local tradition of women's song that likely predated Roman occupation and is still present in Galicia today. These poems are not courtly but common and, in them, concrete images emerge for the first time. In response, I wrote plaints of my own, enacting, mixing and echoing, translating but two or three poems and enclosing them among those that are sheer invention, and attributing my own poems impulsively to whichever troubadour's name was most proximate in my notebooks.

▲●▲

The forms and plaints of the *cantigas* thus seeped into my work, unseating forms, compelling variegated sounds and capacities, irregularities. Now, I hope, the cantigas, rife with ambiguities and errors, can resonate for us, too, in Canada, in English. With the *cancioneiros* as *fond* from which to draw sounds and layerings of interpretation, transcription, my sole aim was to transpose a tone and delicacy, a splendour, a visual pleasure into my own poems. A wandering and turn.

The exchange from one language to another in the work occurs, above all, on the level of tropes, soundscapes. At the same time, my poems incorporate formal structures of archive (use archival numbering, and the names of troubadours, as part of what I wrote), the material substrate of the *cantigas*. Related texts and textures also enter the poems, pushing at or revealing aspects not of the original text but of my own transcription of the transcription in the photograph, printed on a printing press, of the transcription of the now-lost apograph we have never seen that we so confidently call the *original*. And subject to noise, to the noise of my own being and experience and language. They are, simply, poems.

In a reverse tide, understandably, the troubadours started to infiltrate my other reading. In Jacques Derrida's *Mal d'archive*, which I read wandering the steep streets of Lisbon in the February rain, I discovered an *archive ache* that his words do not anticipate, one which in *tone* approaches the Galician/Portuguese untranslatable word *saudade*. Derrida "sounds like" the medieval *cantigas de amor*. It is as if the *cantigas* also, secretly, bear something of the Hebraic.[7] As I worked, I began to corrupt and invent Derridean lament into the text'ure of the paper, creating three-dimensional readings, volumes, and even performances, interactions with other people, with stone walls, with spaces and texts and voices. As if I could learn better how the poems could work on the page by disturbing what we know of page itself. What I give the reader of these poems is a synchronic band of libidinal space-time where *writing itself scratches the lyric* and where the thread of speech itself is palpable, illumined.

In *The End of the Poem*, Giorgio Agamben wrote:

> the troubadours want not to recall arguments consigned to a *topos* but instead to experience the very event of language as original *topos* … an absolute proximity of love, speech, and knowledge. The *razo*, which lies at the foundation of poetry and constitutes what the poets call its dictation (*dictamen*), is therefore neither a biographical nor a linguistic event. It is instead a zone of indifference, so to speak, between lived experience and what is poeticized, an "experience of speech" as an inexhaustible experience of love. *Amor* is the name given by the troubadours to this experience of the dwelling of speech in the beginning: and for them love is therefore the *razo de trobar* par excellence.[8]

Such was the place where I fell. It became "place" in the act of falling. A place where I could fall and keep falling. Where I wrote poems that were palimpsests, markings, and echoes bearing the shiver of the archive. Origin is always already lost here, lost again and again, and its very losing makes origin possible. And if this fallen trajectory of origin stabilizes at all, it is somewhere far ahead of it. At the time of reading. No wonder we trip and fall.

As Derrida urges: "The question of the archive is the question of the future, of the future itself, a question of a response, of a promise and a responsibility for tomorrow. If we wish to know what the archive is trying to tell us, we cannot know but in the time to come. Perhaps."[9]

Perhaps. Poetry is a remnant that moves toward a future people, says Chus Pato (my translation, paraphrased from her *Secesión*).

Is this the reason why I find myself, again, and ever, in the falling-down place? The place poetry is made. The "not-yet." The very falling poses the question of the future. The Peninsular – Iberian or other – is not an island, but part of the Maine. In its turning from the certainties of God to a human insufficiency, it is a promise and a responsibility for tomorrow, *Mâine*. And this, "peu importe qui parle."

What I hope my poems open to readers, as they did to me, their first reader, is that a subjectivity, an I, an *eu*, in entering and being altered by words, fallen, befallen, enters the *saudade* of world. Enters Agamben's "whatever singularity." Enters Norma Cole's "body of expectation." Fred

Wah's "music at the heart of thinking." Robin Blaser's "image nation." Or his "cry of Merlin." Fanny Howe's "full heart." Lisa Robertson's "stuttered accoutrements." Chus Pato's "infinite of language." Choral. *Nin sen chorar*.

6

By the Numbers: Jackson Mac Low's Light Poems and Algorithmic Digraphism

MICHAEL O'DRISCOLL

The End(s) of Chance

There's a certain irony that emerges when the author of what are often understood to be the greatest examples of twentieth-century aleatoric poetry is himself the victim of the cruel indifferences of chance. In June 1968, while at work on the final stages of his latest volume, *22 Light Poems,* which was forthcoming from Black Sparrow Press, Jackson Mac Low wrote of delays to publisher John Martin, explaining that he'd been unable to complete his afterward to the volume because the ceiling of his study had fallen in, covering his materials and workspace in plaster, and forcing him to relocate to the adjacent bedroom.[1]

Mac Low, it seems, had in the process misplaced the famous light chart that governed the production of those poems and the whole process ground, temporarily, to a halt (BSP 47.12.C).[2] Two months later, after some meticulous haggling between poet and publisher over typographic placement and diacritical marks, a clutch of galley proofs went astray in the postal system, forcing further delays (BSP 47.12.E), which were then compounded by the following event in September of that year, as Mac Low writes to Martin:

> Then Sunday morning – I know you won't believe it but the painting rack over the bed fell on us at 7 AM & we both nearly got

> killed. I got a terrible hitna head from the heavy shelf that had overhung the bed or from one of the stretchers – dunno which – & several bad bruises & cuts on my arms and legs. Iris got away with a cut elbow. So I wasn't in any shape to do proofreading until about the middle of the week. (BSP 47.12.I)

These highly random, certainly painful, and all too quotidian occurrences conspired to delay the project, but *22 Light Poems* did, eventually, go to print in October of 1968, resulting in a visually stunning and formally innovative collection of the light poems that Mac Low had begun writing some six years earlier.

It might be no more than idle speculation, but one could presume that Mac Low had had, for the time being at least, enough of chance. Aside from the relatively minor PFR-3 computer poems written the following summer in California, his next major project, the *Odes for Iris*, saw Mac Low producing a body of much more conventional verse – strict syllabic quatrains of unrequited love – that, as Jerome Rothenberg has noted, "out-confesses the 'confessionals.'"[3] Of course, what is much more likely here is that Mac Low's failing marriage – the central subject of the *Odes* – forced him to turn to an expressivist representation of his own emotional turmoil. In the 64th Ode he writes:

> I'm not much surprised to find
> "existential poetry"
> the only kind I seem to
> want to write.
>
> Objective, systematic
> chance operations gave me
> many poems & pieces
> in the past
>
> fifteen years or so, but now
> I only feel like writing
> living subjectivity:
> –inwardness!

is all I write, despite years
of so-called "egoless art"
–chimera! noble daydream
of the proud

who disdain to dump soul-shit
on unwary customers
& think they're Boddhisattvas
thru restraint! (*TB*, 154)

Mac Low's being unjustifiably critical of himself and his fellow experimental artists here – the paradox of self-aggrandizing practitioners of egoless art really overstates the case – and the fact is that Mac Low did not ultimately abandon "objective" operations in the composition of his poetry and, what's more, he had long before this moment, and even more regularly after, made use of much more conventional verse forms as well.

Nonetheless, one can trace throughout Mac Low's career an increasing restlessness about the precise definition of "chance," and a growing skepticism about the role the aleatoric might actually play in the composition of his works. While Mac Low speaks unselfconsciously about his use of the "objective chance operational method" in his 1961 publication "Poetry, Chance, Silence, Etc.," in the 1980 note added to the text, he offers the following corrective to his earlier statements: "I think I used to believe more strongly in the nonegoic nature and origin of aleatoric art than I do now … the artist's motivation is inevitably mixed, at best – and the ego's not really evadable. Besides, nothing would get done – the work would never get written or performed – if the artist's ego – including, of course, the body – didn't get it done."[4] Similarly, in a 1993 interview with Kevin Bezner, Mac Low notes that the "ego is inevitable. It's always there, in one way or another. The more I've worked with nonintentional methods, the more I've seen that the ego is manifested and effectual in anything you do."[5] Mac Low's sense that the artist's ego is always at work to some degree, and that chance is inevitably, in one fashion or another, tempered by choice, leads him ultimately to distance himself from John Cage's famously aleatoric compositional practices and to repeatedly point out that his "algorithmic work is often mistakenly thought to be chance-generated."[6]

By 2001, in a response to Kristin Prevallet titled "The Terminology" and published in *Open Letter,* Mac Low declares that "the terminology has not always seemed adequate" and makes a further and more particular effort to distinguish "systematic chance operations" and "deterministic methods" from each other and those from the liminal writing process (i.e. intuitive and only partially conscious) he calls "gathering."[7] While Mac Low, in such later statements, limits his use of chance, for the most part, to works composed in the mid and late 1950s, he's also careful to insist that he never rejects any of his former methods; indeed, it is the case that chance still plays a subordinate role in his later compositions, albeit always in relation to other practices. He also notes, even more importantly, that it "has been borne in on me that the last half-century of my artmaking has been the 'site' of a dialectic between making and letting be."[8] In view of such very clear statements, one might contend that what most generally characterizes Mac Low's writing career is explicitly *not* the use of chance in the composition of his poetry, but rather the persistent questioning of the limits or purity of the twin poles of subjective, intentional writing (or "making") and objective, aleatoric/deterministic methods (or "letting be") through the deployment of a wide range of competing and interdependent authorial practices in which each challenges and gives shape to the other.

Indeed, and this is part of my point in citing the above highly confessional passage from the *Odes,* Mac Low's poetic corpus is best described as "numerous," in the sense of "multitudinous" or, as Charles Bernstein has called it, "pluriform."[9] While aleatoric/deterministic operations do account for an important dimension of Mac Low's poetic output, overtly intentional and what Mac Low calls "quasi-intentional" methods – such as the above-noted practice of "gathering" – also prevail, and enjoy an equivalent status across the breadth of his career. As Bernstein suggests in a commemorative note published in a 2005 issue of *Bookforum*: "The multiplicity of Mac Low's forms and his rejection of any hierarchy among the forms of poetry – objective or subjective, expository or nonrepresentational, lyric or epic – as well as his refusal to identify poetic composition with a characteristic poet's 'voice,' are among the most radical aspects of his poetic practice (SP, 7).

Bernstein doesn't pursue this astute observation, but I'd like to do so in what follows. It is the case that Mac Low employs everything from an expressivist voice of social conscience and personal affect, to strictly deterministic methods (specifically, his systematic processes that "write through" chosen source texts and result in unanticipated content such as we find in the acrostic *Stanzas for Iris Lezak* or the diastic *Words nd Ends from Ez*) to the kind of middle-ground that Mac Low calls his method of "working from nuclei" in which chance and choice most clearly converge. The problem I'd like to put on the table is that there is a widespread critical tendency to over-emphasize the role of aleatoric/deterministic methods in Mac Low's corpus at the expense of attention to his use of more egocentric, overtly intentional forms of writing.

Louis Cabri's arguments about the politics of Anarcho-pacificism rooted in the crisis of representation Mac Low engenders in his non-intentional writing, Barrett Watten's focus on Mac Low's ethics of reading and notions of community produced through the overdetermined constructions of limited "poetic vocabularies," and Steve McCaffery's demonstration of the manner in which the irrecuperable excesses of Mac Low's compositional methods critique capitalist economies of language (that is, those based on consumption, striated positions of exchange value, and so on) are *all* insightful and important readings of this dimension of Mac Low's work.[10] What is consistently demonstrated in such analyses is the political and ethical import of Mac Low's writing practices: the manner in which the paragrammatic disposition of his compositions either model or make possible alternative forms of self- and social-fashioning. That is, Mac Low's aleatoric/deterministic methods of composition subject source texts to various "objective" procedural operations that result in what Mac Low calls "target forms" unanticipated by the poet. These paratactic, disjunctive fragments of text disavow an author-centric model of textual production in favour of allowing the reader to participate in the generation of meaning and affect. That process of signification, then, is understood to be analogous to various alternative formations of intersubjective relation – i.e. Anarcho-pacifism, communalism, Marxism, and so on.

"Paragrammatic" is McCaffery's term (from Kristeva), and by that he means "the infinitesimal combinations of letters and phonemes that always escape conventional reading habits," a kind of hermeneutic attention produced through Mac Low's use of aleatoric/deterministic strategies of composition.[11] McCaffery, like Cabri and Watten, is well aware of the bifurcated tendencies of language to which Mac Low's art responds:

> What Mac Low orchestrates are two radically divergent orders of meaning. One, a conventionally articulated meaning that describes itself through a linear order, i.e. a syntactic chain of discrete, detectable units. The other, a saturated, cryptonymic meaning, essentially trans-phenomenal, hidden as a latent signification within other word chains, errant, evasive and beyond an immediately legible appropriation. This second meaning is released through a particular reading-writing procedure, one that disengages language from representation and writing from an intentionalist imperative. (*NI*, 223)

While acknowledging elsewhere in a footnote that it "would be misleading, however, to exclude ego-based composition from Mac Low's writing," McCaffery's own tendency is to attribute the latter order of meaning, the trans-phenomenal and cryptonymic, to Mac Low's poetry, while situating forms of "conventionally articulated meaning" outside of Mac Low's own compositions and in the manipulated source texts that the poet employs.[12] Typically, then, while each of these critics does note the consistent presence of more conventional writing practices throughout the duration of Mac Low's career, their central arguments, as is almost universally the case in critical estimations of Mac Low, proceed without also considering the manner in which the intentional components of Mac Low's poetry participate equally in what Bernstein describes as a non-hierarchical relationship with the aleatoric and deterministic.[13]

I don't plan to repeat what I see as a limiting critical gesture in reverse – that is, by making general claims about Mac Low's poetry that extend from only the subset of his overtly intentional works – but I do want to stress what gets missed in any attempt to produce a more narrowed reading of Mac Low's literary, political, or ethical import. That is, by emphasizing one or another aspect of his poetics, what is overlooked is the crucial "dialectic," in Mac Low's words, at work here – across his pluriform corpus – in and around the competing trajectories of poetry that Barbour has usefully called "lyric/anti-lyric." What Barbour attempts to delineate is a long-standing tradition of writing in which certain poetries, of both extended and abbreviated lengths, "interrogate the form and concept of lyric even as they apparently display them," and those instances in which we might witness "lyric straining against itself."[14] Barbour quite rightly points out that "one way of defining lyric/anti-lyric is to note that such definitions can only occur in contrast to a rather sentimental definition of lyric," and as a result his understanding of "lyric" is ultimately limited to "what we conventionally call a short poem full of physically apprehended details of perception and sensuous rhythms" that privileges what Robert Kroetsch has called "its ferocious principles of closure."[15] However, as Rachel Blau DuPlessis argues fully in her essay included in this volume, such definitions, sentimental or otherwise, are neither neutral nor transhistorical, and, as she points out following Derrida's "The Law of Genre," "any genre can only be constituted in our critical imagination comparatively – only by existing alongside the shadow of its opposite, only by presenting phantom alternatives, only by articulating the markable presence of a 'counter-law.'"[16]

While thus far taking in the larger scope of Mac Low's poetic output rather than any individual poem, my point in raising such discussions of lyric and its undoings is to suggest that it is the larger dialectic he demonstrates between lyric and anti-lyric, and *not* aleatoric/deterministic methods of composition alone, that renders Mac Low's poetry radically open and *undecidable*. His is, indeed, a poetry of "phantom alternatives," of law and counter-law, that draws its energies and its critical force from such generic hauntings and shadowed sites of formal contest. It is this movement between these provisionally and only heuristically distinguishable poles that makes it impossible to say that Mac Low's poetry is *this* or *that*. I'm using the term "undecidable" here in a Derridean or de Manian sense, in order to draw out the implications of what I'll be calling a *digraphism*, or doubled-writing, that includes *both* the aleatoric/deterministic conjoinment of letters as a method of composition focused on the non-expressivist effects of language for the sake of its own objective sense and sound, and the more conventional and subjective function of the poet as one who names, and in doing so speaks from an at least provisionally centred consciousness. Viewed more comprehensively, Mac Low's poetic corpus confounds the distinctions we would make between the anti-lyric tendencies of aleatoric/deterministic composition and the lyric tendencies of expressivist forms of verse making. Another way to consider this is to follow Patrick Durgin's insightful description of the Mac Low corpus as an "arc of liminality," a body of works that produces a "continuum," rather than a "purgation," of intention.[17] Focusing on any point along that continuum, one might demonstrate the manner in which Mac Low's poetry challenges our categorical assumptions about the discreteness of the poles marking the ideal-extremes of what Durgin calls "an impossibly pure robo-poetry and an impossibly pure self-expressed motive."[18] For the purposes of this essay, I will focus on the evident, even exemplary, digraphism of Mac Low's *22 Light Poems* and the subsequent light poems that follow in the mode of that publication.

Algorithmic Digraphism

The relationship between the literal and the numeric is one of the things I find intriguing about Mac Low's writing. Aside from the fact that Mac Low's corpus is numerous in the sense of pluriform and multitudinous in the manner one might expect of a prolific and highly creative author over the duration of an almost seven-decade writing career, the titles of some of his key poetic works themselves suggest the importance of the numeric to Mac Low – think, for example, of poetic series such as *Asymmetries 1-260* or *42 Merzgedichte in Memoriam Kurt Schwitters* or *Twenties: 100 Poems* or *Pieces o' Six: Thirty-Three Poems in Prose* or *20 Forties*. I could go on here, and certainly I should mention, in this grouping, the numbered light poems as well, given that they provide my central example. Aside from the consistent accounting for, or of, his own output, there is also Mac Low's tendency to date individual poems – locating their production in the numbered temporalities of passing days, months, and years. Mac Low's methods of composition are also keenly dependent on the numeric – his deployment of aleatoric/deterministic operations at times draws from, amongst other sources, the Rand Corporation's publication of *A Million Random Digits and 100,000 Normal Deviates* (a favourite of John Cage as well). Throughout Mac Low's career he often relies on numbered playing cards, the correlation of letters and their numeric equivalents, the careful enumeration of characters or pages in a given source text or the painstaking measurement of typographic placement in the resulting poems or target forms.[19] Finally, one might point to the surprising and often deft use of poetic meter, measure, or quantity in Mac Low's poetry – this observation perhaps serving as a reminder of the manner in which all poetry is, and has always been to some degree, indebted to the numeric. Beyond, however, any notion of musical quantity, or recognizable meter such as pentameter – broken, in Ezra Pound's famous formulation, or not – Mac Low's methods of composition make that indebtedness evident.

Mac Low is always careful to describe in very specific terms the methods of composition employed in the production of any given text. He consistently describes the process of his compositional methods in head notes to the various poetic sequences, laying bare quite deliberately those unspoken rules that govern discursive formations and that usually go unremarked in both conventional verse and everyday speech. As Bernstein notes, "Mac Low's work embodies an ethics of sincerity and responsibility" in that he renders his own practices transparent and thereby disavows both the authority and mystique of the poetic function. What Bernstein is pointing to here, explicitly, is Mac Low's "use of predetermined structures – procedures or algorithms – for generating poems" (SP, 7). It is important to recognize that "algorithmic" is a term that Mac Low himself used regularly to describe the procedurally governed or thoroughly rule-bound production of certain poems, and his tendency was to restrict that designator to those poems understood to be strictly deterministic, such as his *Stanzas for Iris Lezak* or his *Assymetries*. As already noted, Mac Low has been careful to distinguish such deterministic poetics from what is perceived as purely chance-generated work, emphasizing that "whatever gets into the poetry is determined by the generative method & lies there waiting in the source texts."[20] While such deterministic methods certainly constitute a kind of "writing machine," as McCaffery has described them, Mac Low's rejection of chance here should signal even more clearly that his algorithmic poetries – even in the most extreme cases – are not entirely without authorial direction (*NI*, 222). While the "writing machine" might produce unanticipated results, that generative technology is itself a function of authorial intention and is designed to produce certain effects.[21] Keeping in mind Mac Low's insistence that even fragmentary phonemes bear meaning, as well as his delineation of chance and determination, it might be overstating the case to say, as McCaffery does, that his poetries emphasize "the elimination of a conscious intention, the removal of the writer as a subject 'responsible' for the texts it 'writes,' diminished reference and the absence of the subject from the productive aspect of meaning" (*NI*, 222).[22] While Mac Low's writing clearly throws into question conventional assumptions about signification and an author-centric production of meaning, it does so on the basis of a dialectic between lyric and its antitheses that is immediate to each and every poem as much as it is evident across the breadth of his poetic corpus. As Bernstein contends, Mac Low's corpus "reflects intention writ large" (SP, 7). In other words, Mac Low would in no sense abjure responsibility for the texts he produces; on the contrary, one might say his poetic output is designed specifically to instigate a kind of crisis, a foregrounded set of problematics, around the very question of intentionality that the poet recognizes one can never entirely avoid.

To extend Mac Low's own late hesitations around the very possibility of non-egoic art, I would point out that even the term "algorithmic" – regardless that Mac Low himself might restrict the term to rule-based, thoroughly deterministic methods of composition – belies a confluence of the literal and the numeric, and their associated oppositions of expression/ disinterestedness, subjective/objective, lyric/anti-lyric, intentional/deterministic, and so on – or what I will call here the *nomological* and *numerological* practices of the poet. Indeed, the somewhat tortured history of the term "algorithm" emphasizes that complex relationship. That is, the word derives from the name of the ninth-century Arab mathematician who transposed the use of Hindu numerals into his own cultural milieu. Al-Khwarizmi thereby set the precedent for developing sets of rules or instructions that result in the solution to a problem – the mathematical or logical procedures that now bear his name. Interestingly, while the English "algorithm" is derived from the French "algorisme" – an approximation of the Arab name – the term earned its intrusive digraph – the "T-H" of "algorithm" – in English through a mistaken association – what the OED calls (perhaps oxymoronically) a "learned error" – with the Greek "arithmos," meaning number. For that reason we say "algorithm," rather than the more archaic yet derivatively appropriate "algorism," and commonly associate the term with the numerological, rather than its more accurate derivation as a result of historical attribution – an act of naming or the nomological. One might say, then, that the numerological and nomological functions come together in this term as an errant performance of digraphism – both in the intrusion of the "T-H" into the term itself and in the recognition of the algorithmic as a doubled writing that both numbers and names, that is both calculated and referential. Given that Mac Low defines poetic form as what he calls in his postscript to *The Pronouns*, "the general framework & set of 'rules' given by the poet," and given the replicable procedural logic of his deterministic compositional strategies, it is certainly understandable that we might designate the formal schema of Mac Low's poetry as "algorithmic."[23] However, the term itself emphasizes that there is no such thing as a purely numerological or rule-bound practice of poetry. Indeed, one might also think of Mac Low's poetic methods as a kind of *algorithmic digraphism* in the sense that a digraph (any combination of two letters that produce a single sound, such as "ph" indicating /f/) suggests a kind of hidden or secret grapheme – neither the "p" nor the "h" in their usual enunciation are evident in the vocalized text. But what Mac Low does, effectively, is make apparent the duplicitous rules of composition that constitute his poetry; that is, by foregrounding the competing trajectories of the numerological and nomological that permeate his writing practices, he lays bare the doubledness, or digraphic quality, of all writing, including the algorithmic. The phrase "by the numbers" in the title of this essay, then, is intended both to acknowledge Mac Low's emphasis on the modes of composition that rely on the numeric and to open up a consideration of the "para-numerological" dimensions of his work.

The Digraphic Light Poems

In order to explore this para-numerological, doubled, or digraphic, dimension of Mac Low's poetry, I'm going to focus on what is a prime example of his quasi-intentional poetries and the method of "gathering" or "working from nuclei" that complements and confounds the aleatoric/deterministic operations that are evident in his "light poems." As already noted, in June, 1962, Mac Low began work on the series of light poems that he would continue over many years and that resulted in dozens of such compositions. Aside from their early appearance in various small press or magazine publications (including such landmark venues as Jerome Rothenberg's serial anthology *Poems from the Floating World*, Ed Sander's *FUCK YOU: A Magazine of the Arts*, Clayton Eshleman's *Caterpillar*, and the Clark Coolidge/George Palmers collaboration *Joglars*), the first sizable collection of these was published as *22 Light Poems* with Black Sparrow Press in 1968 – a volume that has been largely overlooked in critical engagements with Mac Low, although Bernstein does note that the light poems should be counted among "Jackson's most beautiful works" (SP, 7).

CARBIDE=LAMP LIGHT

MASER LIGHT

~~LASER~~ LASER L…
LUMINOUSNE…
LUMINIFEROU…
LAMBENC…

EDITORIAL DEPARTMENT

PAYROLL DISTRIBUTION

SHEET NO.__________

A	R	C	M TOTAL	E REF. EDIT	W NEW INTER YEAR BOOK	O NEW STAND YEAR BOOK	L DICT'NARY
A	2	3	4	5	6	7	8
ARC=LIGHT	RADIANCE	CANDLE=LIGHT	MATCH=FLAME	ECLIPSE=LIGHT	WAXING LIGHT	OIL=LAMP LIGHT	LIGHT
AURORA BOREALIS	REFLECTED LIGHT	CHEMICAL LIGHT	MOON=LIGHT	EYE LIGHT	WANING LIGHT	OWL=LIGHT	LUCENCE
ACTINIC RAYS	RAINBOW	CORAL LIGHT	MIDNIGHT SUN	ELECTRIC LIGHT	WATER LIGHTS	ORANGE LIGHT	LAVENDER LIGHT
AURORA	RED LIGHT	COLD LIGHT	MARSH LIGHT	EMERALD LIGHT	WILL-O'-THE-WISP	OLD LIGHT	LILAC LIGHT
AURORA AUSTRALIS	RUBY LIGHT	COLORED LIGHT	MERCURY=VAPOR LAMPLIGHT	EARTHLIGHT	WHITE LIGHT	ORGONE RADIATION	LEMON LIGHT
ATOM BOMB LIGHT	RADIATION	CINEMATOGRAPHIC LIGHT	MAROON LIGHT	ETHER	WHALE=OIL LAMPLIGHT	ORGONE LUMINATION	LUMINANCE
ARTIFICIAL LIGHT	RAYS OF LIGHT	CINEOGRAPHIC LIGHT	MAGIC FLAMES	ETHER LAMPLIGHT	WATCHING=CANDLE LIGHT	OUTDOOR FIRELIGHT	LUMINATION
ANNEALING=LAMPLIGHT	RAYS	CRESSET LIGHT	MAGIC LANTERN LIGHT	ELECTRIC ARC=LIGHT	WATCH=CANDLE LIGHT	OIL=GAS LIGHT	LUMINESCENCE
ALCOHOL LAMPLIGHT	READING=LAMPLIGHT	COOPER=HEWITT LAMPLIGHT	MAGNESIUM LIGHT	ELECTRIC LAMPLIGHT	WATCH=LIGHT	OLIVE=OIL LAMPLIGHT	LAMPLIGHT
ARGAND LAMPLIGHT	ROOF=LAMPLIGHT	CLUTCH=LAMPLIGHT	MAGIC FIRELIGHT	ENAMELING=LAMP LIGHT	WOOD=OIL LAMP LIGHT	AMETHYST LIGHT	LUMINOSITY
ADVANCING IGNITION	REICHSANSTALT's LAMPLIGHT	CLEAR GRAY LIGHT	MINERS LAMPLIGHT	ENLIGHTENMENT	WINESTONES OIL LIGHT	AGATE LIGHT	LANTERN LIGHT
AFTER-GLOW	ROSE LAMP LIGHT	CAMPFIRE LIGHT	MERCURY LAMPLIGHT	ELUCIDATION	WAXLIGHT LIGHT	ACHROITE LIGHT	LUSTER
AUFKLÄRUNG	ROSE LIGHT	CORUSCATION	MOONSHINE	EFFULGENCE	LUMINOUSNESS	ALEXANDRITE LIGHT	LIGHT RAYS
AUREOLA	REFLECTED LIGHT	CAMPHOR=OIL LIGHT	MECHANICAL LAMP LIGHT	EARTH=SHINE	LUMINIFEROUSNESS	ALMANDITE LIGHT	LUMINIFEROUS ETHER
AUREOLE	RADIOACTIVITY	CASTANHA=OIL LIGHT	MAKE=AND=BREAK IGNITER LIGHT	EXPLODING STARLIGHT	LAMBENCY	AMAZONSTONE LIGHT	LIMELIGHT
AZURE LIGHT	REFULGENCE	COCONUT=OIL CANDLELIGHT	MOONBEAM	EXIT=LIGHT LIGHT	ROSEOPAL LIGHT	AMBER LIGHT	LUMINESCENCE LAMPLIGHT
LUMINOTHERMIC LIGHT	RESPLENDENCE	COLOR	MIDNIGHT OIL	EQUINOCTIAL LIGHT	MILKY WAY	AQUAMARINE LIGHT	LIGHTNING
ACETYLENE LIGHT	REFRACTED LIGHT	COMMON LIGHT	MELON=OIL LAMPLIGHT	EARLY LIGHT	SATELLITE LIGHT	OPALESCENT LIGHT	LIGHT OF DAY
ACTINISM	RELUCENCE	CARNELIAN LIGHT	MUSTARD=OIL LIGHT	EVANESCENT LIGHT	MOVIE LIGHT	ORDINARY LIGHT	LAMBENT FLAME
[illegible]NDA=OIL	RHODOCHRO-	CARMINE	METEOR [illegible]	EXTRALIGHT	WINKING	OPAL LIGHT	LUCIDITY

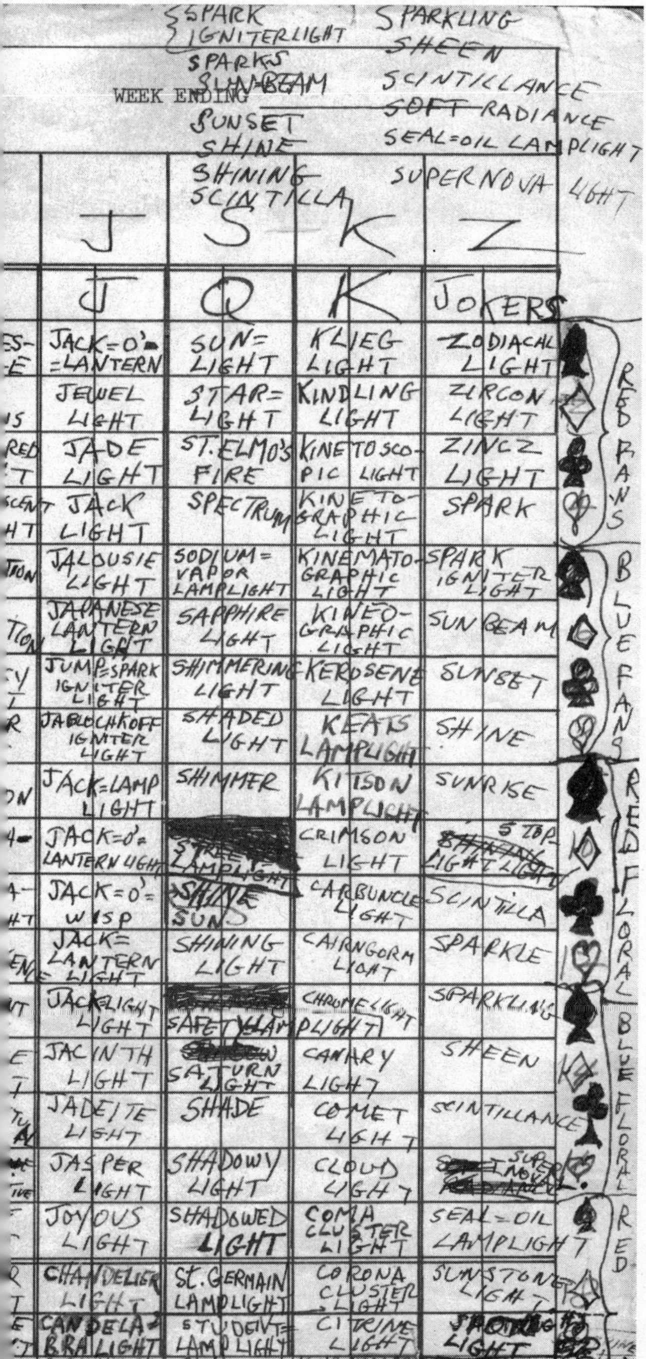

6.1 Jackson Mac Low, *Light Poems Chart* (original version), 1962. Image used by permission of Anne Tardos for Jackson Mac Low in trust.

Mac Low produced the "nuclei" of the light poems by way of an algorithmic method governed by a table of 288 different kinds of light. The original hand written chart has fourteen columns and twenty rows, laid out on a Funk and Wagnall's Editorial Department payroll form – a conceptualization of practice that requires, it should be noted, that one enter names where conventional use of the form would primarily make use of numbers. Each vertical column is headed by one of the letters appearing in the names of Jackson Mac Low and his wife at the time, Iris Lezak, as well as the denomination of a playing card. The columns below include names of light beginning with the appropriate letter heading the column, although a paucity of letters under certain headings ("Z" for example) required that Mac Low flesh out the column with light names beginning with similar letters ("crimson light" appears under "K"; "spark" appears under "Z"). The light names themselves were identified by paging through a copy of a Funk and Wagnall's dictionary, with Mac Low selecting the names as he encountered them. Although there is no indication of what principle of selection governed this process, the light names themselves vary from the philosophical ("Aufklärung) to the quotidian ("sunshine"), from the historical ("wood-oil lamplight") to the scientific ("actinism"), from the poetic ("resplendence") to the idiomatic ("new light"). The chart was designed to be used with five differently backed packs of cards (as along the far right margin) so that the suit and the image on the back of the card would determine the row, and the denomination from ace through king, and including jokers, would determine the column. Mac Low also numbered the rows 1-20, and could thereby make further selections through use of *A Million Random Digits*.

According to the procedural rules of composition – at least as initially set out – shuffled and selected cards would determine the appearance of a light name in the poem. These names of light provided the "nuclei" of the text, and Mac Low would then, through his process of liminal gathering, intuitively or semi-consciously follow the lead of the nuclei (in relation to his immediate environment, ongoing concerns, the dedication of the poem, and other associations) and compose that text appearing between the names of light. However, as Mac Low himself points out in the afterward to *22 Light Poems*, only the first poem followed this method precisely. Otherwise, a number of the poems were chosen without aleatoric/deterministic means at all (for example, light poems three and four) or followed other dictates: the letters in the name of a dedicatee, or phrases and words drawn from other "seed" texts might designate columns, while various other strategies might determine rows. The result is an example of a sporadic or limited use of aleatoric/deterministic methods of composition, but as a simultaneously "quasi-intentional" text, *22 Light Poems* is a series of poems in which chance is most overtly tempered by choice, logic is subject to the imagination, and the algorithmic takes shape as an aesthetic.

Consider, for example, the "7th Light Poem: for John Cage." Mac Low describes the process of producing this poem in the following manner:

> In writing the 7th, I began to use as a supplementary source a numerology booklet entitled *Your Lucky Number*. Chance determined which source was drawn from each time. Triplets of random digits drew phrases from the booklet; cards & random-digit couplets drew light names from the chart. Connecting words & verse lines were freely composed, but indentations were usually determined by placing a letter (or whole word) in one line directly under its appearance in a line (not necessarily the preceding one) above it. (LP, 76)

If we look at the first few lines of the poem, we can discern the results of Mac Low's particular method here.

> Put off an important decision
>   in mechnical-lamp light.
> Success in a new project will bring lumination.
> An exchange of courtesy in the zodiacal
>   light reminds you that expenses can
>   run high when you insist on light
>   from almandites.
> For almandites are iron-alumina garnets
> $Fe_3Al_2(SiO_4)_3$.
> When of a fine deep red or purplish red,
>   from India,
>   and transparent,
>   they are
>   "precious garnets."
>
> (LP, 19)

Phrases like "Put off an important decision," "Success in a new project," and "An exchange of courtesy" are clearly drawn from the prognostications of the numerology booklet, while phrases such as "mechanical lamp light," "lumination," and "zodiacal / light" are drawn from the chart of light names. The chemical formula for "almandites" and the language used to describe "precious garnets" are, I suspect, drawn from S.E. Tillman's *A Text-book of Important Minerals and Rocks*, published in 1908 – a source text that Mac Low does not acknowledge. Tillman writes the following:

> *Almandite*, or *Almandine*. – Various shades of light red to brown. Those with clear color and considerable transparency are the *precious garnets*. Almandite is an iron-alumina garnet … It is also called *precious garnet* when it is fairly transparent and has a pure color.[24]

The poet's task is to bring these fragments of source text together, freely or intuitively composing between these phrases to produce something that approximates conventional syntax, and at times to follow his own inclinations in working from or around those various "nuclei."

Such inclinations lead Mac Low to an intriguing self-reflexive moment in which he describes the composition of the poem itself. This might well be a spontaneous response to the line "Say what you really think," perhaps itself drawn from the numerology booklet:

> The lamp I have clamped to the kitchen
>   table beside the
>   notebook I am writing this in
>   gives a sort
>   of student-lamp light although
>   it is not a student lamp but
>   a PENETRAY.
>
> (*LP*, 19)

This spontaneous incursion of authorial ego here – that is, the self-referential "I" of the lyric voice declaring what it really thinks – is mitigated by the competing aleatoric/deterministic elements of the poem, by the intuitive inclusion of the writer's immediate environment (the PENETRAY lamp is not drawn from the list of light names, but is presumably physically present during the composition of the poem), by the strictures of typographic placement (note the rule-bound alignment of letters with their preceding occurrences), by what constitutes, effectively, a paratactic or open field poetics that at the same time asserts and refuses the stable subject position we might associate with Mac Low's contemporaries, for example Charles Olson or Allen Ginsberg. Nonetheless, many of the elements of conventional lyric verse are also present: musicality, the monologic voice, brevity, the focused perception of the ego, the address of the "I" to the "You," and even the well-worn lyric themes of illumination, ambition, fate, and cosmic determination find a place in this poem. One can see immediately how the numerological and nomological become indistinguishable here: numbers produce names of light and other textual elements, but the names also produce numbers in the sense that their typographic placement on the page governs prosody and therefore controls lineation and the poetic measure of the poem. The source text *Your Lucky Number* is actually a repository of nomological content, while Tillman's nomological textbook yields up numerological formulae. In every instance of this poem, names and numbers converge in a performance of algorithmic digraphism.

When one considers the larger scope of the light poems, this digraphic tendency becomes even more apparent, albeit in a variety of ways. Take, for example, the personal polemic of the "16th Light Poem: for Armand Schwerner," written in August 1962. This occasional text constitutes a response to Schwerner following his mocking performance and public ridicule of one of Mac Low's poems – in the author's presence, and during a gathering at the New York City home of Jerome and Diane Rothenberg. What is particularly intriguing about this poem – beyond the prurient interest sparked by what appears to be a superficially light-hearted but clearly damaging personal clash – is that Mac Low here employs the form of his light poems, but abandons the use of aleatorically or deterministically derived names of light in favour of a free composition that effectively parodies his own quasi-intentional practice:

In what light
do you read a poem
you wish to demolish?

An unsympathetic light.

In what light
do you wish to appear
when you read a poem
with the intention of demolishing it?

A superior light.

In what light
do you wish to appear to be reading a poem
when you read it
with the intention
of demolishing it?

A critical light.

In what light
do you appear
to one who tho suffering
from an ugly reading
of a poem with the intention of demolishing it
see that this reading
arises from a suffering of the one
who reads it
with the intention of
demolishing it?

An 'insecure' light.
(*TB*, 208–9)

Here, the names of various kinds of light – unsympathetic, superior, critical, insecure – appear to function in much the same manner as the nuclei of Mac Low's similarly formalized poems; however, for the purpose of expressing personal affect and a confrontational invective, Mac Low here merely mimics that form otherwise derived from a mixture of aleatoric/deterministic and quasi-intentional methods. That is, Mac Low provides a pastiche of the formal properties of a numerologically derived text in a nomological undertaking that names, that answers the question "in what light?" Indeed, none of these "kinds" of light are actually derived from the light chart; they are, rather, chosen quite deliberately by the poet. That the poem itself – which continues on for another seven pages or so – focuses on matters of intention, interpretation, taste, and the politics of poetry (Mac Low makes an impressive case for the "necessary" affront of publications such as Sander's *FUCK YOU* magazine, in which the mocked poem appeared), furthers the relevance of this performative gesture. In other words, the "16th Light Poem" thoroughly problematizes the distinction we might make between intentional and non-intentional methods of composition by demonstrating the manner in which the effects of aleatoric/deterministic methods can, in fact, be feigned, and foregrounding the kind of socio-cultural issues of interpretation and aesthetics that result from such dissimulation.

Another variant of the digraphic arises in the "32nd Light Poem: *In Memoriam* Paul Blackburn – 9–10 October 1971." In the instance of this overwhelmingly beautiful and sad poem, the stunning elegiac voice of the poet finds poignant light imagery in various terms not available to the determinations of the light chart:

> Let me choose the kinds of light
> to light the passing of my friend
> Paul Blackburn a poet
>
> A pale light like that of a winter dawn
> or twilight
> or phosphorescence
>
> is not enough to guide him in his passing
> but enough for us to see
> shadowily his last gaunt figure.
> (*TB*, 220)

Here, the task of the poet requires – as he himself tells us – deliberate choice; while certain names of light in the poem do acrostically spell out "Paul Blackburn," the proper sequence is often haphazardly interrupted, suggesting that there is no real possibility of relinquishing intention when it comes to the responsibilities of commemorative performance. Furthermore, while certain kinds of light in the poem can be found on Mac Low's chart ("lightning" and "amber light" specifically), others are conjured purely for this moment ("pale light," "twilight," "phosphorescence," "umber light") and ultimately the poem acknowledges the utter absence of light that results from the pure circumstance or contingency of death:

> but when Jerry telephoned me of your death
> the lightning that destroyed
> the illusion you were safe
>
> led thru dreadful amber light
> not to friendly car light
> & welcoming kitchen light
>
> but to black light of absence
> not ultraviolet light
> revealing hidden colors
>
> but revelatory light that is *no* light
> the unending light of the realization
> that no light will ever light your bodily presence
> again
>
> Now your poems' light is all
> The unending light of your presence
> in the living light of your voice.
> (*TB*, 222–3)

This poem reads, in these closing stanzas, not unlike any other of Mac Low's light poems (the repetitive cadence of the word "light," occurring fourteen times in fifteen lines, creates a typical effect); however, such striking reiterations not only reinforce the elegiac mood of the piece, but curiously both announce and denounce the presence of light in the same gesture. Ultimately, one might say, "the revelatory light that is *no* light" can only be found in poetry – that is, the metaphorical light that is nomologically attributed to the acts of naming that are poetry cannot be quantified or empirically measured in numerological terms. For Mac Low, Blackburn's poetry is exemplary here, but that claim might be extended to the light that any verse might offer as testimony to the "presence" and "voice" of the poet. Elegy, in this instance, restores lyric to our attention, but curiously Mac Low retains the markers and constraints of a procedural poetics against which the lyric voice must strain.

At such moments of high affect – anger, mourning – Mac Low seems to turn firmly away from the numerological determinations of the algorithmic, but while emphasizing the nomological retains the form of the light poems that serves to signify the constraints of such determination. This, however, is not always the case, and as a final, and perhaps telling, counterexample I'll turn to the "58th Light Poem: For Anne Tardos – 19 March 1979." This wonderful love poem (dedicated to the woman who would be Mac Low's partner from then on) shows the poet at the height of his ability to work in and around the algorithmic determinations of various nuclei. The poem announces, at several moments, its own methodology, including in its opening lines:

> I know when I've fallen in love I start to write love songs
> Love's actinism turns nineteens to words & thoughts in love songs
> as your "A" & the date made "actinism" enter this love song
> (*TB*, 228)

The first letter of the dedicatee's name, and the day of the month, results in the selection of "actinism" as the first light name of the poem (on the light chart, "actinism" appears in the nineteenth row under the "A" column). Mac Low incorporates the concept of actinism (that is, the radioactive property that produces photochemical effects) into the conceit of these opening lines; and then repeats the name "Anne Tardos" almost silently, that is paragrammatically, without typographic markers or other obtrusions, three times throughout the text (e.g. "actinism" is followed, in various contexts, by "noon light," "northern lights," and "evanescent light, spelling out A-N-N-E; "tranquil light," "aureole," relucence," "deflected light," "ordinary light," and "sun" spell out T-A-R-D-O-S). Other than the light chart, the poem's central source text seems to be an unidentified astrological guide, selections from which confirm the rightness of this romantic match – an older Virgo man and a younger Sagittarian woman:

> O ingratiating
> astrological light may you never prove false
> even to one who has often decried you as no light
> but superstitious darkness natural light would dispel
> or the electric arc light of empirical science.
> (*TB*, 230)

In the poem's extended engagement with both the aleatoric/determinist methodology and its central thematic of astrological divination, the "58th Light Poem" explores the interanimations of fate and intention, chance and choice, in the context of new love. Here, the names of light are used specifically to mediate in a contest of discourses (the astrological and the scientific) that might be said to provide competing models of nomological and numerological illumination. Interestingly, however, the "no light" of poetry celebrated in the Blackburn poem, now rendered in the form of the "no light" of astrology, is here suspect given the poet's stated preference for the quantifiable evidence of scientific empiricism. This shift of allegiance, one might suspect, is emblematic of the algorithmic digraphism at work throughout this poem, the collection of light poems, and the Mac Low corpus in general – providing precisely the kind of "dialectic," between "making" and "letting be," Mac Low understands to be central not only to his poetry but, indeed, to his life, to every life.

If we return to Bernstein's suggestion that it is the pluriformity of Mac Low's career – that is, the engagement of Mac Low's writing with a multiplicity of competing and non-hierarchical forms – that is its most radical quality, then further questions are called for. If Mac Low's paragrammatic poetry enacts or draws out what McCaffery has called the "built-in critique" of conventional models of textual production – that is, the tendency of normative sign systems to create their own destabilizing excesses – what, we might ask, is the object of that critique when we attend not just to Mac Low's use of important and influential aleatoric/ deterministic methods, but also to Mac Low's deployment of the more obviously lyric elements of his poetry?[25] What happens when we shift our attention from the numerological to the nomological – and back again? One may, then, just as legitimately ask how lyric might challenge, or push back against, assumptions about the production of anti-lyric in a manner that might modify, without necessarily undermining, what the critical consensus tells us is the ethico-political program of Mac Low's poetry. The object of critique, as detailed above, remains the same; however, recognizing the method that results in the successes of Mac Low's ethico-political program requires a slight shift in critical focus. In answer to those specific questions, my argument has been that this version of the "built-in critique" is best located in the *interminable dialectic* of Mac Low's texts – that the deployment of *both* lyric and anti-lyric, law and counter-law, produces a set of dynamic, irresolvable tensions that *not only* refuses the sensibilities of normative models of communication, value, and subjectivity in language *but also* subjects the presuppositions and recuperability of a purely aleatoric/deterministic writing to scrutiny by describing those methods' own limitations. What is ultimately evident, then, in the algorithmic digraphisms of Mac Low's poetry is a transformative awareness of authorial responsibility, a performance of the necessary ethics and politics of choice, and a demonstration of the unavoidable, but always modified and modifiable, role played by intention in a world of chance and determination.

7

Better Living through 'Pataphysics: The Biosemiotics of Kenneth Goldsmith

ADAM DICKINSON

Things explain each other, not themselves.
George Oppen

Part A: Things

In early March of 2008, two environmental activists, Rick Smith and Bruce Lourie, sequestered themselves in a Toronto apartment for four days in order to perform an unusual experiment. They deliberately exposed themselves through daily activities to a variety of common household substances, such as personal-care products, plastic food containers, and furniture treated with stain repellent. In addition to taking regular blood and urine samples, they passed the time watching cable news and playing "Guitar Hero." The purpose of this unorthodox experiment, which the authors likened to a science fair project, was to measure levels of common pollutants in their bodies, pollutants that have received little study in the context of quotidian human use, despite, in some cases, being known carcinogens. Inspired by the "body burden" testing initiatives of the US-based Environmental Working Group in the late 1990s, Smith and Lourie's experiments, outlined in *Slow Death by Rubber Duck*, focus on their own bodies as sites of environmental contamination. The goal of their science project is to change the way people think about pollution, emphasizing how "We have all become guinea pigs in a vast and uncontrolled experiment" where we marinate daily in a cocktail of chemicals through food we eat, surfaces we touch, and creams we absorb.[1] By making their own bodies guinea pigs in this experiment, the authors redefine conventional notions of toxicity, making pollution a matter of not only acute, external, geographical concern, but also one of chronic, internal, biochemistry.

The unconventional and highly personal methodologies practiced by the authors represent a political intervention into the systematic science that governs environmental regulation and corporate interest.[2] Where traditional science depends on anonymity, the whole point of "body burden" testing is to be public and personal (*SD*, 11). Moreover, there are significant gaps in existing scientific testing on these chemicals: "For some chemicals, like bisphenol A (BPA), there are virtually no human data available at all" (*SD*, 5). Consequently, these authors were inspired to create an alternative scientific practice, one which proposed an imaginative solution to a question no one had thought to ask: what happens if we try intentionally to raise and lower the levels of certain chemicals in our bodies?

Such questions evoke the pseudo-scientific methodologies of 'pataphysics, where science and art intersect as research practices and mutually engaged discursivities.[3] 'Pataphysics, which traces its roots to the early twentieth-century writings of Alfred Jarry, is variously the science of imaginary solutions, the science of the particular, and the science of exceptions.[4] Jarry's numerous definitions (a 'pataphysical ploy itself) coalesce around the idea that 'pataphysics seeks to uncover marginalized and unique perspectives by controlling for unusual frames of reference and signification. By attending to exceptions, 'pataphysics is ultimately a deconstructive project inasmuch as it exposes the irreducible gaps that haunt ostensibly totalized systems. While 'pataphysical works include intentionally useless or impossibly realized forms, such as ready-made sculptures for preventing snow accumulation (Robert Fones), or archaeological reports on the twenty-two-letter alphabet (bpNichol), 'pataphysics is, as Karl Jirgens points out, "no joking matter. It is the product of minds who have recognized aspects of reality that others have failed to."[5] Smith and Lourie's self-described "cuckoo" science experiment is 'pataphysical inasmuch as "what began as a joke, an offhand thought," has become, through the imposition of unusual constraints, a scientific and political intervention into the metaphysical assumptions of corporate science and government health regulation (*SD*, 6).

The implications for environmentalism are obvious in the case of Smith and Lourie. What are we to make, however, of the implications for literary environmentalism – or, ecocriticism – of 'pataphysical experiments that, while textual, bear some similarities to the experiments performed by these activists? Take Kenneth Goldsmith's *Soliloquy*, for example.[6] During a week in 2001, this American poet strapped a hidden microphone to his body and recorded his daily conversations. The resulting poem, published in 487 pages and seven "Acts" corresponding to the days of the week, presents only Goldsmith's side of his conversations, splicing comments together in a catalogue of the various communicative environments he experienced that week. The constraint-based, 'pataphysical poetics applied to the gathering of "data" in the poem suggest the methodological strategies of scientific experimentation, where variables are controlled in order to apprehend a particular environment in a particular way.

Smith and Lourie's concern with body burden testing and with the subjective engagement of environmental chemicals is complemented in *Soliloquy* by Goldsmith's exploration of membranous subjectivity in the semiotic environment of New York City. In fact, semiotic activities might be said to be fundamentally involved in both projects – both involve controlling frames of signification for alternate perspectives. Moreover, semiotic issues are implicit in the concern with endocrine disruptors in Smith and Lourie's experiment – phthalates signify as estrogens in various biochemical circumstances, which can lead to toxic effects on the body. Such explicit links between semiotics and biology are the focus of the developing discipline of biosemiotics, which is the study of biology as a function of semiosis, or sign systems and processes. It is an emerging, interdisciplinary field linking biology and linguistics by asserting the importance of interpretive modulation over deterministic mechanisms in life processes. As a reaction against Cartesian dualism, biosemiotics owes its modern shape to Thomas Sebeok and more recently Jesper Hoffmeyer, both of whom rely heavily on insights from and connections between C.S. Peirce's "triadic logic" in semiotics, Jakob von Uexküll's *Umwelt* theory, and Gregory Bateson's work in anthropology and cybernetics.[7] For biosemiotics, the semiosphere (the environment of signs and signification) rather than the biosphere is the locus of biological concern. Hoffmeyer points out in *Signs of Meaning in the Universe*, that "all plants and animals

– all organisms, come to that – live first and foremost, in a world of signification. Everything an organism senses signifies something to it: food, flight, reproduction – or, for that matter, despair."[8] The focus on signification is further extended to the cellular level where hormones, for example, act to induce semiotic interpretations.

Like 'pataphysics, biosemiotics deconstructs the metaphysics of objectivity by underscoring the importance of subjective perspectives in biological science. In fact, unlike in traditional biology, the question of subjectivity is a dominant concern. Hoffmeyer emphasizes in *Biosemiotics* that "a decent biology must search for the evolutionary root forms of *what it is to be* an 'I,' or a first-person *singularis*. A key to answering this question … lies in a sufficiently rich concept of *semiosis*."[9] As I will discuss shortly, by eliminating traditionally expressive poetic elements from his work, Goldsmith 'pataphysically controls the variables of his compositions to reveal unusual perspectives on the semiotic relationships that both surround and constitute an emergent subject.

Ecocriticism has paid little attention to 'pataphysical texts, despite increasing interest and deference to scientific principles in literary analysis. In this article I propose an alternative conception of the relationship between experimental artistic and scientific epistemologies by considering the link between poetry that imagines itself as science ('pataphysics) and science that imagines itself as poetry (biosemiotics). I want to make an argument for Kenneth Goldsmith's work as a form of ecopoetics, inasmuch as *The Weather*, *Soliloquy*, and *Fidget* are all examples of environmental texts in which the poet, as a self-described "information manager," becomes a kind of environmental scientist filtering, collecting, and archiving in order to illuminate the membranes and structures through which information from and about the environment is channeled and interpreted. I wish to focus in particular on the importance of subjectivity and the role of interpretative membranes, as well as on the interplay between analog and digital codes, in Goldsmith's work in order to demonstrate that his 'pataphysical projects offer an example of a subtle and complex interrogation of the contemporary self – the self that is both product and producer of environmental writing. Because of their emphasis on scientific realism, neither nature writing nor ecocriticism have been able to deal adequately with the question of subjectivity.

Part B: Explain

Realist aesthetics and the associated recourse to scientific materialism have typically been privileged in ecocriticism for their capacity to offer faithful environmental representations. In *The Truth of Ecology,* Dana Phillips laments what he perceives as the failure of ecocritics to see that "art can be Green without literally being green."[10] This emphasis on realism has accompanied an ecocritical devotion to singular, individual accounts of nature. In their introduction to the *Norton Nature Book of Writing*, Robert Finch and John Elder propose that "The personal element – that is, the filtering of experience through an individual sensibility – is central to what we view as the nature writing tradition."[11] Ecocriticism and nature writing frequently rely on and endorse subjective experiences of nature and yet often universalize these experiences, under the implied assumption that the self is a transcendent entity. We see this, for example, in David Abram's *The Spell of the Sensuous,* where phenomenological methodologies are evoked loosely as a means to rescue the contemporary subject alienated from nature.[12] After all, the environmental crisis is frequently characterized as having its cause in a form of the human self in need of renovation (Jack Turner quoted in *TE*, 208). Phillips, Timothy Morton, Lawrence Buell, and others have argued that ecocritics cannot "simply brush the self aside as an object of study: we have to meet it head on" (*TE*, 196). Despite a desire to focus on the surrounding environment, individual sensibility looms large in nature writing. Indeed, Phillips observes that "nature writing has a fundamentally contradictory character: at critical junctures, it swerves inward, erasing the world it has been at such pains to describe, and abandoning the physical for the metaphysical" (*TE*, 230).

The difficult and contradictory position of the "self" in ecopoetics is illustrated in J. Scott Bryson's introduction to *Ecopoetry: A Critical Introduction*. For Bryson, ecopoetry represents a subset of nature poetry marked by an ecocentric perspective, humility in the face of wilderness, and skepticism towards technological thinking and practices.[13] According to this definition, the ecopoetic self is torn between downplaying the individual ego and yet drawing attention to its own particular humility. Moreover, the self maintains an objectively situated ecological perspective that is selectively skeptical of "hyperrationality" and technology.[14] The self is at once aligned with science, and the amorphous category of ecological relations, but also opposed to science and its particular, idiosyncratic technological manifestations. Consequently, within ecopoetics itself, there remains the need for a more developed sense of the self. In asking what it means to be an emergent "I," biosemiotics is fundamentally concerned with subjectivity as a function of biological processes (*B*, xvi). Moreover, as I will explain, 'pataphysics challenges conventional notions of the subject and, through its literary experiments, reveals the articulated subject at the heart of objective observation.

What 'pataphysics investigates scientifically in the realm of culture, biosemiotics investigates culturally or socially in the realm of biology – though, as we shall see, easy distinctions between culture and nature are challenged by the semiotic implications of these approaches. Both might be called "nomad sciences," in Deleuzian terms, where a "royal science is a standardized metaphysics" and a "nomad science is a bastardized metaphysics."[15] Both are concerned with "bastardizing" or subverting reified scientific assumptions by asserting the fundamental semiotic nature of science. Despite a shared anti-metaphysical stance, however, the mischievous, humourous element so present in 'pataphysics is clearly not as pronounced in biosemiotics, which yearns to be taken seriously. Notwithstanding its high jinks, 'pataphysics cannot simply be reduced to a joke; both Bök and Jirgens, for example, represent attempts to take 'pataphysics seriously. Bök laments that only a few critics have recognized the centrality of 'pataphysics to contemporary art and philosophy. Moreover, as he asserts, "'Pataphysics reveals that, like poetry, science has an avant-garde with its own history of dissent."[16] Biosemiotics, we might say, is one such example of dissenting science, an avant-garde biology. 'Pataphysics may celebrate the supreme ruse, but there are serious consequences to its humour. In fact, biosemiotics is more intimately concerned with the seriousness of jokes than it might at first appear. A fundamental paradox underlies contemporary biology. The "genetic code" is the foundation of life, but because there can be no *meaning* in modern science, the code, with all of its associated interpretive and semiotic implications, must be understood to be a metaphor and not *real*: "it is perfectly right to mention the genetic code practically in every single problem of biology, provided one keeps in mind that *it is not meant to be serious*."[17] Therefore, both 'pataphysics and biosemiotics ask us to take seriously what might seem like jokes, like wildly preposterous claims and associations. In fact, the unlikeliness of the connections between 'pataphysics and biosemiotics is as potentially humorous as it is profound, as I think the work of Smith and Lourie and Goldsmith demonstrates.

In the case of biosemiotics, the fundamental semiotic nature of science is reflected in the emphasis on sign processes and emergent identities as conditions for life itself. In the case of 'pataphysics, attention is drawn to the repressed semiotic dimension of science in order to correct the historical interest in "stabilizing the *signified* within a restricted economy of monosemic enunciation."[18] Consistent with this 'pataphysical resistance to reductive science, biosemiotics seeks to overturn the bias that attributes undue influence to genetic codes at the expense of environmental influences. It is membrane structures such as the skin and cellular surfaces that actively use DNA to direct life processes, not the other way around. The fertilized egg is an example of such an interpretive surface: it deciphers the genetic code of DNA idiosyncratically and converts or translates it into a physically coded version (mistakes can always be made which, of course, affect the viability of the translation/organism). In this way each generation is an ongoing experiment in flesh of a deep genetic memory that extends back to the origins of life. Similarly, each generation of flesh can affect subtle changes in this genetic memory through the selection of reproductive partners: "Through procreation, temporal and three-dimensional aberrations are translated into one-dimensional code; the (genetic) directory available to the next generation has been altered" (*SM*, 22).

The important idea here is that interpretive agency is always involved. There is no random natural selection; rather, subjective engagement exists at the cellular or cytoplasmic level as well as at the community level. As a consequence, in this biosemiotic environment there are always two forms of code in continual relation: digital and analog. A digital code is any code that is based on discontinuous symbols (like fingers, *digitus*); this would include alphabets, numbers, or any other sort of writing system. Hoffmeyer points out that binary code has become synonymous with digital coding, but in fact the invention of the book represents a far earlier employment of digital coding (*B*, 78). An analog code is based on the principle of analogy and continuity. So, a thermometer goes up or down with the temperature, and a piece of clothing codes for the shape of the body. Think of language as digital and body language as analog. Think of not understanding the digital code of someone requesting to see your train ticket in an unfamiliar language, but of understanding the analogically coded hand gesture to see the ticket peeking out of your breast pocket. Digital codes are for memory (they depend on learned conventions or systems resistant to quick change) and analog codes are for action (they depend on the dealings of immediate bodies). As a function of evolutionary memory, the genetic code, Hoffmeyer points out, is a "clear case of digital coding" (*B*, 79). In fact, "if organisms are not natural units of selection, they are at least natural units of communication. Via the digitally coded messages in their genome, they are literally in a line of communication with both their ancestors and their eventual offspring. And via the multiple analog coded messages of their current bodies, they take part in the local semiosphere and interact with other creatures, whether specific or not" (*B*, 103). While analog codes can consist of the physical experiences an organism undergoes in ecological space, Hoffmeyer pushes the idea a bit further and argues that the organism itself represents a unique analogically coded version of the digital DNA recipe. This code-duality is fundamental to life, according to Hoffmeyer; to survive organisms must constantly be involved in "a recursive and unending exchange of messages between analog and digital coding surfaces" (*B*, 80).

Any organism as such is a veritable mise-en-abyme of surfaces inside surfaces. It is skin (and the various skins of which we are composed) that makes us who we are. "On the one hand," Hoffmeyer observes, "the skin thus serves us as a kind of topological boundary; while, on the other hand, its semiotic capacity opens up the world to us" (*B*, 25). Just as 'pataphysics is interested, through methodological constraints, in exposing frames of cultural and linguistic signification, the biosemiotic concern with surfaces and skin interprets intentionality or "aboutness" in the context of membrane thresholds. As Hoffmeyer argues, "the biological orchestration of an organism is created by a well-tuned symphony of biosemiotic relationships across the membranes, which in each instant of an organism's life controls and coordinates the biochemical, physiological, and even cognitive processes that together constitute life" (*B*, 31). Organisms are made of messages and live among messages. For example, a dog's sudden pursuit of another dog is not wholly explained by physical, chemical, and genetic accounts; rather, the scent of one dog constitutes a message to the other. Similarly, a ring dove must coo not only as an act of courtship but also as a sign to her own ovaries to release eggs (*B*, 118). Furthermore, the life cycle of the locust is such that in an un-crowded state it exists as a harmless grasshopper; however, as soon as environmental conditions force greater concentration, a pheromone is released which signals all fertilized eggs to produce what amounts to an entirely different creature – a ravenous, migratory locust with a more powerful body that in turn releases a substance to attract more locusts (*SM*, 21). The locust, as Hoffmeyer observes, "'has taught itself' to read the environmental conditions and report back on them (via a chemical signal) to its reproductive cells, its gametes, ensuring that they shape the members of the next generation to suit the prevailing conditions" (*SM*, 21). Consequently, the analog code of a locust's body is entirely dependent on how the digital code is read in any particular environment.

The metaphor of the well-tuned symphony echoes Jakob von Uexküll (1864–1944), one of the principal forebears of biosemiotics, and his *Umwelt* theory of biological analysis. For Uexküll, ecological dynamics within an ecosystem are best characterized as symphonic, contrapuntal engagements between the different *Umwelten* (subjective universes, or worlds of signification) that constitute each creature's perceptual frame of reference. In "The Theory of Meaning" he proposes that "The properties of the animal and the properties of its fellow actors harmonize in every case like point and counterpoint of a polyphonic choir."[19] Uexküll spends a great deal of time mapping the finely-tuned, harmonic interactions between organisms as morphologically diverse as ticks and humans, spiders and flies, and bees and snapdragons: "their developmental melodies mutually influence each other; the snapdragon's melody appears as a theme in the bumble-bee's developmental melody, and vice versa ... [the bee's] development would be unsuccessful if its body were not 'flower-like'" (SCA, 74). As a means of providing insight into nonhuman *Umwelten*, Uexküll offers what can only be called 'pataphysical descriptions of the imagined worlds of various creatures. In "A Stroll Through the Worlds of Animals and Men," suggestively subtitled "A Picture Book of Invisible Worlds," we are presented, for example, with images of a "village street, seen a by a mollusc," and a "Chandelier as seen by man" versus a "Chandelier as seen by fly."[20] He speculates at one point in "The Theory of Meaning" on the loss of a nocturnal moth species and imagines what shifts in sensory perception would be required to "retrain a day moth" to take its place (SCA, *78*).

Any *Umwelt* involves a continuous feedback between creature and environment. Organisms build their own *Umwelten* through a "functional circle" that links perception and operation.[21] As Thomas Sebeok notes, "Any observer's version of his/her *Umwelt* will be one unique model of the world, which is a system of signs made up of genetic factors plus a cocktail of experiences, including further expectations."[22] While Uexküll explicitly asserts that that "no two human *Umwelten* are the same," it is possible to make claims for larger culturally specific or species-specific *Umwelten* – and their consequent mutability, as I will later argue in the context of environmental ethics.[23] Thus, at the end of "A Stroll Through the Worlds of Animals and Men," he undertakes a series of "ethograms" that detail the worlds of signification particular to different cultures of scientific study. The astronomer, for example, is depicted in an accompanying drawing seated in a tower extending high above the earth, his field of vision dominated by exaggerated orbiting spheres.

Uexküll's poetic pictures of the perceptual worlds of organisms contributed to the view held by other early ecologists that his work was overly vitalistic.[24] Contemporary biosemioticians have endured similar charges. Hoffmeyer, however, insists that while biosemiotics does not share the mystical associations of vitalism, its interest in the interplay between mechanical forces and self-determination in biological systems allies it with broader strands of vitalist thinking (*B*, 12). Jane Bennett has similarly advocated for a "vitality of matter" which she acknowledges has affinities with older discredited animist and vitalist theories. However, like Hoffmeyer, she is not arguing for bodies infused with divine spirit; rather, she worries that we have ignored the lively effects that foods and chemicals have on our bodies and on other creatures around us. Part of her larger project in *Vibrant Matter* is to consider how patterns of consumption might change were we to acknowledge that trash is not simply a disposable object, but a volatile, "lively and potentially dangerous matter."[25] This kind of reconsideration is certainly the object of Smith and Lourie's experiment – the plastic rubber ducky and sippy cup are actively interfering with the semiotics of human biochemistry and need to be seen in this light. I would also argue that Goldsmith's projects have similar political implications when seen in the context of biosemiotics, given that the signifying surfaces of the environment come to constitute the self and its activities. The subway, the park, the weather, his lunch, even his eye virus are not inert entities, but lively forces that interfere with and affect the semiotic processes of the emergent subject in *Soliloquy*.

While biosemiotics is not vitalist in the mystical sense, it does posit, according to Hoffmeyer, a potential driving force behind evolutionary change: semiotic freedom. Semiotic freedom is defined as "the depth of meaning that an individual or species is capable of communicating" (B, 186). Rather than explaining evolution as the emergence of ever more complex morphological structures, it is understood instead as a matter of increasing semiotic freedom – bodies have changed relatively little over the course of evolutionary history compared to the increasing sophistication of communicative capacities. Language, consequently, becomes another complex layer in the evolution of semiotic activity and not a supernatural miracle or the result of a "hopeful monster hypothesis." Wendy Wheeler has extended this idea into a renovated socialist politics and claimed that "Flourishing, we might say, is about how much semiotic freedom you have."[26] The degree to which we signify or do not signify socially affects not only our interpersonal relationships but also our health. A rich semiotic world has both social and environmental implications. Stacey Alaimo writes about how the sensitivity to chemicals that characterizes "environmental illness" implies a co-extensive relationship between humans and the outside world that serves to recast "human health as a matter of environmental health."[27] This transcorporeal space, she argues, is the site of emerging forms of environmentalism that must take into account more complex notions of materiality and subjectivity in order to propose "an ethics that is centred neither in individual humans nor in the imagining of a pristine nature, but instead in the flows and interchanges between them."[28] Similarly, Morton proposes that nature writing has been too quick to create separations between wilderness and humans. Like Buell, Phillips, and others, he proposes addressing this problem by examining the role of subjectivity in nature writing: "Instead of looking at the trees, look at the person who looks at the trees."[29] To ask about the person who looks at trees is to ask about interpretive membranes; it is to refocus attention not on the object of nature writing but upon the subject who writes, on the membranes that filter and read. Goldsmith focuses on such frames and filters in his work. As an information manager of translated texts and medial language, as well as analog and digital codes, his 'pataphysical projects offer a different approach to environmental writing – one whose relevance to ecocriticism must be appreciated for its capacity to increase semiotic freedom.

Part C: Each Other

In *The Weather*, the New York City weather reports, transcribed word for word from hourly radio bulletins for an entire year, become one of the membranes through which interaction with the environment is regulated. As Craig Dworkin notes, *The Weather* "exhibits Goldsmith's signature mode: remediating found texts and crossing artifice with everyday life by metrically regulating the flow of the quotidian through 'pataphysically measured intervals."[30] Given that certain rhetorical patterns emerge, the weather report is never simply elemental information; it is, rather, a living and breathing event that reflects various cultural concerns with, among other things, violence and community – Carolyn Merchant goes so far as to suggest in *The Death of Nature* that weather reports in general can reflect repressive attitudes towards nature.[31] The most obvious examples of culturally inflected forecasts are those that open the "Spring" section of the book. In 2003, the first day of spring was 21 March, one day after the beginning of the invasion of Iraq by US forces. Consequently, the weather for Baghdad begins to signify in the context of New York's weather. In fact, what qualifies as "good" weather becomes recast as favourable conditions for battle:

> As for Middle East weather, it continues to be favourable for military operations, and that'll remain the case through Sunday, but Monday and Tuesday, there may be another episode of strong winds, poor visibilities, and, uh, even some sandstorms. Right now fifty-seven and cloudy in Central Park, temperature going up to sixty-two.[32]

In addition to mediating larger geopolitical concerns, and more local escapist concerns (baseball games are mentioned a number of times), the weather report is a membrane that mediates and determines interior intentions (such as dress codes and travel) according to exterior impediments (heat waves and blizzards). The assumptions and interpretations archived and juxtaposed in the text illuminate the expanded fields of signification at work in the negotiation between subjective and environmental surfaces.

For example, while David Antin praises the book on the back cover as "a classical narrative of New York's four seasons," "a kind of Vivaldi without the birdcalls," the narrative in question is not an objective account (despite the disinterested tone of the meteorological details). Rather, as Marjorie Perloff argues, *The Weather* is actually "Kenny's weather, witnessing his comings and goings in the course of a year."[33] Not every day of the year is represented in the book; the omissions suggest occasions when Goldsmith was out of town or otherwise away from the radio. Moreover, Goldsmith tells Perloff in an e-mail that the act of transcription is not an objective science: "no matter what we do, we leave our imprint – and a very personal imprint at that – on our work."[34] The mechanical process of transcription inevitably deterritorializes into something more personal. This underscores the subjective "aboutness," in biosemiotic terms, of the membranes of transcription and of the weather report itself. Weather reports are transcriptions of meteorological interpretations, and Goldsmith's text is a partial transcription of those transcriptions. *The Weather*, filled with repetitions of phrases such as "we're in for a nice day" and "you should hold off your outdoor plans until Sunday," underscores the way in which processed meteorological data is inevitably personalized and interpreted within larger cultural frames of signification.

"The weather" is a text that we write in the act of transcribing. This is precisely Goldsmith's point in defense of his poetics more generally. He admits that he often asks himself if what he is doing is really writing. His answer is yes: "in the expanded field of appropriation, uncreativity, sampling, and language management in which we all habit today ... Each and every word was 'written' by me ... [and] without my intervention, slight as it may be, these works would have never found their way into the world."[35] Transcription is not a neutral practice. In describing his discussions with students who have been assigned the task of "uncreatively" transcribing texts, Goldsmith points to all kinds of questions that might normally fall to the periphery of writing discussions. Such questions include: "What kind of paper did you use? Why is it on generic white computer paper when the original edition was on thick, yellowed, pulpy stock? What does it say about you: your aesthetic, economic, social, and political circumstances?"[36] *The Weather*, retyped, raises the same kinds of questions – not just for Goldsmith, but for readers who encounter the forecasts in their resonant materiality and semiotic variability.

"Transcription" may not be the best word to describe the operative mechanism of Goldsmith's poetics. In fact, in light of Steve McCaffery's writings as part of the Toronto Research Group (TRG), I would like to suggest that what Goldsmith calls transcription is better understood as translation – or, more specifically, geomantic translation. "Rational Geomancy" for the TRG represents a 'pataphysical activity that is concerned with the semiotics of the environment. It is concerned with "rearranging existing elements in nature" in order to "augment and focus the yin/yang energy currents that flow over the earth's surface" (TRG, 33). Geomancy is the art of interpreting earthly signs (for example, the patterns revealed by dirt thrown down upon a surface) (TRG, 53). While Goldsmith's works are not translations in the conventional sense, they are all nonetheless found poems (texts taken from various discursive environments), which, according to the TRG, makes them a species of translation inasmuch as they represent "an activity upon a source text and a transportation of selected material into a new context" (TRG, 56).

Soliloquy, for instance, is a geomantic act given the perceptual realignment that it creates. By controlling for the first-person perspective, Goldsmith's text succeeds in affirming the ontological status of the relational activity of phatic language and interpersonal exchange. (The phatic dimension of language is something that Morton believes ecocriticism has regrettably neglected; see *EWN*, 37.) He prefers the term *medial* to phatic for its emphasis not only on speech, but on the communicative medium, such as page, lettering, and other paralinguistic elements in printed texts.) By a kind of translation, *Soliloquy* puts into relief the embodied gestures, discourse markers, and speech disfluencies that take place alongside, or within, the conversation:

> Yeah. Yeah. Yeah. Yeah. Uh huh? Oh, I, you know, professional what is, you know, I know you don't have to explain that. Oh well, yeah. I I understand. No, really, you know… Oh, Christ! Can you hold it a sec? Al, can you hold it a sec? Yes, I agree. Wait. This is interesting let me maybe Cheryl, hold on. Hello? Hey Bruce, how you doin'? Good where … good. Where are ya? OK, um, quick or you wanna yak a little bit? OK. Yep. Yeah. Great. Great, um …[37]

This sequence, abounding with phatic particles, draws attention to the material environment of language and, as Dworkin notes, to its deeply social nature.[38] It has ecopoetic implications as well. As Morton argues,

"Avant-garde and experimental artworks that are not directly ecological in content are environmental in form, since they contain medial elements" (*EWN*, 38). The whole book draws attention to the medial materiality of this voice – the stutters, references, tones, locations, and implied futures and pasts suddenly exist in the forefront. Such a focus is consistent with the biosemiotic aim of countering "The tendency of natural science to deny the ontological reality of relations" (*B*, 51). Biosemiotics stresses the role of "process organization," where relationships and not simply individual parts can be said to exist as drivers of causality (*B*, 46, 49). The relational and semiotic dynamics of systems alter the mechanical processes within any organism or organization.

The "ums," "ahs," and stutters also serve to mark the integration of digital and analog codes in Goldsmith's work. Gregory Bateson, one of the important precursors to biosemiotics, was interested in the paralinguistic aspects of communication (the modulation of pitch, the *way* things are said) and in this way brought attention to the "much overlooked importance of analog coding in natural systems" (*B*, 88). Goldsmith is often described as a "digital poet," which is an appropriate label given his interest in the web (as both a source and site for his art), as well as his interest in procedural poetics. However, the analog dimension to his work, generally neglected in such terms by critics, is just as important.[39] In fact, Goldsmith's work might be said to express digital-analog code duality in a manner relevant to biosemiotics. The digital codes of his texts, the genetics of his 'pataphysical project, so to speak, are the conceptual methodologies he employs (his constraints) that recall the memory of avant-garde medial art – techniques previously used by Cage, Warhol, and others. The analog codes are the unique manifestations of these conceptual methodologies – the actual real-life interpretations. The analog codes are the textual bodies: the final results as well as the physical interactions with various environments and predicaments that go into making them. In order for these texts to have been written, a body had to experience everything, as Goldsmith is all too happy to point out – even cutting and pasting becomes a sensual experience for him: "physical, and as sexy as, say, carving stone."[40] The importance of analog codes and membranous surfaces is underscored by the offhand remarks Goldsmith makes about his experiences. For example, in undertaking *Fidget*, a book that transcribes every physical movement the author made for a day, he talks about how he could no longer withstand the tedium of his practice and consequently sought relief in drunkenness. This particular detour is not in the conceptual methodology of the project at all; however, it reflects an interpretive intervention by an affective dimension. It reflects a particular emotional aspect, or filtering membrane, that inflected the fundamental result of this project.

The privileging of digital codes in Western culture is synonymous with capitalist industrial modes that emphasize plans over execution. Hoffmeyer points out that "industrial production is supposed to follow deterministically from the prescribed plan, there is left little or no space for *interpretation* at the level of execution" (*B*, 79). The innovative interpretations of workers are subordinated to larger corporate directives. This hierarchy extends to traditional evolutionary theory and its emphasis on the master plan of DNA over the subordinated role of membranes as agents of interpretation. Goldsmith himself falls into this prejudice as well when he claims that his books are fully explained by their concept; they do not even have to be read.[41] His claims for "uncreative" writing, however, ring a bit hollow when in fact he is quite literally creative not only with the bodily execution of his plans, but also with his willingness, as I mentioned above, to share important details about the experience that would not have been evident from the purely digital (textual) result. In fact, it is clearly the point that his projects be realized, that they demonstrate, according to McCaffery, the spectacle of their labour, "the activity of labourious transcription as information portage."[42] Similarly, as Molly Schwartzburg insists, the "performance of his experiments is not just the story behind his works, it *is* the Work."[43] If the 'pataphysical catalogue of Darren Wershler-Henry's *The Tapeworm Foundry*, for example, includes imaginary but unrealized works of art, Goldsmith, like a good scientist, sees his experiments through to completion. The often absurd labour of his projects is a literal creativity that, despite his claims to the opposite, draws undeniable attention to the analog coding of the digital concept.

Code duality is important in biosemiotics because it allows for interaction between genetics and environment, between the recipe for the organism and its real-world manifestation and behaviour in ecological space – without reducing the organism to a deterministic explanation by way of either code. The implication is that "the organism cannot be the privileged unit in biology and neither can the genome. Life is a semiotic process carried forward in time by the lineage in its interaction with changing environments."[44] The contingencies of the execution in *Soliloquy*, for example, reveal a body signifying in various contexts, be they artistic, familial, or dog-walking spheres. A day or a week in this life – like any life – is a composite of evoked personae depending on circumstance. In *Soliloquy* Goldsmith says hypocritical and unflattering things about friends. He is occasionally mean – sometimes even in explicitly biochemical terms, such as his critique of the hormonal chemistry of a homely acquaintance: "She's so unattractive! Like she's kind of like an excess of male hormones."[45] He is paradoxical in his treatment of "nature," which he encounters variously as a moment of wonder at blooming trees, as something to be dismissed in his talks with Perloff, and as a pastoral retreat to France and upstate New York. Indeed, despite the distaste he obviously shares with Perloff for the words "environmentalist" or "ecology," this text underscores repeatedly the influence of the environment of New York City on his identity: Goldsmith constantly re-writes himself depending on where he is. As Craig Dworkin observes, "Manhattan itself is an important character in *Soliloquy*, with its cabs and subways not just providing transportation but also mapping discourse networks and lines of communication."[46] The soliloquizing subject of this book is not a discrete entity, but a membranous figure composed of composite interpretive surfaces that constantly re-transcribe or geomantically re-translate subjectivity according to the diversity of the semiotic environment.

Similarly, in his analysis of *Fidget* (in the essay belonging to this volume), McCaffery implicitly draws attention to the importance of the environment for the manifestation of the body by remarking that "Goldsmith's itinerary perversely celebrates a single locale: Manhattan, present in its referential absence, a metropolis imploded into body parts and movements."[47] In *Fidget*, Goldsmith effectively creates a new semiotics of the body, one in which digital language can be only roughly adequate to physical, analog experience. Here is Goldsmith urinating:

> Extracts testicles and penis using thumb and forefinger. Left hand grasps penis. Pelvis pushes on bladder, releasing urine. Stream emerges from within buttocks. Stomach and buttocks push outward. Stream of urine increases. Buttocks push. Sphincter tightens. Buttocks tighten. Thumb and forefinger shake penis.[48]

The result is a kind of "body language," which Christopher Schmidt defines in terms reminiscent of biosemiotics as the text's capacity to express "the body's inter-organ communication as well as its semaphoric messages to other subjects."[49] This "new language field," as Perloff calls it, is most readily revealed in the closing chapter where Goldsmith (drunkenly) reprints the first chapter backwards with slight alterations to reflect a mirrored experience (for example "pinch" in Chapter 10:00 becomes "etarapes" (separate) in Chapter 22:00). The ubiquitous word "and" becomes "dna," as if to suggest that the rendering of this emotionally distressed body will call for an expansion of the rules and recipes – "the genetic code" – of this language. The chapter in reverse represents, moreover, a recursive intervention of analog coding into the digital code of the published text and of the memorialized occasion – it feeds the analogical body back into the digital code of the day. If *Fidget* is a recording of a life, then its digital memory (the unfolding text of the book) is constantly being written over (and into) by the analogical codes of the experiencing body. We see this in *Soliloquy* as well through the shifts in stories and the duplicitous comments that unfold over the course of the week – Perloff, for example, is an important recurring element of Goldsmith's week. However, his historical (recorded and archived) account of his lunch with her varies depending on who he is talking to and reflects his increasing confidence that he has impressed her, that he has come to signify as someone important for this significant literary critic.

If *Soliloquy* and *Fidget* express biosemiotic code-duality, does that mean that the books are organisms? Does Goldsmith's decision, outlined in "Being Boring," to reprise his experiment with *Day* using the 11 September 2001 edition of the *New York Times* reflect the evolutionary influence of his analog experiences on the digital code of his conceptual art? Is this the evolution of the textual organism before our very eyes? There is a long history in ecocriticism of making webs and chains into models for the ecological dynamics of poems. William Rueckert, for example, proposes that "A poem is stored energy, a formal turbulence, a living thing, a swirl in the flow. Poems are part of the energy pathways that sustain life. Poems are a verbal equivalent to fossil fuel."[50] Goldsmith's work is important to ecocriticism because it does not rely on organic metaphors but literally enacts the biosemiotic principle that semiosis is life. A day or a week in the life of the organism of Kenneth Goldsmith is a constant exchange of messages between inside and outside, between affect and defect, between the limits of emotional and physical worlds, and between a body and the city that both surrounds it and reflects it. While it is true that Goldsmith is a digital poet, he is also importantly an analog poet; he puts his plans into action, he turns words into affective substances (how much does a week's worth of speaking actually weigh?), he literally reminds us that language is part of the environment. The job of the writer, Goldsmith declares in the film *Kenneth Goldsmith: Sucking on Words*, is to be a filter, to "become an intelligent agent," a membrane, in biosemiotic terms, that is attentively and broadly tuned to the semiosphere, actively building an expanding *Umwelt.*

Goldsmith's texts revel in their paradoxes rather than trying to escape them. In this way, they could be called "darkly ecological." For Morton, dark ecology proposes that to clean the world we need to make thinking dirtier. For example, "Instead of trying endlessly to get rid of the subject-object dualism, dark ecology dances with the subject-object duality" (EWN, 185). Ecocritics presuppose unproductive distinctions when they worry about a self divorced from nature. From a biosemiotic perspective, the interplay between digital and analog codes in Goldsmith's texts reveals the subject to be an emergent and contingent form always in relation to and constituted by semiotic feedback from its environment.

Goldsmith's 'pataphysical works need to be seen in the context of ecopoetics because they draw particular attention to the role of the writer as a species of environmental scientist, collecting and ordering forms of communication in the semiosphere. Just as Smith and Lourie draw attention to the body as an internal engagement with external environmental pollutants, Goldsmith presents the body as a semiotic environment engaged with and responsive to its immersion in the external circulation of signs and messages. If semiosis is life, then Goldsmith's conceptual poetics function as a kind of natural history project, identifying unusual *Umwelten* through the imposition of 'pataphysical filters. For all of their transcribed predictability, *The Weather*, *Soliloquy*, and *Fidget* are, in the end, highly unpredictable texts in terms of the juxtapositions they effect and the responses they elicit: they are outrageous works of environmental writing (who would do such a thing?). If Goldsmith's work does not need to be read, then it throws into question the very nature of reading itself, as Robert Fitterman speculates.[51] Is *not-reading* a form of reading? Given that Goldsmith acknowledges his interest in engaging a "thinkership" rather than a readership, what alternative form of reading might this require? These kinds of questions lead us back into the nature of semiotics itself, into the nature of what it means to communicate. It is precisely these provocations that make Goldsmith's work an example of increasing semiotic freedom.

What Morton calls for in his description of "dark ecology" is consistent with 'pataphysics and biosemiotics – both are interested in "reframing our view of the ecological" so that "what was 'outside' yesterday will be 'inside' today" (EWN, 195). The implicit question raised in *The Weather*, *Soliloquy*, and *Fidget* is, as Joshua Schuster asks of Goldsmith's work more generally: "What is it like to live in these textual environments? Could a different management of language create a better way of living?"[52] Rachel Carson reminds us powerfully in *Silent Spring* of the disquieting specter of a world without birdsong, a world of diminished signification.[53] If life depends on semiotic processes, then environmentalist politics must surely depend on listening at the edges of the semiosphere, it must depend on an information management that pushes the boundaries of *Umwelten* so that what does not matter might begin to matter.

8

Getting Every Word In: A.R. Ammons's *Garbage* and the Corpora

J. MARK SMITH

In an annunciative essay of 1973, Harold Bloom set the work of his friend A.R. Ammons squarely in Emerson's line.[1] Those with something to say about the poet since have generally taken the Emerson-derived quality to be perfectly self-evident. In an essay published some thirty years later, for instance, Marjorie Perloff in one stroke summons and dismisses the side of Ammons's work she considers tired and trite: "[the] willed air, as if to say, yes, I *am* an Emersonian poet and should therefore talk of the mysterious 'radiance, that does not withhold itself …' I should present the epiphany that makes 'the heart move roomier.'"[2] Now this critical situation is interesting. Perloff finds mannerism rather than thought in the lines of the poem she deprecates – "The City Limits," probably Ammons's best known lyric. And yet her disappointment could very well serve as an example of what others (Richard Poirier, Stanley Cavell) consider the most characteristic Emersonian movement of thought: namely, its resistance to formations or formulations too facile or close at hand, or to what in the long poem *Garbage* Ammons himself calls "a real stick in the fluencies: a leftover light / that hinders the light stream …"[3]

In his compositional approach to the long poem and in his commitment to a lexical "open field," Ammons works with a continuum of utterance whose central furrows are the most frequently repeated words and phrases in the contemporary American vulgate, but whose far outcastings register the faintest traces of anomalous use. In this poem, moreover, Ammons explores – through such figures specific to *Garbage* as primate "accommodation" and "the blabbermouth" – the process by which any phrase or expression may be used, used up, ignored, discarded, taken as exemplary, rediscovered, lost again, transformed, even "revitalized." *Garbage* is the record of a series of "one-time events," a throw of utterance.[4] Its lines record historical-linguistic contingency and conformity, but also a speaker's partial freedom. To bring into highlight Ammons's interest in "events of sense" and the saliences that can be discerned in them, I turn to a contemporary philological instrument, the linguistic corpus, and consider what such a database has in common with a garbage dump, and what with a published long poem.[5]

Garbage, published in 1993, works outward from a central image of great mounds of burning landfill seen by Ammons one day "down by I-95 in / Florida" (G, 18). It's a poem about things fallen out of use, and out of mind; about transformations entirely material, but also about degradations and recuperations of interest, attention, and relationship ("garbage is spiritual" [G, 18]). Ammons's premise is that the process of sorting and grouping (or abstracting) that produces what we commonly call "garbage" also powers the appearances, disappearances, and re-appearances of words. The physical contents of an American landfill as imagined by Ammons – "knickknacks (knickknackatery), / whatnots (whatnotery), doodads, jews-harps, / belt buckles, do-funnies, files, disks, pads, / pesticide residues, nonprosodic high-tension / lines, whimpering-wimp dolls, epichlorohydrin / elastomotors, sulfur dioxide emissions, perfume / sprays, radioactive williwaws ..." [G, 108] – one can only hope will, in mid-range geological time, be turned over to "the bacteria, the tumblebugs, the scavengers" of his dedication.[6]

As for the words, the poem also gets in its sights "the garbage-heap of used-up language."[7] Ammons goes a distance down this tropological sidecurrent of Romantic tradition, one where we find Emerson too. Both wonder about the part to be played by the poet, over a differently calibrated (historical) span of time, in revitalizing or transfiguring – perhaps even rematerializing – the "dead-material concentrate" in speech and thought. The poetic act, Ammons writes, is itself "like an installation at Marine / Shale," for it

reaches down into the dead pit
and cool oil of stale recognition and words and

brings up hauls of stringy gook which it arrays
with light and strings with shiny syllables and

gets the mind back into vital relationship with
communication channels: but, of course, there

is some untransformed material, namely the poem
itself; the minute its transmutations end, it

becomes a relic sometimes only generations or
sets of countrywide generations can degrade:

a real stick in the fluencies: a leftover light
that hinders the light stream: poems themselves

processing, revitalizing so much dead material
become a dead-material concentrate time's

longest actions sometimes can't dissolve ...
(G, 108–9)

What exactly is this "dead pit" of language that by deft rearrangements can be reanimated?[8] And what - since the qualification is almost twice as long as the affirmation of future restoration – is the "dead material" that "time's / longest actions sometimes can't dissolve"?

Ammons's source for the notion of poetry being opposed to "stale recognition and words" is, of course, Shelley's well-known formulation in "A Defense of Poetry": "Their language is vitally metaphorical; that is, it marks the before unapprehended relations of things and perpetuates their apprehension, until the words which represent them, become through time signs for portions or classes of thoughts instead of pictures of integral thoughts; and then if no new poets should arise to create afresh the associations which have been thus disorganized, language will be dead to all the nobler purposes of human intercourse."[9] The sedimentation that forms shale is Ammons's further figuring of what happens to successful metaphors over time. The death of a metaphor is really a "disorganizing" of thought; large areas of a language become a "dead pit" when its readers have no hope of representing and organizing thought and feeling in it. Metaphor "revitalizes" insofar as it realigns living minds with the apprehensible world in which they dwell.

As for "material," Ammons allows the word, as in ordinary usage, a range of meaning between the physical and the semiotic. But the lines from *Garbage* quoted above point primarily to the phrasings and combinations of words themselves. Ammons's installation at Marine Shale has some sort of genealogical relation to Emerson's famous remark in "The Poet": "The etymologist finds the deadest word to have been once a brilliant picture. Language is fossil poetry. As the limestone of the continent consists of infinite masses of the shells of animalcules, so language is made up of images or tropes, which now, in their secondary use, have long since ceased to remind us of their poetic origin."[10] Emerson has in view the histories of roots and cognates uncovered by nineteenth-century philology, and perhaps also (a little before that) John Horne Tooke's inclination to find a concrete root buried in every abstract meaning.

And yet, despite the metaphor of shale and oil, Ammons is not drawn to etymology – not at all; there's not a nod anywhere in *Garbage* towards the late medieval Anglo-French contexts (hunting, preparation of game, early cook books) out of which "garbishe," noun and verb, first emerges into modern English usage.[11] The sort of "relic" or "dead-material concentrate" Ammons contemplates does not necessarily date from the beginning or origin-time of any language. Rather, these sticks in the fluencies are thrown up by current usage itself (Emerson's "secondary use") – they are, in the main, culturally prestigious instances of use, since these are most available for thoughtless repetition. Ammons's dead-material concentrate shows up not in the shells of Indo-European animalcules, but is an entirely contemporary phenomenon.

With this qualification in mind, I would like to consider again the riverine vehicle and tenor of Ammons's phrase "a real stick in the fluencies." If it's a metaphor, what is the stick? And what are these "fluencies" exactly?

First, the stick. It presents an image of protrusion or salience that belongs both to the realm of *physis* and of human meaningfulness. The word "saliences" appears frequently in Ammons's mid-phase poetry. John

Ashbery, in an essay of 1973, notes acutely that in Ammons's idiolect "saliences are pertinent and outstanding but not necessarily to be confused with meaning."[12] According to *Webster's Third*, "salient" (adj.) includes such senses as [4a] "projecting above or beyond a general line, surface, or level: jutting upward or outward" and [4b] "standing out conspicuously." A salient (n.) is "something (as a promontory or cape along a shoreline or an abrupt change in the profile of a stream course) that projects outward or upward from its surroundings." A stick pushed up above the horizontal surface of a stream is a salient. Now why did Ammons have a preference for the plural form of the noun? I think the reason is that salien*ces* are many such projections; and that saliences produce a perceptual or aesthetic effect of roughness, of complex orderings that challenge traditional notions of congruency and shapely form.

Next, the fluencies. Something central to *Garbage* is its representation of linguistic "ongoing" or "the central current" – its figuring of usage broadly and synchronically understood, what lexicographer John Landau defines as "any or all uses of language, spoken or written."[13] Any or all uses in (what was) the present moment, that is. Ammons values the currency of use rather than the historical might and magnitude of language, hence avoids almost all reference to Europe while seeming indifferent to processes of lexical differentiation or absorption.[14] The lexicography of past usage interests Ammons considerably less than the way that, as he phrases it in the poem called "Saliences," contemporary "events of sense / alter old dunes of mind"; and the way these "changing weathers" – the constantly ongoing but mostly unnoticed pressure of linguistic drift and transformation – enter into the speech patterns of individual speakers, sometimes into their awarenesses.[15]

Now, what is "a real stick in the fluencies"? It is obvious that in some general way Ammons is referring to cliché, to the over-used expression. In what way, then, are clichés like sticks – saliences – in a river? To answer that, we first need to say something about the method of the poem's composition, which is to say how these words and clauses and sentences came to the page as "events of sense":

... I think of this tape

(this is another tape, a little wider, just about
pentameter) as the showboat churning down the

Mississippi with the banks, the fast currents,
the sandbars, drenchings; that is, it is going

down, like it or not …
(G, 63–4)

Ammons employed similar improvised, no-stopping, "one-time event" compositional procedures – first in *Tape for the Turning of the Year* (1963) and in later long poems.[16] The procedures themselves were not original with Ammons: in the background were widely shared mid-century reference points such as the "free association" of psychoanalytic method, Jackson Pollock's drip paintings, Jack Kerouac's experiments in typing (as Truman Capote dubbed them), and John Cage's "happenings." Nevertheless, the way Ammons followed out the implications of those procedures in each long poem, as well as in the group of such works produced over more than three decades, was singular. They allowed him to steer a poetic showboat down "the fluencies" in such a way that the throw of utterance in the moment would register historical-linguistic contingency and conformity, in addition to a speaker's partial freedom to seek out or swerve away from "the sticks" in the fluencies.

I follow a distinction once made by Hugh Kenner in preferring to call the words recorded in *Garbage* "utterance" as opposed to soliloquy or monologue. In a little-known 1982 essay, Kenner begins by arguing that "the closed field" – a term from number theory – is "the dominant intellectual analogy of our time."[17] By excluding elements from a system of numbers, one sets up a closed field. A literary closed field, by analogy, might constrain the lexical elements in the system. A dictionary – the print edition of one anyway – presents a closed field: "[the dictionary] implies that the number of words at our disposal is finite; it also implies that the process by which new words are made has been terminated" (ACF, 207). Kenner notes how Flaubert's interest in the isolated word or *mot juste* was "the residue of nearly two centuries of lexicography, which had virtually transformed the vocabulary of each written language into a closed field" (ACF, 207). The modernist experiments of Joyce and Beckett turned upon a closed field of words or other literary elements; the constraint-driven exercises of the Oulipo group still more so. But, Kenner, goes on, for the most part twentieth-century American poets – led by William Carlos Williams – rejected the closed field:

> American literature … has always tended to reject [the analogy of the closed field]. That is one reason, I think, why so much American poetry has patterned itself aggressively on speech, not print, and furthermore not the speech of conversation, which is always in danger of falling into a closed set of patterns, as Flaubert saw, but rather the speech of what is sometimes called spontaneity but is actually just naked utterance, spontaneous or premeditated. That is because it cannot afford to imply an answer, which implies a counter-answer, which implies a conversation, which implies a game with rules and so … a closed field. (ACF, 212)

The sentences set down in each section of *Garbage* – whether they were spontaneous or, as seems likely, partly premeditated – have this quality of "naked utterance." The rules of its game commit this poem, in the way Kenner suggests, to the idea of an open field.[18]

Ammons typically declines to figure his idea of an open field exclusively in linguistic terms: he writes of "not getting caught inside"; of bringing to mind fringes, peripheries, edges. And because the writing of *Garbage* draws so much attention to the present moment – to what is happening now – his preferred metaphor for the open field of temporality is generally riverine: The lines of words on the unwinding tape, typed and/or read in the present moment, are "going down"; the poem, as projected into a temporary future, has "a clear space to go" (G, 63). Usage – not "language," which implies a fixed and finite system – is a stream, but within its fluencies are both highly repetitive and anomalous patternings that Ammons figures as protrusions or (inversely) furrows. These verbal patternings are "real stick[s]," with a play on "stick on the mud," itself an example of a phrasal stick in the fluencies. In that such patternings are perceptible as filigree or fringe in the onward flow of a riverine system, they are "sticks"; they have, as I will explain, a fractal quality.

Garbage makes visible a continuum of utterance between the patternings of high frequency repetition and the faint outcastings of the anomalous and the singular. These two poles I will call – without implying any simple binary such as correct vs. erroneous speech – "representative" and "anomalous" utterance. By representative speech, I mean the word choices and combinations that, at a particular historical moment, in certain commonplace communicative situations, most speakers of a language, most of the time, draw upon frequently. Common usage authorizes all claims about representative speech, and about anomalous utterance too. By anomalous, I mean a broad and neutral category that includes eccentric, odd, non-conforming, and poetic uses. Examples of representative speech have been statistically analyzable since the 1990s in lexicographical databases, also known as *corpora*, which catch anomalies as well as dense aggregations of representative use.

In *Garbage*, representative and anomalous traces of speech amount to two kinds of salience. On the one hand are the always amassing instances of "main current" speech; on the other, the outliers of use. In the poem "Saliences," Ammons pictured "events of sense" as the apparently chaotic, always changing patterns of sand dunes. More recently, a digital equivalent to the drifting dunes of speech presents itself in the corpora that have been repositories for mass instances of speech and writing. *The Corpus of Contemporary American English* (COCA), a searchable online database that contains some 410 million words of text gathered from instances of writing and speech published or recorded between 1990 and 2010, is an instrument that I have found helpful for discerning the two sorts of salience.[19] That COCA includes no published poems in its representative collection of texts (it does include some literary and commercial fiction) makes singular and striking instances of use even less likely to occur. There are no records in COCA, say, of "saliences," "spread firmingly," or "not a single single thing endures." In contrast, a search of COCA turns up many occurrences of "factor" or "variable" or "overall" or "not a single thing."[20] The bar-graph saliences of representative speech, in effect, tower over those of low-frequency words and phrases. These linguistically unremarkable congruencies attest to the collective speech habits of the moment. High-frequency usage is, by definition, representative. Everything else is statistically insignificant. The question of how poetic instances of use – those that present the language with "another need for the word," as Wilhelm von

Humboldt once put it – can be distinguished, or come to distinguish themselves, from odd and infelicitous uses brings us to the theme of the exemplary, which I will discuss in the latter part of this essay.[21]

COCA is typical of corpora in that it archives a very large number of actual instances of language use as produced by what its creators consider to be a representative cross-section – hence by no means a predominantly literary sample – of writers and speakers. As with a concordance, one can search through corpora to determine the frequency of occurrence of particular phrases, or of the syntactically undetermined groupings of words known (in the jargon of corpus linguistics) as collocations. Corpora store text in not quite the same manner as landfills hold material; their digital spaces are filled with citations or duplications of recorded acts of speech or writing. More to the point – and here the analogy breaks down – each string of text in a corpus is multiply tagged and searchable. A landfill is not as easy to search through. Corpora, however, may well be our best example of what Ammons calls the textual "disposition" of words: garbage, out of mind, lies silent and "disposed" of; and so too do these instances of use.[22]

In book 10 of *Garbage*, Ammons records his own unsatisfactory encounter with a digital library catalogue that he was attempting to harness as one might twenty years later have employed the search engine of a corpus. That is, he was in pursuit of words and collocations ("garbage disposal," for one) rather than of treatises on the subject of garbage disposal:

> … I punched
>
> out Garbage at the library and four titles
> swept the screen, only one, Garbage Feed,
>
> seeming worth going on to; and that was about
> feeding swine right: so I punched Garbage Disposal
>
> and the screen came blank – nothing! All those
> titles, row on row, of western goodies, mostly
>
> worse than junk, but not a word on Disposal: I
> should have looked, I suppose, under Waste Disposal

but, who cares, I already got the point: I
know garbage is being "disposed" of –
...
(G, 49)[23]

One thing quickly discovered upon browsing in any corpus is the massively repetitive, tedious, unimaginative quality of most instances of speech and writing, especially (and not surprisingly) in the cases of high-frequency words and collocations. Sidney Landau explains the difference between the "citation files" collected in traditional lexicographical practice (by the OED's early editors, for instance, and their teams of readers) and the text files stored in corpora: "As James A.H. Murray had occasion to remark in connection with the OED files, citation readers all too often ignore common usages and give disproportionate attention to uncommon ones, as the seasoned birder thrills at a glimpse in the distance of a rare bird while the grass about him teems with ordinary domestic varieties that escape his notice."[24] The "ordinary domestic varieties" of speech do not escape the scanning equipment used to stock the corpora. An information feed of that sort is not, of course, dependent upon any one reader *noticing* the saliences of common usage. Self-conscious diction and syntax, stylish speech, mindful speaking – however highly literary judgment rates such attributes, the evidence of the corpora suggests that these outliers may be, like consciousness itself, an over-rated phenomenon.

The corpora are charged with banalities and oddities that perhaps would have pricked Ammons's sense of humour, which was sustained by the incongruity of expanses and fringes, ridiculously local ("these bitty / events" [G, 95]) and absurdly or terrifyingly universal perspectives. To be more precise: incongruity is humorous; but the sensation of the sublime, in Edmund Burke's formulation, narrowly, and hence pleasurably, avoids terror. The vastness of the man-made world is itself enough to overwhelm and inflict pain upon the mind. It is perhaps fortunate that, as Ammons writes, "Words, which attach to edges, cannot represent wholeness" (G, 114). As for the immensity of the physical universe, Ammons allows himself a humorous (rather than sublime) sketch of what the representation of wholeness would call for:

> … but think what it would be like to get
> every word in, to trickle every rhythm in and
>
> the overrhythms curling, lagging, eddying along
> a network of motional obbligatos: imagine
>
> getting all the elements in (including the
> element of surprise), the axis each philodendron
>
> leaf takes to the window, gathering it up round
> and dumping it where it belongs in the sweeping,
>
> the unheard, the unspent, that which is around
> the edges of whatever may be: everything
>
> assimilated to star-ypointing song: would that
> not ease the mind, if discommode breakfast,
>
> unhinge federal taxation …
> (G, 104)

This fantasy of "getting every word" and "all the elements" in involves, crucially, getting all the rhythms, and rhythms within rhythms, in too. Ammons, unlike Borges, having "got in" an infinity of verbal *and* non-verbal detail would not have us proceed to the universe-size map, since he diagnoses in himself – and all humankind – a drive instead towards the sublime ease of "higher assimilations." Our anxious prosodies crave "star-ypointing song": trickling every rhythm in would exacerbate rather than assuage anxiety, even if the bitty events (and their representations) are more likely to be amusing.[25] Digital mnemo-technologies make possible "higher assimilations" of a computational sort. Repositories of vast quantities of linguistic information such as COCA make a plausible claim to representativeness. (Federal taxation relies on it too.) But the presumption of completeness or wholeness, even exhaustiveness, is illusory. If anything, the technologies of computer science in combination with theories of communication seem to "dump" the larger part of linguistic reality out with "the sweeping, / the unheard, the unspent, that which is around / the edges of whatever may be ..."

Even so, the fantasy of "getting every word in" finds an unexpected correlate in the information management networks that make sense of – and make technically possible – Kenneth Goldsmith's conceptual poetics. For instance, Goldsmith's *The Weather* project (published 2005; commented on by McCaffery and Dickinson in this volume) is a transcription of the vocal stagings of a year's worth of hourly one-minute weather bulletins broadcast by a New York radio station. These localized texts bear a family resemblance to larger corpora in that accumulative and open-ended citation of whatever sort depends at present on digital technologies of reproduction and storage.[26]

Now if, as I hold, COCA's data stores as much as Goldsmith's transcriptions point to hard truths about usage – namely that literary combinations of words scarcely even graze the great drifting mass of high frequency collocations – a question that soon follows is whether any dichotomy between mass and literary uses of language can be sustained. Some would say it cannot. For its part, COCA pretty clearly shows that there *are* differences in patterns of usage, though such evidence merely shifts the terms of the question. And corpus linguists value their databases, and mistrust traditional lexicographical sources, precisely because the former are not distorted by the outcastings of literary usage.[27] Moreover, literary usage is not the same as anomalous usage; as Wordsworth observed more than two centuries ago, clichés that appear only in literary contexts are still clichés. Why defend that special sub-class of anomalous use that is "original" or "creative" or "poetic," especially when successful – what I have called here *exemplary* – instances are by definition subsumed into a common speech? Is it something other than linguistic perversity or elitism or plain orneriness that turns a poet's utterances away from harmonious congruence with the "uncreative" saliences of mainstream speech?

I think Ammons's answer to such a question can be found at a number of points through *Garbage*. It seems likely he would have declined to champion human creativity, or even the "thinking" part of the mind, if it required claiming that "language" confers some special status upon *homo sapiens*. "[G]rooming does for baboons / most of what words do for us" (G, 52). Which is to say, mostly we use words for pre-verbal social purposes

– to bond, to hierarchize, and to arrange "accommodation" (G, 26). The corpora reaffirm Ammons's observation regarding what words do for us, as do Goldsmith's works.[28] Both are full of instances of speech that were not intended to be repeated, listened to for their semantic content, or thought about. Those utterances, prior to being transcribed and repeated in print, were doing other things for us – namely, helping us to accommodate and be accommodated.

But do words never help us to think? To represent the world and our relation to it clearly and distinctly? Ammons, though with many qualifications, evidently supposes that sometimes they do. Moreover, certain orderings of words will help us to think better about complexity. From Ammons's perspective, the best hope for poetry and thought is a compositional situation in which the "clarity" of representational thought will not disallow the motional "complexity" of everything that does not think – including ourselves, most of the time, and our usages – but nor will the motional complexity swamp the noetic possibility that is clarity:

> I want to see
>
> furrows of definition, both the centerings of
> furrow and the clumpy outcastings beyond: I do
>
> not want to be caught inside for clarity: I
> want clarity to be a smooth long bend
>
> disallowing no complexity in coming clean: why
> do I want this, complexity without confusion,
>
> clarity without confinement, time in time, not
> time splintered: …
> (G, 92–3)

The image of graph or schematism that comes to Ammons at this moment in the poem is a way of talking about the difficulties that arise in representing the "roughness" of natural phenomena.[29] Like saliences, "furrows of definition" are not necessarily to be confused with meanings, for the "centering / of furrow and the clumpy outcastings beyond" describes both natural and linguistic phenomena. That said, the image of "furrows of definition" pictures word frequency and usage as a phenomenon characterized by complex discrepancies in "scale" (that is, again, by "roughness"). The task of the poet – "not to be caught inside for clarity" – would seem to be at least two-fold: to find a way out of the formal regularity or containedness of lyric; and to take on the complex linguistic and social determinants of a measure such as lexical frequency *not* as the problem of how to "get every word in" but as an always localized instance of the problem of vision ("clarity").

The now celebrated mathematician Benoit Mandelbrot, by his own account, first noticed ordered patternings concealed in various sorts of "roughness" when he reviewed George Kingsley Zipf's early twentieth-century studies of word frequency (*MBM*, 151–2). Zipf had found that the most frequently used words in a language occur in a diminishing series that can be quantified by a formula that mathematicians call a "power law." The incidences of most other words are so rare as to form what are known statistically as "fat tails."[30] One could, then, to various ends (some fatuous or reactionary), use such a formula to measure differences in the lexical richnesses of texts or individuals' utterances (*MBM*, 152). Despite sharing the view with Mandelbrot and Zipf that language is a natural phenomenon, Ammons diverges from this sort of thinker in that their effort is directed towards understanding and eventually managing "irregularity."[31] Ammons, on the other hand, aspires to set the transitory sightings made possible by a poetic sequence of words into a "motion" that holds the fact of roughness or irregularity within its literary smoothness. The striking image (already quoted) of an unrepresentable whole is of a complex fractal in motion: "the over-rhythms curling, lagging, eddying along / a network of motional obbligatos ..."

That is, as Ammons writes in the passage above, "I want ... time in time, not / time splintered ..." We should pause to consider the phrase "time in time," for it implies that the primary frame of Ammons's poetics is temporality, not language. The problems associated with the "government of large tracts" (*G*, 113) in a long poem have to do with the embodied movements of poetic lines and sentences, the temporary clarities and sight-lines they may allow of the represented universe. As those movements are set into a "smooth long bend" – curvature, sweep, arch – time is set in time.

Even from within speech, Ammons takes temporality to be more basic than language. That is another way to describe his valuing the currency of use more highly than the historical might and magnitude of language. Ashbery notes in that same early essay how Ammons's struggle with the transcendental "tends to turn each poem into a battleground strewn with scattered testimony to the history of its making."[32] Ammons puts great stock in the power of action "to turn and turn back" (G, 54), even to turn back the "aberrant" (G, 24) motions of speech.[33] Equally important is the capacity in a speaker "brought low" by "the grief of failure, loss, error" (G, 21) to be "turn[ed] around" – to fail to move or speak well, that is, and to discern it. And so to discard, abandon, let go (the object); or (for the subject) to avert one's interest. For Ammons, that means working through, and leaving traces of, motions of thought and speech in poems themselves. It also means that the philological history "disposed" of in dictionaries, lexicons, etc., does not compel Ammons; he is scathing about the diachronic way that "history" ("all that antedated western slop" [G, 104]) most often gets understood.

That "we are there in / the form of apes" is, in contrast, a fact that Ammons continues to find remarkable, one congruent with the fact that language does not belong exclusively to *homo sapiens*. Human languages are primate languages, and for that reason function always in a dialectic with the primate "name of [the] game" – accommodation:

> … tongue, crotch, boob, navel,
> armpit, rock, slit, roseate rearend and
>
> consider the perfumeries of slick exchange,
> heaving breath, slouching mouth, the mixed
>
> means by which we stay attentive and keep to
> the round of our ongoing: you wake up thrown
>
> away and accommodation becomes the name of your
> game: getting back, back into the structure
>
> of protection, caring, warmth, numbers …
> (G, 25–6)[34]

How does this mix of primatology and mild libertarianism connect to word frequency and "power laws"? Or, for that matter, to "time in time"? George Zipf hypothesized that the power law drop-off in frequency beyond the hundred or two hundred most commonly used words in a language could be explained by a quasi-economical "principle of least effort."[35] Most of us most of the time will not expend energy remembering and calling up extra words when a handful will suffice. Then again, one might ask: suffice how? Ammons supposes that *homo sapiens* uses language primarily to enable a movement toward accommodation – in order to "get back, back into the structure / of protection, caring, warmth, numbers …" So far, so primatological. The saliences, or furrows, of what I have called representative word-use are built up, or grooved out, by this drive to accommodation. It is also the reason why those "outcastings" of exemplary use almost always end up being statistically inconsequential. Why speak in non-representative ways that will push you away from that "structure / of protection," etc.? The poet in the post-Romantic era "wake[s] up thrown / away" *every* day.

To welcome (back) the words of those out on the aberrant peripheries, Ammons imagines a seemingly harmless figure he names "the blabbermouth" – tempter and comforter at once, and by no means other or alien. The thirteenth chapter of *Garbage* commences with a natural history of this figure:

> the real trouble with a blabbermouth is that when
> he talks and keeps talking, pretty soon he's
>
> talking *around*, and pretty soon he's
> *on the other side*! of where he was …
>
> … a fool blabberer cannot believe all the
>
> things he says himself, indeed he believes nothing
> except the wisdom of agreeing with whomever he
>
> meets: he can present a scaffolding exfoliation, a
> splaying network of words that will accommodate the color

of any man's opinion, or woman's ...

... a blabbermouth, wandering around

in disquisitional irresponsibility, can sashay
by your one or two words and contextualize them ...
(G, 78–9; Ammons's italics).

Fittingly, this sequence follows hard upon pages 76-7 of chapter twelve, where the Ammons voice drifts itself into the speech of a blabbermouth. The drift is minimally signposted – only a "what" wedged between colons – but it seems safe to say the passage that follows, with its fantasy of humans in spaceships seeding the stars, would have struck Ammons as foolish or adolescent.[36] It is not, however, another voice; nor is it the staging of a dialogue or a polyphony. It is Ammons's own disquisition sashaying, as he might put it, right on by its preceding words to the "other side" of what he believes ("one goes out to see if / it is there" [G, 92]). He has allowed himself a blabbermouth moment, almost as if to try it out. It is an example of how human language, even when operating at a high level of abstraction, conversationally deployed, can "accommodate the color of any man's opinion." Moreover, if the blabbermouth is the one who contextualizes, then we need the blabbermouth (the blabbermouth position, let's say) since "words and twos" (G, 78) of laconic utterance require contexts in order to be understood. In fact, Ammons's characteristic clauses joined and/or separated by colons make themselves particularly vulnerable to the splaying networks and scaffolding exfoliations of contextualization.

Nevertheless, this drift, under the genial pressure of blabbermouthery, is not entirely admirable. Accommodation is the beginning, not the end, of how words can set us primates right (or wrong). The star-seeding passage is an example of utterance that solicits repetition without being exemplary in any positive sense. Emerson famously accused American thinking, speaking, and writing of an inclination to conformity. Stanley Cavell has returned time and again to a curious couple of phrases from "Self-Reliance": "The virtue most in request is conformity. Self-reliance is its aversion." And (a few paragraphs later in Emerson's essay): "... every word they say chagrins us and we know not where to begin to set them right."[37] *Garbage* realizes Cavell's "aversive thinking," not because it celebrates the self-reliant but because its poet sets his own (primate) need for "accommodation" – a need deeply at odds with the determination to distinguish what "they say" from what "we say" or "I say" – at the heart of his compositional proceeding. The fantasy of getting every word in gives way to a wrestling with every word they – and hence that I too might – say.

The Emersonian quality of the poem is intensified by the circumstances of its composition. In the throw of unpremeditated utterance, what is most likely to come to mind – or be presented to mind by various contemporary media – will be words, combinations of words (and so complexes of thought and image), that in the uttering become cause for chagrin, or repulsion, or scorn. At various points in *Garbage*, a reader can retrace the path of sentences that, simultaneous with their own "one-time" unwinding, registered Ammons's unease. Having once tried his best to turn those words, it is the *stance* the poet takes towards main current speech rather than "the battleground strewn with scattered testimony to the history of its making" that is exemplary.

All speakers depend on ordinary words and collocations – the high-frequency ones in the corpora – to think with. For Emerson, as for Ammons, in saying "we know not where to begin to set them right," the bare differentiation of "we" and "they" is the point:

If I'm in

touch, she said, then I've got an edge: what

the hell kind of talk is that: I can't believe
I'm merely an old person: whose mother is dead,

whose father is gone and many of whose
friends and associates have wended away to the

ground, which is only heavy wind, or to ashes,
a lighter breeze …
(G, 22)[38]

In reading through the two colons – from "I've got an edge" to "what the hell kind of talk is that" to "I can't believe I'm merely an old person" – one moves through a mingling of generational differences in usage.[39] Once again, it is not exactly dialogue, nor polyphony. The first idiom is for the speaker not something he can simply reciprocate with a nod of recognition. Those words are not right; they chagrin him. The complaint that follows – "what the hell kind of talk is that" –turns in part, then, upon the matter of individual agency or liberty. Free to acknowledge rightness, rather than correctness, of usage, a speaker may find that these words or this phrase do not speak for him or her.

The passage is also a lament for the fragility of the shared world:

> ... if you are not gone at a certain
>
> age, your world is: or it is shriveled to a
> few people who know what you know: aunts and
>
> uncles with their histories blanked out, the thick
> tissue of relationships erased into one of emptiness
>
> or maybe your cousins, too, are gone, and
> the world has starved to a single peak,
>
> you and what you know alone, with no one
> else in the world to nod recognizing what you
>
> say and recall without explanation: ...
> (G, 93)

The high-frequency saliences of recorded use in the corpora are traces of repetition, accommodation (in Ammons's sense) – of a shared world. While contemporary mass usage can seem monolithic, overwhelming, a ziggurat of conformity, it might better be described as a "thick tissue of relationships" that soon becomes a thin or non-existent tissue. And when "the world has starved to a single peak," accommodation, however much desired, can no longer be the name of the game.

Though "I've got an edge" may be an idiom not quite ready for the garbage-heap, it will be soon enough. Ammons, in one of the poem's opening sequences, pictures the scene at a great burning landfill, "the precincts of flame, the terrifying transformations / the disappearances of anything of interest" (G, 31), and banks his already-swerving Shelleyan metaphor this way:

> wind slams flickers so flat they lose
> the upstanding of updraft and stifle to white
> lingo ...
> (G, 31)

"Dead language" is being "burned down on" this mound. Strictly speaking, that isn't what happens, in single lifetimes, to words, to saliences of use. The objects of interest disappear, yes, but there are no linguistic microbes busily breaking down the most frequently used words and phrases and turning their material into energy.[40] The texts, the ink, the computer screens, the bodies of speakers – all of these degrade. But the possibilities of use do not degrade materially. "White / lingo" is the continuing possibility – now; at this moment – of meanings and motions on "a smooth long bend" of cosmic scale. The disappearances and reallocations of interest alter the instantiations of speech, its saliences. A "burning down" is in process at the very moment of a speaker objecting "what the hell kind of talk is that." A stick in the fluencies loses its "upstanding." But even so, the possibilities of utterance remain: possibilities having to do not only with primate accommodation but with ideality, more broadly speaking.

Ammons wants us to entertain the premise that there is no fundamental difference between "actions, actions, / actions, human or atomic" (G, 54), that "all / motions [are] cousins" (G, 84), *and* that "things are awash in / ideality" (G, 89). The motion enacted by the utterance "what the hell kind of talk is that" participates in ideality by a negation, a turning away from, a deprecation of, another instance of speech. In the same spirit, Ammons points us to "young squirrels playful at dusk" and "their several examples":

> ... these are the motions
>
> we learn from, these are the central figures,
> this is the dance, here attitude and character,
>
> precision and floundering lay out for us to see

their several examples ...
(G, 55)

A watcher finds a young squirrel's motions exemplary, that is, of "precision" or "floundering"; and for Ammons this finding something exemplary is itself a movement more basic than what the philosophical tradition calls judgment.

Although I set out a definition of anomalous use at the start of this essay, exemplary use is my primary quarry. It is certainly possible to think of a closed field of phrases or sentences that are examples of the greater demand any speaker may make of words and sentences. Most of the illustrative citations in Samuel Johnson's dictionary, and many of them in the OED, are exemplary in this sense. We have seen that Ammons was emphatically not drawn to the closed field as method. And yet a paradox emerges when we consider the published result of Ammons's "showboat" (G, 63) sessions at the adding machine tape in the late 1980s, i.e., the book-length poem called *Garbage*. On the one hand, the text reminds its reader almost continuously that the field of things that could potentially be named therein is as open as are America's landfills. On the other hand, his phrasings and constructions, though extended moment by moment in confluence with or avoidance of the stream of contemporary usage, dispose themselves at last in each realized section of the poem as a closed field. The only way that field of utterance can be opened again is along a temporal axis, by the free repetition of component words and phrases in other contexts. That is, if those words are to be spared the inconsequential fate of non-representative utterance, other speakers will have to take them as exemplary – exemplary, for instance, of "clarity ... disallowing no complexity in coming clean." Any instance of use we call "poetic" starts out thrown away but, never leaving the vicinity of blabbermouthery, will rely for its perpetuation on the ideal – free – capacity of all who speak.

9

Day Labour

STEVE McCAFFERY

Light dies before the uncreating word.
Alexander Pope, *The Dunciad*

Let me start at a mid-peak in the Language moment, at Ron Silliman's buoyant proclamation of innovative fecundity in "The Practice of Art," his 1994 afterword to *The Art of Practice*, the poetry anthology edited by Dennis Barone and Peter Gannick to supplement the acknowledged lacunae in Silliman's own *In the American Tree.* That in excess of 160 North American poets, he claims, "are actively and usefully involved in the avant-garde tradition of writing is itself a stunning thought … [W]e in North America are living in a poetic renaissance unparalleled in our history."[1] I wish to discuss against this optimism the emergence of one of several of the new conceptualisms that have escorted innovation out of statistics into the accursed share of *poiesis.* I am hard pressed to find a *vera causa* for the recent conceptual turn in writing. A supersessionary declaration against the stultified disjunctive parataxis that Marjorie Perloff sees as the in-house style of contemporary Language poetry? A belated extension into language of conceptual art and the mundane replications on Andy Warhol's canvasses? A fecund addition to the poetries of the numerous? I personally stand in broad concurrence with Tom Mandel's 2008 claim in Part 7 of *The Grand Piano* that "there is no such 'movement' as Language poetry, although Language poetry is real. Real but not a movement that can be characterized or that has had its 'moment' or that can ever be 'over.'"[2] I see conceptual writing as neither superseding nor expanding upon that historic trend in innovative poetry, nor challenging the inherent political critiques advanced by Language writing. So, *quo vadis*?

Craig Dworkin's account of conceptual writing in general – "writing in which the idea cannot be separated from the writing itself: in which the instance of writing is inextricably intertwined with … the material practice of *écriture*" – applies to Kenneth Goldsmith.[3] In other words, while intransigently non-utilitarian, Goldsmith's conceptual works do not involve a dematerialization of the art object. Quite the opposite. They all inhere as material organizations in space, the worked-through consequence of the idea, the material realization of the concept. This introduces a perversely Kantian inflexion, for if Lyotard is correct in claiming masochism to be the propelling force of the sublime, which Kant derives from a conflict between the "conceptual" and the "presentational," then Goldsmith's conceptual endeavours represent a resurgence of the logic of reflective judgment.[4] Goldsmith has called himself "a collector of language"; in the late 1990s, his self-proclaimed commitment was to become utterly uncreative by the age of forty.[5] So far his accomplishments are increasingly confirming Goldsmith's trajectory: from conceptual projects on the borders of literature to current ones that purportedly evacuate entirely any morsel of the literary. The earlier projects, such works as *Fidget* and *No. 111 2.7.93-10.20.96*, haunt the margins of the literary with an unquestionably aesthetic attraction akin to some works of Oulipo. Indeed *No. 111* can incorporate in its entirety a short story ("The Rocking Horse Winner") by a doyen of literary modernism, D.H. Lawrence, precisely because that story obeys Goldsmith's constraint of phonemic termination, ending as it does with the sound "er" in "winner."

Arguably *Fidget* marks the culmination of the New York School and its cross-cultural syntheses. Updating John Gay's 1716 *Trivia, or the Art of Walking the Streets of London*, Goldsmith's itinerary perversely celebrates a single locale: Manhattan, present in its referential absence, a metropolis imploded into body parts and movements. The work attempts to document Goldsmith's every movement for 13 hours. Recorded 16 June or Bloomsday, 1997, on a small tape recorder and later transcribed and edited, it itemizes a choreography of physical movements and proprioceptive consequences and one instance of autoeroticism (Goldsmith masturbates), offering a paratactic continuum of minimal physical movements. Fundamentally an oral text documenting the passage of actions into words and words into book-form, it stands as the polar opposite of Surrealist automatic writing, recovering a single body's dissipative motions in brief sentences whose cumulative effect Majorie Perloff likens, in her afterword, to the claustrophobic prose of the later Beckett.[6]

> Body turns one hundred eighty degrees. Pushes on top.
> Thumbs press. Fingers push. Press. Body shakes. Thumb
> pushes. Mouth opens. Lips lick. Hands lift. Plunge. Emerge.
> Immerse. Elbow out.[7]

Rubén Gallo perceptively notes that the protagonist of *Fidget* never gets dressed and remains a nude "hero" throughout the impersonal recitation of his own body parts and ephemeral motions.[8] However, Goldsmith's eschewal of the first-person pronoun and the collapse of simultaneous bodily motions onto the temporally sequential plane of language, with a claustrophobic specificity, renders *Fidget* not only a naked text but also a profoundly decentered one. Emerging from the catalog of plural and separate movements is the impression of a morselated corpse, a parade of body parts that Derek Beaulieu likens to a crime scene.[9] It is precisely because Goldsmith's book avoids an ego-logical axis that it illuminates the ontological paradox that an obsessive preoccupation with the details of a "self" actually leads to that self's disappearance.

But need we read *Fidget* as a collapse in lyric centeredness, a contortion of autobiography, or as an exercise in auto-analysis as Gallo does? Read as an epic text of tracking and self-surveillance, *Fidget* inflects a more sinister theme (persuasively outlined by both Foucault and Anthony Giddens), the implosion of an ideological state operation onto the level of a mundane, non-rhetorical, anti-lyrical self. To my mind, *Fidget's* greatest triumph in negativity lies in its inability to complete itself; its ultimate "achievement" is to end up as, if not a failed, then a radically compromised formation. For Goldsmith's project of boredom instigated an unbearable ennui in the artist himself. The curious subtext of his narrative can be constructed from the numerous paratexts and related interviews and articles that discursively frame (and contaminate by elucidation) all his projects. The anecdote of him buying a bottle of Jack Daniel's sour mash to ease the monotony of his *Fidget* project is now near legendary. Progressively intoxicated, Goldsmith starts to slur his speech, blurring words to such a degree that they become impossible to transcribe in the sober surroundings of his Manhattan scriptorium. His decision is to end the book at hour 22:00 by retranscribing the opening chapter backwards.

> .etarpes regniferof dna bmuht thgiR. flac thgir sehctarcs dnah thgiR .ydob dniheb tsiF.[10]

In a veritable boustrophedonic flourish Jack Daniel's emerges as the successful hacker into Goldsmith's self-surveillance project; it's booze, that never-failing prosthetic antidote to ennui, rather than the tape recorder, that finally and deliciously subverts the project.

Goldsmith has been keen to distinguish his practice from the potential literature of Oulipo, seeing in their work an end product of "blandly conservative … fiction."[11] His more recent work additionally throws the category *literature* into contingency, and in this lies the challenge to all emergent poetries. I choose Goldsmith's *Day* as a gesture towards a limit text within the multiple projects we name "poetries," a limit that challenges our situating it within the domains of the poetic. Since *Day*, Goldsmith's work in many ways signals the revenge of the *Dunciad* and its litany of values excoriated by Pope: uncreativity, dullness, bathos. It equally instantiates that condition pertaining to the character in Ronald Sukenick's *The Death of the Novel* who is led by "the blank nothingness of uncreation" into a self-inflicted choreography of spasms, pains, and resistances.[12] It's useful to reflect on Goldsmith's adoption of the techno-mechanic persona of a word processor (a cyborg identity radically different from Stelarc's) as the mundane fulfillment of Eliot's high modernist call for a poetics of the impersonal, attaining a radical non-egotism that defines itself as an uncreative obsession. Where *Fidget* stages the tedious and meticulous accumulation of data, *Day* presents a radical instance of information management. The mammoth project of *Day* implicates a poetic of the "uncanny replica," or "imperfect clone," while throwing down the gauntlet to the potential literature of procedural constraint by taking on two of the most difficult constraints of all: to be "uncreative" and "unengaging." If Foucault claims the "event" of literature to be "a spreading forth of language in its raw state, an unfolding of pure exteriority," then *Day* is the pure exteriority of the newspaper.[13]

Day is a document of truly sumo proportions, occupying the entirety of an 866-page, 10″ x 6½″ book (purposefully chosen, I might add, to be the identical format to the Harvard edition of Benjamin's *Arcades Project*). It testifies to a single mundane act: the transcription of all the words and numbers found in the *New York Times* edition for Friday, 1 September 2001. Joshua Schuster succinctly summarizes the work as "one long quote."[14] Yet *Day* attains to Francis Ponge's poetics of transport – a transport less celebrative of sublime *ekstasis* than of mundanity, of the humble, everyday object rescued from oblivion and positioned within the uncertain and contested domain of the modern art project. *Day* instantly evokes Cage's enigmatic definition of poetry: "I have nothing to say and I am saying it and that is poetry." It also ranks as an egregious instance of Pound's quip that poetry is the "news that stays news," and stands as a laborious refutation of the adage that today's news wraps tomorrow's fish and chips.

Thought otherwise, *Day* is dictation spectacularly disembodied and confined within the banal choreography of drudgery. Accurately reflecting the current status of labour in advanced (and now reducing) economic zones of the global scene, *Day* records the activity of labourious transcription as information portage, implementing a poetic of forwarding, quantitative reiterations and data replication. Indeed, *Day* offers itself as the very emblem of a pure transference offered minimally (in its magnitude) without distraction or controversion, and in so effecting this Goldsmith proffers a profoundly secularized *anamnesis* as well as an elitism available to everyone.

Day has two mythopoetic mentors: the uncreative repetition of Echo, the nymph in love with Narcissus; and the backward gazing Orpheus. The creative/non-creative crux of *Day* lies in Blanchot's interrogation that registers the aporia at the heart of any Orphic recuperation. "How can I recover it, how can I turn around and look at what exists *before*, if all my power consists of making it into what exists *after*."[15] *Day* has more recent and non-mythic antecedents. Indeed, the project historically situates itself within Modernism's embrace of the quotidian. (It's Baudelaire after all who redirects poetry away from its aspirations to the universal and toward the local, quotidian, and ephemeral.) *Day* similarly and instantly evokes the old Dada legacy of recycling. Schwitters' *merz* is precisely an art constructed out of heterogeneous cast-offs, and marks less the elevation of mundane implements prone to appropriation to the level of art than a reclamation of the already discarded. Goldsmith is close to this spirit, yet not entirely. Where Schwitters sublates the refuse of the city to an aesthetic order (however controversial that aesthetic), Goldsmith resists this move, submitting the quotidian cast-off to exhaustive replication. The ecopoetic ramifications of Goldsmith's practice are thus ambivalent. On the one hand he implements a practice of recycling and conservation, an eco-friendly recirculation of texts, avoiding the toxic heap of spam. On the other, he inscribes and preserves "nutritionless" data.[16] While Schwitters instantiates an ecological aesthetic of recycling, Goldsmith endorses a scatophilial poetics. As a vast copying, *Day* also calls to mind Barthes' *scriptor* reduced to a servile absurdity; its method similarly evokes the fictional Pierre Menard's abandoned attempt to write Cervantes' *Don Quixote* verbatim. There is, however, a crucial difference. Whereas Borges's character reproduces identical passages of text that are different precisely because the historical context of the transcription is different, Goldsmith reproduces his identical source text within a commonly shared historical ethos.

It's similarly tempting to compare *Day* with Duchamp's readymades, but anything beyond a superficial comparison will elicit three significant differences. First, Goldsmith adds the category "work" to "art" thus combining the appropriative act of the readymade with the drudgery of transcription. Secondly, where Duchamp chooses his *tout faits* from the commodity world of hardware stores, plumbing shops and restaurant suppliers, Goldsmith chooses mediated data – less the readymade than the already read. Thirdly, while Duchamp deracinates his readymade, radically recontextualizing its manifestation, he never strips it of use-value; its instrumentality is always nascently retained. (It's possible, of course, to read *Day* but the act of reading would not yield the news *per se* as would the source text on its day of publication; its use value as instant information is of necessity temporally denied.) If Goldsmith introduces the category of labour back into the avant-garde work of art, it's a paradoxical manoeuver. Goldsmith, in fact, pulls off an effective atavism, resuscitating the humble activity of the medieval scribe in the cause of the archive and in so doing foregrounds an ambivalent history of volatile origins in reappearance.[17] This mobilization of the past for avant-garde ends in the age of informatics is itself an echo of Khlebnikov's own Orphic glance to the past: his discovery, in Jan van der Eng's words, "of forgotten but never completely lost archive resources of construing, which leads to unexpected significations of the language structure."[18] (There is also something reminiscent of Jack Spicer's desire to facture poems out of real objects, but whereas Spicer might conceive of a real newspaper as potential material to be taken up by *poiesis*, Goldsmith seizes it instead as a text that can be transported into a different discursive space.)

Falling outside the utilitarian imperative of the newspaper, *Day* transposes, transcribes and enlarges its original. At the same time the work's format remains an intelligent terminal: it is the book, though obtaining to a gross monstrosity. The significant aspect of the project is not simply its quasi-absurdity, but its elevation of a useless item to haecceity, like Jacques Prévert's collection of empty matchboxes (of which Lacan speaks).[19] Goldsmith believes *Day* to be unreadable owing to the boredom largely induced by the shift in format.[20] Newspapers offer modular detachable sections and page continuation cues that not only allow for, but actually promote, skimming. A reader moves perhaps from the front-page banner headlines to the Sports and Weather sections carefully avoiding the mountains of statistics in the Stock market reports, casually perusing the photographs and visual ads along the way. The supreme paradox of *Day* is to preserve the unit of the book by shattering the ephemeral performativity of the newspaper. *Day* exposes the nakedness of its initial concept while at the same time actualizing that concept – making it "real" by not "making it new." Indeed, Goldsmith exacerbates the info-commodity he is apparently attacking, contributing to commodity culture a quizzical instance: a book born from a newspaper, destined to be marketed and sold to a readership that will not read it and sold for twenty-three dollars (a price far greater than that of a copy of the *New York Times*). The "reader" is, of course, a function assumed by the singularity of the one who is reading – but who will read *Day*? For *Day* is a practically useless text offering none of the instantaneous information of the newspaper. It is as if with *Day* Goldsmith anticipates Tan Lin's 2007 call for more books with fewer readers.[21]

Day is, and splendidly so, the regurgitation of *the New York Times* as a trace inscription, a supplement, radically removed from the category of instant news and thereby from the category of value. Notwithstanding the problematics of readership, *Day* nevertheless situates inside the contingent and virtual paratextualities that constitute literature's social space. For what does Goldsmith's name signify on the cover of *Day*? Authorship? Hardly. His rearrangement or editing, his completed act as scribe? Perhaps. But the key aspect is the registration of intellectual property installed within commercial, commodity culture: "Kenneth Goldsmith" is now an "author" and can sign copies of his book (and that way increase their collectability and market value). For their part, readers can add marginal comments and critics respond with a fulguration of encomia or a fusillade of excoriation.

Where *Fidget* offers a nude protagonist, *Day* presents a text stripped of all the familiar multi-media features of the newspaper's voco-visual arrangement; it presents a raw, naked format of unmitigated uniformity without the relief of typographic variation. In Goldsmith's denuded non-creativity, the concept alone is clothed in the spurious "ornament" of its own realization. *Day's* obvious value as boring, nutritionless writing is its effective social exposé of human habit and expectation, pointing out along the way that we *don't* read a newspaper – rather we read *in* it. It would appear that *Day* defamiliarizes precisely in its recontextualizing. A newspaper presented as a mundane object complicates the Gricean implicature: an author (KG) offers the transcribed words of others (and many anonymous) as that author's (KG's) text. Where Russian Formalist *ostranenie* aimed to undermine the routine relation of humans to objects, Goldsmith defamiliarizes the act of reading itself by implying its cultural constitution as a social, quotidian habit.

But does *Day* offer anything more than an alienation effect carried out upon the category of the quotidian? If literature is "the act of writing that specifically addresses those who should not read," as Rancière avers, then *Day* is a curious literature of reversal offering to a literate constituency an unreadable tome.[22] Goldsmith's concern in *Day* is not with aesthetic defamiliarization but with obdurate exemplarity – carrying out a totally useless labour, with the attendant consequence of transcribing an immense and theoretically unreadable tome whose value is admitted to be zero. Actually to read *Day* seems beside the point (as Goldsmith himself admits). And if "thing" is that which is not open to interpretation, as Pessoa claims, then Goldsmith's *Day* is certainly not a thing; its mode of existence is at the same time material and interrogative, and its primary task is to raise questions as to what precisely it is. (Goldsmith's informative paratexts precisely undermine this mode of existence by addressing such questions and framing his conceptual works within a personal complexity, revealing less a vaporization of the self than a recognizable protagonist behind them and a highly efficient mode of self-fashioning.) To repeat, Goldsmith's *telos* in his information shifting is not to transform information from one domain of utility to another, but rather to recontextualize it so that its former functionality is rendered unworkable and that way made available for contemplation and scrutiny. The critical desire his books excite is conceptual rather than interpretive.

"Conceptual" writing, however, presupposes a conceptual mechanism. The procedure of conceptual art is a process of matching an indeterminate "art" object to a preexisting, or constructable, conceptual context; the trajectory is thalamial: the marriage of art and discourse in the form of the "perfect fit." One arrives at the latter via numerous imperfect fits, a chain of "not quites" or "no longer but not-yets," which allows us to situate *Day* as "no longer a newspaper" but "not yet art." Goldsmith's "conceptual reader" or receiver must perforce become "pagan" in Lyotard's sense of that term – thrust into judgment *without criteria.*[23] Indeed, in its unreadableness, the work proposes itself for cognitive encounter *at a distance.* In other words *Day* should be taken much the same as Duchamp's readymades; i.e. as provocation to a line of interrogation: why produce this in the first place? What happens to the information in its recontextualization? Why is reading *Day* a different experience from reading *The New York Times*?

This ineluctable trajectory to speculation on the reader-thinker's part has interesting consequences. If Celan and Jabès envisioned the exile and orphaning of poetry, Goldsmith solicits its absolute death. His projects carry a universal admonition against *poiesis* and literature in general and seem to remark upon both the exhaustion of literature and the profound anxiety of art in information culture. In Goldsmith's practice, the writer is precisely the one who doesn't write (if writing is to be considered an original inscription). As such it argues against Mallarmé's magisterial formulation of dance as "a poem set free of any scribe's apparatus."[24] Uncreative writing is profoundly gravitational, stultifying any dance of the intellect while at the same time repositioning the creative principle *inside* the concept. (In this sense Goldsmith's paratexts are best considered as "leaks" into exegesis from an uncreative core.)

The abnegation of a recognizable aesthetic situates itself too under the shadow of a catena of precedents starting with Rimbaud's own rejection of poetry as a poetic act, a rejection repeated by Breton, Éluard, and Laura Riding Jackson. Goldsmith also seems to respond to Nietzsche's call for an artistic Socrates (the philosopher who claimed his wisdom was based on the fact that he knew nothing). This epistemological paradox surely underlies Goldsmith's method of transcription, or put more bluntly, *Day* seemingly offers the quintessential antidote to poets and poetry alike. The implications of *Day*, however, do not escape the Platonic postulate of the *nature* of poetry. For Plato, who banished poetry from his philosopher's state, poems do not transmit discursive thought (*dianoia*) so much as petition it. As Badiou puts it, "The poem is … an offering, a lawless proposition."[25] By contrast, *dianoia* is the act of intellectual advance towards concatenation, i.e. a move to an intelligible matheme.[26] Moreover, if *Day* (over and beyond Goldsmith's intention) does indeed insinuate a poetry without poetry, then it parallels felicitously Derrida's mature (later) thematizing of a messianic religion without religion. In *The Truth & Life of Myth* Robert Duncan observes of poetic vocality that "When the 'I' is lost, when the voice of the poem is lost, the matter of the poem, the intense information of the content, no longer comes to me, then I know I have to wait until that voice returns."[27] Duncan's comments register a poetic platitude, yet to read *Day* against a broader poetics of desertion and return, we note how Goldsmith's tome is a consequence of precisely that abandonment. However, that space of loss is not abandoned to waiting but seized upon as the time and space for mundane labour. The intellectual distance between Duncan's poetic and Goldsmith's conceptual writing reiterates the cultural distance between Hesiod's *Theogony* and Adam Smith's *Wealth of Nations*, between a non-productive time of abiding and time seized and partitioned by labour.

To the features of uncreative writing, boredom, and zero nutrition should be added that of unoriginality, for there are antecedents to almost everything Goldsmith has produced so far. The intimate connection of art and uncreativity was first noted by Hegel, who believed art offered an invitation to intellectual engagement, not to the production of further art objects.[28] The debts owed by *Day* I have already noted. *Fidget*'s ghostly, intertextual dependence on Joyce's *Ulysses* is transparent. Composed on Bloomsday, both texts record one man's movement through a city on the identical day, and both contain masturbatory episodes. *Fidget*'s method also finds a precedent in Andy Warhol's own uncreative practice in his novel *A* (a verbatim transcription of the group conversations and comments from a tape-recorded evening). *Soliloquy*, Goldsmith's transcription of every word he spoke over the course of a week, encourages comparison with David Antin's shorter and more socially appealing talk-poems. The poetics of eavesdropping (Goldsmith's chosen method in *No. 111*) can be traced back through Marianne Moore to Apollinaire's café poems such as "Les Fenêtres" and "Lundi rue Christine," both of which originated in snatches of overheard conversation. His 2005 work *The Weather* (a transcription of an entire year's one-minute hourly weather bulletins from the New York radio station 1010 WINS) has its august precursor in the concluding section of Tobias Smollett's 1778 *Travels through France and Italy* where the author offers a fastidious daily register of a year's weather in Nice. Goldsmith's attempt to facture an unnamable object is in the same spirit as Joyce's *Finnegan's Wake*, and his proud claim to be "a collector of language" conjures up the great antecedent spectre of Walter Benjamin. Goldsmith's works are palimpsests and eavesdroppings, the contorted echoes of former texts and practices.

Nevertheless, Goldsmith's work is as successful in its own way as is Duchamp's, effectively constructing an institutional oxymoron by which a vast project of uncreativity is generating a plethora of critical and nutritional exegesis (including my own). Goldsmith's oeuvre establishes an effective double-bind: to write about it is to write about nothing of worth, a writing degree zero in which the relation between physical expenditure and aesthetic merit is fundamentally undermined. Like Duchamp, Goldsmith situates the issue of art outside the formal aspects of the artwork itself (it's in this sense that he can be called a "conceptual" writer). To evaluate Goldsmith's work in a strictly literary dimension is unproductive, precisely because Goldsmith's conceptualized labour has more pertinence in the production and discourse of twentieth and twenty-first century art. Critical engagement must focus not *on* but *around* his work. Does Goldsmith sense this as a limitation on his oeuvre, that its ultimate fate is to be tied down by a useful and normative critical discourse of legitimation? If he does perhaps his crowning project will be to sabotage this paradox by an act of unsurpassable, uncreative disappearance, a project so successful that it will attract no critical attention, passing by the institution of the avant-garde completely and generating a posthumous tomb to the unknown non-creator.[29]

So where does Goldsmith's originality lie? In an e-mail exchange with A.S. Bessa (published as the prefatory material to his book *6799*) Goldsmith makes clear his material ambivalence toward the book as an inherited, traditional, and ideological format now situated in an age of alternative linguistic transportation both actual and virtual. Indeed, perhaps Goldsmith's truly vanguard contribution to the ongoing discourse of the avant-garde is his UbuWeb project, whose ideology can be traced to a paradigm switch in pluralistic practice from formal innovation on the level of the object to innovation in distribution.[30] "[T]he new avant-garde" remarks Gene Youngblood, "is all about creating autonomous social worlds that people can live in. Art is central to that but the art is not what's avant-garde. What's avant-garde is metadesign, the creation of context."[31]

The web in its variant offerings of the open book and of the hard-copy archive affords such a context. So perhaps Marcos Novak is correct in conceiving the internet and its attendant new media as the belated realization of Constant's *New Babylon*: a vast ludic space open to delirious psychotextual geography and flaneuristic *dérives* through an entanglement of photo-linguistic data. In addition, the Internet also renders operative the Mallarméan dream of all existence ending in a book, for what is the Internet if not an open and continuously expanding book available for paragrammatic engagements, festive appropriation, and imaginative reconfigurations?

If genius resides inside the poem rather than the poet, as Robert Duncan once claimed, then not only do Goldsmith's projects stand as a solid refutation of this assertion, they further offer themselves as thoroughly exorcized materialities.[32] Goldsmith extends Barthes's historicizing project first developed in "The Death of the Author" to underscore how "genius," like "author," is a historically contingent term in both its emergence and disappearance; both are finite notions, a passing in a passage, a product and victim of historical mutation. Christian Bök claims Kenneth Goldsmith to be "our James Joyce of the 21st century," a judgment that is beguiling and even defensible.[33] For if Lyotard is correct in asserting Joyce's greatest achievement to be that of rendering the unpresentable presentable inside the signifier (PMC, 80), then this fact is pertinent to Goldsmith's work when we install the latter within the "sublime" (unrepresentable) and untotalizable condition of informatics. Today's Apollo perhaps needs a tenth muse, "Data," as custodian of materially and hyperspatially embodied information, to conflagrate finally the history of the archive and of information management so it can emerge the phoenix of information transport – a veritable messianic anabasis.

However, if Goldsmith, in his crusade against value, is addressing the sedimentary condition of hypertrophic information, the heaps of unproductive, obsolete, unyielding facts and statistics that characterize the eschatolic side of information culture, then his uncreative writing is best explained through Baudrillard's critical engagement with Saussure's paragrams. Informatics is itself symptomatic of more encompassing contemporary techno-capitalist formations, a vast disemboguing of commodities and language into irreducible and inescapable sedimentation. Baudrillard elucidates the sepulchral side of this "affluent utopia" when considered in the broader context of production. "Just as every commodity, that is to say, everything produced under the sign of the law of value and equivalence, is an *irreducible residue* that comes to bar social relations, so every word, every term and every phoneme produced and not symbolically destroyed accumulates like the repressed, weighs down on us with all the abstraction of dead language."[34]

It would seem that *Day,* along with Goldsmith's other uncreative writing, is preeminently a symbolic rather than conceptual action, a ritual cancellation of meaning and the *poetic* extermination of value along the lines of archaic composition that Saussure investigated (unsuccessfully) in his *Cahiers d'anagrammes.*[35]

Notes

CHAPTER ONE

1 Douglas Barbour seems to have invented this formulation. See "Lyric/Anti-Lyric: Some Notes about a Concept" (1984) in *Lyric/Anti-Lyric: Essays on Contemporary Poetry* (Edmonton: NeWest Press), 2001.

2 Marjorie Perloff, *Unoriginal Genius: Poetry by Other Means in the New Century* (Chicago: University of Chicago Press, 2010), 58.

3 Passages representative of the critical stances I mention: "the tired dichotomy that has governed our discussion of twentieth-century poetics for much too long: that between modernism and post-modernism" (*21st-Century Modernism: The 'New' Poetics* [Malden, MA: Blackwell, 2002], 4); "the thesis that the contemporary avant-garde is no more than a recycled version of Dada revolt, that it can do no more than spin, so to speak, its Duchampian wheels, returning again and again to the 'scene of provocation' of the early 20th century but devoid of that scene's inherently political motive, has become a commonplace of pomo theorizing" (*Radical Artifice: Writing Poetry in the Age of Media* [Chicago: University of Chicago Press, 1991], 4–5); "the real fate of first-stage modernism was one of deferral … [until] this second wave of modernism" (*TCM*, 4).

4 Both Hannah Weiner and Erin Moure, for instance. According to Moure, "In 1976, Susan Penner showed me *The Collected Books of Jack Spicer*, which changed my life really" (personal e-mail communication; 20 Nov. 2011).

5 I follow Wayne C. Booth's use of the term. Rhetoric makes something public: "Regardless of how we conceive the core of any literary work, will it be entirely freed of a rhetorical dimension? On the contrary, at the very moment of initial conception, at the instant when [Henry] James exclaims to himself, 'Here is my subject!' a rhetorical aspect is contained within the conception: the subject is thought of as *something that can be made public*, something that can be made into a communicated work" (Booth's italics; *The Rhetoric of Fiction* [Chicago and London: University of Chicago Press, 1961], 104–5).

Indeed, a trace of rhetoric in this sense may be all that differentiates avant-gardist work (say, Hannah Weiner's *Clairvoyant Journal*) from the "outsider" art in an archive such as UbuWeb. In a recent essay, Terry Castle notes "the apparent lack of rhetorical intent" (22) in outsider art: "the archetypal outsider work is not a statement addressed to a viewer. It is not 'rhetorical,' not meant as communication. It is not produced to impress or charm or teach or convince" ("Do I Like It? Outsider Art," *London Review of Books* 33, 28 July 2011).

6 Edgar Allan Poe, *Poems and Essays on Poetry*, ed. C.H. Sisson (New York: Routledge, 2003), 88.

7 Rachel Blau DuPlessis, "Lyric and Experimental Long Poems: Intersections," 37.

8 Ibid, 27.

9 José Saramago, *All the Names*, trans. Margaret Jull Costa (San Diego and New York: Harcourt, 1999), 180–207. In a five-page section ("*O Meu Cadoiro – Os Nomes*") of the "*O Cadoiro* Postface," Moure lists the names of 161 troubadours but does not link them to any of the 1693 known poems of the period (http://bit.ly/OCadoiro; accessed 24 Sept. 2012).

10 Giorgio Agamben, "The Dictation of Poetry," in *The End of the Poem: Studies in Poetics*, trans. Daniel Heller-Roazen (Stanford: Stanford Univ. Press), 79. Quoted phrases in the preceding two sentences are also from page 79.

11 Louis Zukofsky, *Prepositions +: The Collected Critical Essays*, ed. Mark Scroggins (Hanover, NH: Wesleyan University Press, 2000), 20.

12 Rachel Blau DuPlessis, *Blue Studios: Poetry and Its Cultural Work* (Tuscaloosa: University of Alabama Press, 2006), 238.

13 Zukofsky wrote in the essay "Poetry" (1948): "a case can be made out for the poet giving some of his life to the use of the words *the* and *a*: both of which are weighted with as much epos and historical destiny as one man can perhaps resolve. Those who do not believe this are too sure that the little words mean nothing among so many other words" (*Prepositions +*, 10).

14 Presumably, DuPlessis has in mind Oppen's *The Materials* (1962), the title of which is not "Some Materials" or "A Collection of Materials."

15 Barbour makes a similar point in *Lyric/Anti-Lyric*: "the power of lyric in its myriad forms is too great [to be broken entirely with]"; 15.

16 In *Radical Artifice*, Perloff quotes Joan Retallack's account of a performance of Cage's *Lecture on the Weather*: "the room, the performance, the concept of weather, as Cage presents it to us, including the 'weather' of coincidences, voices, ideas – all combin[e] to cause the kind of storm that occurs in a particular … climate. That particular experience of that particular weather … in Rockville, MD, May 5, 1989 at approximately 9 p.m. could only assume its particular and variable character with the kind of permeable boundaries – between the inside and outside of his pieces – that Cage structures into all of his work" (*RA*, 25).

Compare Ammons, commenting on his own practice in *Garbage* (New York and London: W.W. Norton, 1986), a compositionally constrained long poem of the late 1980s:

I do
not want to be caught inside for clarity: I
want …

clarity without confinement, time in time, not
time splintered … (92–3)

17 Doyle draws as well upon the work of Julia Kristeva, whose writings on "the semiotic" and the paragram were published in the late 1960s and early 1970s.

18 Cited in Astradur Eysteinsson and Vivian Liska, "Introduction: Approaching Modernism," in *Modernism*, Vol. 1. Edited by A. Eysteinsson and V. Liska, (Amsterdam, The Netherlands, and Philadelphia: John Benjamins, 2007), 2.

19 Tyrus Miller, *Singular Examples: Artistic Politics and the Neo-Avant-Garde* (Evanston, IL: Northwestern University Press, 2009).

20 Charles Altieri, "Modernist Innovations: A Legacy of the Constructed Reader," *Modernism*, Vol. I, 67.

21 See Edward Możejko, "Tracing the Modernist Paradigm: Terminologies of Modernism," *Modernism*, Vol. I, 11–33.

22 Badiou, *Handbook of Inaesthetics*, trans. Alberto Toscano (Stanford: Stanford University Press, 2005), 8.

23 Lyotard's critique of "the presumption of the mind with respect to time" makes a similar diagnosis. See *The Inhuman: Reflections on Time*, trans. Geoffrey Bennington and Rachel Bowlby (Stanford: Stanford University Press, 1991), 107.

24 Perloff, *The Dance of the Intellect: Studies in the Poetry of the Pound Tradition* (Cambridge: Cambridge University Press, 1985), 21, 23.

25 "Language poetry had as its explicit aim to oppose such 'natural' expressivist speech, such individual voicing and accessible syntax [as found in the poems of Elizabeth Bishop, Allen Ginsberg, Sylvia Plath, James Wright, Denise Levertov, and A.R. Ammons]. But for the most part – and this has been insufficiently recognized – the poets represented in, say, Ron Silliman's *In the American Tree* did accept their predecessors' trust in invention, in the poet's power to create a unique *parole* from the language pool of the culture – a *parole* framed to *resist* what Adorno had defined as the culture industries" (*UG*, 11).

26 Gérard Genette, *The Architext: An Introduction*, trans. Jane E. Lewin (Berkeley: University of California Press, 1992), 28.

27 Barbour, *Lyric/Anti-Lyric*, 19.

28 Marjorie Perloff, *The Vienna Paradox: A Memoir* (New York: New Directions, 2003), 74.

29 Perloff, *The Vienna Paradox*, 74.

30 Perloff notes that the intersection of European political catastrophe with her own family history produced in herself an array of literary antipathies and attractions highly compatible somehow with those of Goldsmith, a subur-

ban Long Islander thirty years younger. See "A Conversation with Kenneth Goldsmith," *Jacket*, vol. 21 (Feb. 2003), http://jacketmagazine.com/21/perl-gold-iv.html (accessed 14 Sept. 2010).

31 Recent editions of *The Dunciad* amend "the" to "thy" in the line McCaffery quotes: "Lo! Thy dread Empire, CHAOS! is restor'd; / Light dies before thy uncreating word: / Thy hand, great Anarch! Lets the curtain fall, / And Universal Darkness buries All" (IV, 653–6).

32 The OED's first example of the use of "creative" [a.] to describe a person rather than the Deity is from W. Thompson's *Sickness* [1745]: "Creative bard [Spenser]…" OED *Online* (accessed 24 Sept. 2010).

33 Jean-François Lyotard, *The Postmodern Condition: A Report on Knowledge*, trans. G. Bennington and Brian Massumi (Minneapolis: University of Minnesota Press, 1984), 75.

34 A.S. Bessa, "kenneth goldsmith and as bessa | 6799" [Interview], *zingmagazine* 11, http://www.zingmagazine.com/zing11/bessa/ (accessed 8 Sept. 2010), n.p.

35 The phrase describing the collection is Goldsmith's in "kenneth goldsmith and as bessa | 6799."

36 Benjamin, *The Arcades Project,* trans. Howard Eiland and Kevin McLaughlin (Cambridge, MA, and London: Belknap Press of Harvard University Press, 1999), 203-11. Chapter H is titled "The Collector."

37 Kenneth Goldsmith, "Being Boring," in *American Poets in the 21st Century*, eds. Claudia Rankine and Lisa Sewell (Middletown, CT: Wesleyan University Press, 2007), 362. Goldsmith describes himself as "an OCR demon."

38 Main page, www.ubu.com (accessed 1 Dec. 2011). "UbuWeb was founded in November of 1996, initially as a repository for visual, concrete and, later, sound poetry. Over the years, UbuWeb has embraced all forms of the avant-garde and beyond." (www.ubu.com/resources/faq.html#6, accessed 1 Dec. 2011).

39 Jackson Mac Low, "The Terminology," *Open Letter*, 11, no. 3 (2001), 87. See O'Driscoll's essay in this volume.

40 Alexander Pope, "An Essay on Man in Four Epistles," Epistle 1, line 33; *The Major Works,* ed. Pat Rogers (Oxford: Oxford University Press, 2006), 273.

41 Bessa, "kenneth goldsmith and as bessa | 6799," n.p.

42 Thomas de Quincey, *Collected Writings*, Vol. 13, ed. David Masson (Edinburgh: A. and C. Black, 1896), 43–4.

43 Steve McCaffery, "*Day* Labour," 185.

44 Between 1990 and 2009, the phrase "more of a good thing" occurs at a frequency of 0.01 per million words, or four times in the entire corpus. The instances archived by COCA came from *Men's Health* magazine (1994); the academic journal *Agricultural Research* (1997); the *Chicago Sun-Times* (2003); and NBC *Today* (2007).

45 Oppen, "Of Being Numerous," 87.

46 McCaffery, "*Day* Labour," 179, 181.

47 Alain Badiou's gloss on one of Plato's key terms for theorizing the relation between poetry and philosophy (*IN*, 17).

48 "*Day* Labour," 182.

49 Ibid., 182.

CHAPTER TWO

1 The writing and consolidation of this paper was aided considerably by my appointment to the National Humanities Center, North Carolina, 2008–09.

2 Louis Zukofsky, "Interview Conducted by L.S. Dembo, 16 May 1968," *Contemporary Literature* 10.2 (Spring 1969), 218.

3 Edgar Allan Poe, "The Poetic Principle," *Poems and Essays on Poetry*, ed. C.H. Sisson (New York: Routledge, 2003), 88.

4 Edgar Allan Poe, 90.

5 Ibid., 88.

6 Robert Creeley, "Introduction to Charles Olson: *Selected Writings* II," *The Collected Essays of Robert Creeley* (Berkeley: University of California Press, 1989), 127.

7 James Williams Johnson, "Lyric," *The New Princeton Encyclopedia of Poetry and Poetics*, eds. Alex Preminger and T.V.F. Brogan (Princeton: Princeton University Press, 1993), 714.

8 Ibid., 714.

9 I have applied to lyric as a whole the term *akra*, which means literally high in space or distance, from Page Dubois' discussion of Sappho # 31 ("To me he seems like a god" / "Peer of the gods" / "Fortunate as the gods …") – the poem of shuddering and physical confusion at erotic desire (*Sappho is Burning* [Chicago: University of Chicago Press, 1995], 66).

10 I use the universal "death" rather than "love" or "the body" as these others open much larger cans of worms.

11 The storehouse of lyric contains figures such as apostrophe and prosopopoeia, as Jonathan Culler has discussed in "Poetics of the Lyric," *Structuralist Poetics: Structuralism, Linguistics and the Study of Literature* (Ithaca, NY: Cornell University Press, 1975), 161–88; "Apostrophe," *The Pursuit of Signs: Semiotics, Literature, Deconstruction* (Ithaca, NY: Cornell University Press, 1981), 135–54; "Changes in the Study of the Lyric," *Lyric Poetry: Beyond New Criticism*, eds. Chaviva Hosek and Patricia Parker (Ithaca, NY: Cornell University Press, 1986), 38–54; and "Deconstruction and the Lyric," *Deconstruction is/in America: A New Sense of the Political*, ed. Anselm Haverkamp (New York: New York University Press, 1995), 41–51. Robert Kaufman discusses the analytic lyric in "A Future for Modernism: Barbara Guest's Recent Poetry," *The American Poetry Review* 29, no. 4 (July/August 2000): 11–16; and "Aura, Still," *October* 99 (Winter 2002): 45–80.

12 Antony Easthope, *Poetry as Discourse* (London: Methuen, 1983).

13 DuPlessis, *Blue Studios: Poetry and Its Cultural Work*, (Tuscaloosa: University of Alabama Press, 2006), 102–4. See also DuPlessis, "Agency, Social Authorship, and the Political Aura of Contemporary Poetry," *Textual Practice* 23, no. 6 (2009): 945–57.
14 DuPlessis, *Blue Studios*, 104.
15 William Carlos Williams, "Portrait of a Lady," *The Collected Poems of William Carlos Williams, Volume I, 1909–1939*, eds. A. Walton Litz and Christopher MacGowan (New York: New Directions, 1986), 129.
16 And other amusing discursive/textural shifts can occur in lyric. One thinks of some shorter poems of Wallace Stevens: "Poet, be seated at the piano/ Play the present, its hoo-hoo-hoo,/ Its shoo-shoo-shoo, its ric-a-nic,/ Its envious cachinnation"; *The Collected Poems of Wallace Stevens* (New York: Alfred A. Knopf, 1954), 131.
17 Tristan Tzara, "To Make a Dadaist Poem"/"Pour faire un poème dadaïste" [1924], Jerome Rothenberg and Pierre Joris, eds. *Poems for the Millennium* (Berkeley: University of California Press, 1998), 302.
18 It is possible that we think of the lyric as having more sound, or more intense sound, because we (as hearers) cannot consistently attend to sound spread over multiple lines, and when there are hundreds of lines – a long Wallace Stevens poem, for instance, we get into the style and thus take the music for granted. (Poe rears his head here, and laughs at my abrupt agreement with his thoughts on attention-span.) Lyrics are therefore musical because we experience them quickly and don't get used to their sound, as we do with a longer unrolling poem. Sometimes lyric poems allude thematically or narratively to music, to instruments, singing voices, or to birds; perhaps this occurs to remind readers of the musicality they might otherwise subsume or ignore.
19 This is why Zukofsky's 1940 translation of Cavalcanti into Brooklyn-ese is so edgy; it took poetic smoothness and made it class rough. See "A Foin Lass Bodders Me," *Louis Zukofsky: Selected Poems*, ed. Charles Bernstein (New York: Library of America, 2006), 152–4.
20 René Welleck and Austin Warren, "Euphony, Rhythm, and Metre," *The Structure of Verse: Modern Essays on Prosody*, ed. Harvey Gross (Greenwich, CT: Fawcett Books, 1966), 26.
21 "The lyric tradition, with its emphasis on the enunciative, on sound, and on subjectivity remains extremely valuable to my poetic concerns"; Charles Bernstein, *My Way: Speeches and Poems* (Chicago: University of Chicago Press, 1990), 10.
22 John Wieners, *The Hotel Wentley Poems: Original Versions* (San Francisco: David Haselwood, 1965), n.p.
23 The shadow of a gender narrative here is consistent with Creeley's speaking about Olson's "In Cold Hell, in Thicket" as "a form of 'lyricism' brought from the instant, or the single and abrupt emotion, to bear on all there is" – and thereby representing "much more than delight." Delight is vaguely femi-

nine; the projective lyric is "much more" than that – it is synoptic and encyclopedic – a version of the long poem ("Charles Olson: 'In Cold Hell, in Thicket,'" *Collected Essays of Robert Creeley*, 100 and 101).

24 George Oppen, *New Collected Poems*, ed. Michael Davidson, pref. Eliot Weinberger (New York: New Directions, 2002), 53.

25 One then needs a particular attention to the apotheoses of female figures, often constructed in lyric modes, at the end of that poem.

26 Barbara Johnson, *The Feminist Difference: Literature, Psychoanalysis, Race, and Gender* (Cambridge, MA: Harvard University Press, 1998), 127.

27 Ezra Pound, *Instigations* (Freeport, NY: Books for Libraries Press, 1967 [1920]), 239.

28 The term seems to have originated with James Joyce for modernism. Although, according to Wim Tigges (1999), there is a full nineteenth-century history of suggestive definitions of such consolidating heightened moments, the term "epiphany" seems to have been solidified in literary criticism by commentary on Joyce. The term emerged from Joyce's own philosophically acute meta-poetic discussions in *Portrait of the Artist as a Young Man* (1916) and *Stephen Hero* (1944), and from there into early critical studies of Joyce. Ellmann and Feidelson excerpted key Joycean passages defining "epiphany" in *The Modern Tradition* (1965; 135–42). One can see the term passing into general use in such titles as Morris Beja's *Epiphany in the Modern Novel* (1971). For its continued prevalence, see this recent anonymous review in *The Economist* (7 Feb. 2009): "The best lyric poems – think of Keats or Shelley, for example – are moments of epiphany, a sudden opening out onto magic casements." This was a clipping given to me, hence has no page number, but the indication that such thought is still with us is important to signal.

29 Charles Bernstein, *My Way: Speeches and Poems*, 4.

30 Pound, *ABC of Reading* (New York: New Directions, 1960 [1934]), 17–18.

31 Even in the post-World War II period, Pound's metaphor of political/ethnic "cleansing" (i.e. destruction) did not self-criticize or self-question: "pity, yes, for the infected,/ but maintain antisepsis,/ let the light pour" (Pound 1987, 635 [Canto XCIV]). Antisepsis – the destruction of micro-organisms that produce disease, putrefaction, fermentation.

32 Theodor Adorno, "On Lyric Poetry and Society," *Notes to Literature*, Vol. I, trans. Shierry Weber Nicholsen (New York: Columbia University Press, 1991), 45. Charles Altieri also evokes the criterion of intensity in his "Taking Lyrics Literally: Teaching Poetry in a Prose Culture," *New Literary History* 32, no. 1 (Winter 2001): 259–81.

33 However, in some of the discussion, Altieri uses "lyric" as a synonym for poem, and thus it's hard to know whether he is defending poetry in general or lyric in specific by offering this sophisticated sense of its functions.

34 How does one identify "lyric materials" if there is no such thing as "the lyric"? The answer is by conventional agreement, which has a snowball effect.

35 As has often been noted, this is precisely the empirical and situational knowledge of a "discrete series."

36 Satya P. Mohanty, *Literary Theory and the Claims of History: Postmodernism, Objectivity, Multicultural Politics* (Ithaca, NY: Cornell University Press, 1997), 221.

37 See Michael André Bernstein's *The Tale of the Tribe: Ezra Pound and the Modern Verse Epic* (Princeton: Princeton University Press, 1980).

38 Nathaniel Mackey, *Splay Anthem* (New York: New Directions, 2006), 78 and 115.

39 Jacques Derrida, "The Law of Genre," *Acts of Literature,* ed. Derek Attridge (New York: Routledge, 1992), 227. Hereafter cited parenthetically by page number and abbreviated *AL.*

40 Peter Middleton, "The Longing of the Long Poem," *Jacket Magazine* 40 (Late 2010). http://jacketmagazine.com/40/middleton-long-poem.shtml (accessed 1 Dec. 2011).

41 Mikhail M. Bakhtin, "Discourse in Poetry and Discourse in the Novel," *The Dialogic Imagination: Four Essays,* ed. Michael Holquist, trans. Caryl Emerson and Michael Holquist (Austin: University of Texas Press, 1981), 285.

42 I will not deal with the opposite proposition – that a ghost of long poem may haunt the lyric.

43 My position differs from what Peter Baker claims in *Obdurate Brilliance* about the long poem insofar as he opposes its "exteriority" to the lyric's "interiority"; he argues that a resistance to the lyric is expressed in long poems by denial or rejection of interiority or the lyric subject, itself postulated as unified and in contrast a long poem is based on "split subjectivity." This might be true sometimes, but it's also true that marks of lyric modes enter the long poem; they are not binary/opposed modes.

44 The same kind of thing can be seen in one of the earliest long poems of modernism – *Tender Buttons* (1914). In "Food," the section called "Roast Beef," Stein breaks into a rhyming, sing-song lyric of praise to the sexual relationship with Toklas. From the middle of the paragraph: "to surrender one another, to succeed saving simpler, to satisfy a singularity and not to be blinder, to sugar nothing darker and to read reader, to have the color better, to sort out dinner, to remain together, to surprise no sinner, to curve nothing sweeter …" See *Tender Buttons* in *Selected Writings of Gertrude Stein,* ed. Carl Van Vechten (New York: The Modern Library, 1962), 481.

45 William Carlos Williams, *Paterson*, revised, ed. Christopher MacGowan (New York: New Directions, 1992). *The Collected Poems of William Carlos Williams, Volume II, 1939–1962*, ed. Christopher MacGowan (New York: New Directions, 1988).

There are several other moments of intensely condensed, occasional, epigrammatic lyrics in *Paterson* as quasi-separable entities though none appears in the *Collected Poems* (either volume). Book IV, iii (P, 192) contains the eight-line celebration of the birth of child, also quite celebratory of the sexual act that proved to be fertilizing: "Here's to the baby, / may it thrive! / Here's to the labia / that rive …" There is also the Zukofskyian play with vowels: "There is no ease. / We close our eyes, get what we use / …" (Book III, iii, [P, 135]). Others use lyric tropes (trees, flowers, birds) – "Who is younger than I" (I, iii [P, 30–1]), "Look for the nul …" II, iii (P, 77), "On this most voluptuous night of the year …" (II, iii [P, 86]), "I love the locust tree / the sweet white locust …" (III, i [P, 95]), "The birds in winter …" (III, iii [P, 141-2]). This list is not exhaustive.

In *Paterson* as well are two important sections that were also published as separate poems. That is, they are switch hitters – they could be lyrics/short poems in one context, or modular parts of a long poem in another. They are both autonomous and joined, mobile and fixed. One of these is, of course, "The Descent beckons … ," which is the lead-off poem in *The Desert Music* (WCW, 245) and functions also as a turning point for the whole of *Paterson* in II, iii (P, 78–9). The second, "Satyrs Dance," which concludes V, ii (P, 219–21), is titled "Tribute to the Painters" in the 1955 collection *Journey to Love* (WCW, 296-8; the latter version adds fifteen lines at its end; the *Paterson* version adds six at the beginning).

46 T.S. Eliot, *Collected Poems, 1909–1962* (London: Faber and Faber, 1963), 131–2; Rachel Blau DuPlessis, *Genders, Races, and Religious Cultures in Modern American Poetry, 1908–1934* (Cambridge, England: Cambridge University Press, 2001), 103–4.

47 Gertrude Stein, "Patriarchal Poetry," *The Yale Gertrude Stein: Selections with an Introduction by Richard Kostelanetz* (New Haven: Yale University Press, 1980), 124.

48 John Ashbery, *Flow Chart* (New York: Alfred A. Knopf, 1991), 186–93.

49 Ashbery calls this "a kind of continuum, a diary, even though it's not in the form of a diary. It's the result of what I had to say on certain days over a period of six months, during the course of thinking about my past, the weather outside. I free-associate and come up with all kinds of extra material that doesn't belong – but does." Cited in John Shoptaw, *On the Outside Looking Out: John Ashbery's Poetry* (Cambridge, MA: Harvard University Press, 1994), 308.

50 The placement of the sestina near (about twenty-three pages from) the end of *Flow Chart* parallels the placement of "Satyrs dance!" in *Paterson* (about fifteen pages from the end of Book V). A number of experimental poems, including "The Waste Land," use several genre-multiplying ending gestures for a genre-multiplying variety of strategies (see BL, 243–6).

51 I will clearly differ from early, and brave, Zukofsky reader Barry Ahearn who qualified "A"-16 with "hardly seems serious." See *Zukofsky's "A": An Introduction* (Berkeley: University of California Press, 1983), 141.

52 Zukofsky wrote "A"-16 in 1963. By 1963, he is coping with his having restarted

the writing of "*A*", but a good deal of it had already been accomplished, about half.

53 Louis Zukofsky, "*A*" (Berkeley, CA: University of California Press, 1978), 376.

54 The poem could fit all of these definitions of inequality: 1. the condition of being unequal 2. social or economic disparity 3. unevenness; lack of smoothness or regularity 4. variability or changeability 5. an instance of a thing unequal 6. in Math(s), an algebraic statement that a quantity is greater than another quantity or that it is less than another quantity.

55 Louis Zukofsky, *Complete Short Poetry* (Baltimore: Johns Hopkins University Press, 1991), 18.

56 This retrospective interview occurred when the poem was not yet completed. It is notable that only after the 1968 musical ending was assembled by Celia Zukofsky – and only after the Dembo interview also in 1968 – did (could?) Zukofsky write sections 22 (1970–73) and 23 (dated 1973–74).

57 Four categories that might appear in a taxonomy of modes of the long poem:

Encyclopedic Hyper-Text "Epic." Those field compositions that have seemed to symbolize the North American long poem in the twentieth century(ies). From *The Waste Land* to *The Cantos*, from *Paterson* to *Iovis*, from *Maximus* (in its first two books) to "*A*" and *The Martyrology*, these are hyper-text (or field) compositions because of the collage correlation, the sense that one moves off via "links" to vortices of material that are not forensically or propositionally argued but juxtaposed with others to occasion oblique inferences. Because they are informational *summae*, sometimes "anthologies" of what the poet considers important, the term "epic" is honorific only.

Odic Logbooks of Continuance. Many of the people writing in this odic mode have a vocation for the sublime aspects of being. By logbook I mean the record of a launching out on a journey in space-time with each stage of the poem: an intense temporal engagement with continuance and retrospection in the ever-changing now. Robert Duncan's intermittent work "Passages" fits here as do Beverly Dahlen's various works called *A Reading*. So too Lyn Hejinian's *The Cell* and *Oxota – a Russian Novel* as well as my own *Drafts*.

New Realist Procedurals. In this category would go *Tjanting* and pretty much anything else by Silliman (although *The Alphabet*'s ultimate basis is serial); Lyn Hejinian, *My Life*; Barrett Watten, *Progress*; Bernadette Mayer, *Midwinter Day*; and Kenneth Goldsmith's *Soliloquy*. Here with Oulipean flair, writers define specific and inventive procedures as plans of action, making some commitment to putting the same world together but differently (which parallels *Spring and All*). The procedure can be something as simple (and challenging) as making up a certain number of varied sentences per prose section, or recording everything you say in a week (but the words of no one else); the obsessive writing with an often documentary goal reduces expressive subjectivity and (perhaps) individual ego in favor of language acts, which is why Jackson Mac Low's work can go here, too. These procedurals, like serial poems, scan the time/space coordinate of now, a now that curiously suspends *telos*.

Long Poem as Essay or Conceptual Text. Stein – say some of the oblique essays, almost poetic prose – is the good-enough parent here. Certainly Bernstein's *Apoetics* could be placed here, but also work by David Antin (whose ethos of "keep talking" might, however, recategorize his work as log-book of continuance …). Kamau Brathwaite's books of conceptual history, Jena Osman's recent work and Juliana Spahr's. Watten's *Bad History*, certain work by Susan Howe (*Pierce Arrow*; *The Midnight*) and again by Beverly Dahlen (*A Reading*) may be proposed here. Definitely some of Bernadette Mayer – *The Desire of Mothers to Please Others in Letters*. Clark Coolidge. Leslie Scalapino. Hannah Weiner. It's not so much that these works are often in prose (that is, poetry lacking linebreaks) but that they make commentary on *poiesis*. In this group of works there is an almost discursive, explanatory impulse, an intervention in critical self-reflection, in tracking consciousness, making the quotidian and thought itself a continuous commentary on its own continuous construction in language.

58 Alice Notley, "Iovis Omnia Plena," *Chicago Review* 44 (1998), 126.

59 The assumption that lyric is "feminine" and epic "masculine" had nothing to do with my sense of writing, though I am quite familiar with those ideas from the point of view of literary history. Susan Stanford Friedman, for instance, has argued that a female poet writing a long poem enters a field already masculinized by convention.

60 I appreciate that several other women were writing long poems when I began *Drafts*, but without this particular passionate rage as a motivator. Beverly Dahlen and Lyn Hejinian and Leslie Scalapino were much more in the essayistic "que sais-je" line of things – how am I situated, in what, through what, and how is my so-called "I." In Susan Howe's *The Liberties* one can find a perhaps comparable investigation of cultural figures and products.

61 Silliman: "Self-conscious of its own difference, the longpoem is thus always the poem designed against innocence"; "'As to Violin Music': Time in the Longpoem," *Jacket Magazine* 27 (April 2005); accessed 3 May, 2008, http://www.jacketmagazine.com/27/silliman.html).

62 Ron Silliman, *The Age of Huts (compleat)* (Berkeley: University of California Press, 2007), 40.

63 Ron Silliman, *The Age of Huts (compleat)*, 42.

CHAPTER THREE

1 Raymond Williams, *Politics of Modernism: Against the New Conformists*, ed. Tony Pinkney (Brooklyn: Verso Books, 2007), 65–6. Williams, who died in

1988, intended to write a book-length study of modernism and the avant-garde. *Politics of Modernism* is a collection of his essays and conference papers on the subject.

2 "Real," as used throughout this essay, is not Jacques Lacan's "Real." Although there is much potential for considering the Lacanian Real in relation to poetry, for instance as that concept is utilized by Julia Kristeva in her theory of the semiotic, in my usage "real" and "apparent" simply point to the way that defenders of both avant-garde and lyric poetry too easily suppose that this by-now conventional division has some incontrovertible theoretical grounding.

3 Ruth E.C. Prince, "A New Way of Being: Helen Vendler on Poetry Past and Future," *Radcliffe Quarterly* (Winter 2000), 2.

4 "A Life of Learning," *American Council of Learned Societies,* Occasional Paper No. 50: 1, http://www.acls.org/Publications/OP/ Haskins/2001_Helen-Vendler.pdf (accessed 13 July 2003).

5 "When we note that in English at least … 'avant-garde' may be indifferently used to refer to Dadaism seventy years after the event or to recent fringe theatre, the confusion both willed and involuntary … becomes less an intellectual problem and more an ideological perspective" (PM, 32). The received notion of the lyric is also grounded in ideology – the ideology of humanism.

6 Gérard Genette, *The Architext: An Introduction*, trans. Jane E. Lewin (Berkeley: California University Press, 1992), 28.

7 As Alex Davis and Lee M. Jenkins, the editors of *The Cambridge Companion to Modernist Poetry* affirm, "Modernist poetry involves recuperations of history *and* Futurist and Dada abandonments of tradition; arcane *and* demotic registers of language; elitist *and* populist forms of literature," (New York: Cambridge University Press, 2007), 1.

8 Marjorie Perloff, *Differentials: Poetry, Poetics, Pedagogy* (Tuscaloosa: The University of Alabama Press, 2004), 158.

9 Marjorie Perloff, *Dance of the Intellect: Studies in the Poetry of the Pound Tradition* (New York: Cambridge University Press, 1985), 16.

10 Marjorie Perloff, *The Poetics of Indeterminacy: Rimbaud to Cage* (Princeton: Princeton University Press, 1981), 33. Perloff argues that a lack of coherence and consistence opens the possibility for a "poetry of indeterminacy" (4), which she opposes to works (by Lowell and Berryman, for instance) that inherit the legacy of the so-called High Modernists (Yeats, Eliot, Auden, Stevens, Frost, and Crane).

11 Marjorie Perloff, *Radical Artifice* (Chicago: Chicago University Press, 1991).

12 Perloff, *Differentials,* 171.

13 Marjorie Perloff, "Revolving in Crystal: The Supreme Fiction and the Impasse of Modernist Lyric," in *Wallace Stevens*: *The Poetics of Modernism*, ed. Albert Gelpi, (New York: Cambridge University Press, 1985), 51.

14 DuPlessis, "Lyric and Experimental Long Poems: Intersections," 24.

15 Robert Sholes, "Introduction," in *The Architext: An Introduction,* by Gérard Genette, trans. Jane E. Lewin, (Berkeley: California University Press, 1992), viii.

16 Ibid., ix.

17 Perloff, *Differentials*, 171.

18 See Mikhail M. Bakhtin, "Discourse in the Novel," in *The Dialogic Imagination: Four Essays,* ed. Michael Holquist, trans. Caryl Emerson and Michael Holquist (Austin: University of Texas Press, 1981), 287.

19 I follow Raymond Williams, who refused the conflation of avant-garde, experimental, and modernist. We can find experimental poems in any historical era, as well as experimental modernist poetry not aligned with the politics of the avant-garde. Further, even "conventional" forms, rhetoric, or figures can be used experimentally in order to challenge static/symbolic/monoglossic language.

20 "Lyric and Experimental Long Poems: Intersections," 41.

21 Ibid, 41.

22 Ibid, 41.

23 Kristeva, "Word, Dialogue, and Novel," in *Desire in Language: A Semiotic Approach to Literature and Art*, ed. Leon S. Roudiez (New York: Columbia University Press, 1980), 66.

24 Julia Kristeva, "Word, Dialogue, and Novel," in *Desire in Language*, 74. See Tzvetan Todorov's *Mikhail Bakhtin: The Dialogic Principle,* trans. Wlad Godzich (Minneapolis: The University of Minnesota Press, 1984) for a sustained comparison of the differences between the early and later works of Bakhtin.

25 Tyrus Miller, *Singular Examples: Artistic Politics and the Neo-Avant-Garde* (Evanston, IL: Northwestern University Press, 2009), 72.

26 "Revolution in Poetic Language," in *The Kristeva Reader*, ed. Toril Moi (New York: Columbia University Press, 1986), 93.

27 Mikhail M. Bakhtin, "The Problem of the Text in Linguistics, Philology, and the Human Sciences: An Experiment in Philosophical Analysis," in *Speech Genres and Other Late Essays*, trans. Vern W. McGee, eds. Caryl Emerson and Michael Holquist (Austin: University of Texas Press, 1986), 110.

28 Wallace Stevens, "Notes Toward a Supreme Fiction," in *The Collected Poems of Wallace Stevens* (New York: Vintage / Random House, 1990), 387.

29 "Artifice … is less a matter of ingenuity and manner, of elaboration and elegant subterfuge, than the recognition that a poem or painting or performance text is a *made thing* – contrived, constructed, chosen – and that its reading is also a construction on the part of its audience" (*RA*, 27–8).

30 Marjorie Perloff, "Visionary Company," *Boston Review* 23, no. 3–4 (Summer 1998), http://bostonreview.net/BR23.3/perloff.html (accessed 18 August 2003).

31 Bakhtin, quoted in Todorov, *Mikhail Bakhtin*, 48.

32 Wallace Stevens, *Opus Posthumous*, ed. Milton J. Bates (New York: Vintage Books, 1990), 204.

33 Much of Perloff's argument is a critique of readings of the poem by Roy H. Pearce, Frank Kermode, Helen Vendler, Frank Doggett, Harold Bloom, and Joseph Riddle.

34 Mikhail M. Bakhtin, "Response to a Question from the *Novy Mir* Editorial Staff," in *Speech Genres and Other Late Essays*, 4, 5.

35 Ibid., 3.

36 Bakhtin, "Toward a Methodology for the Human Sciences," in *Speech Genres and Other Late Essays*, 169.

37 Bakhtin, "Response to a Question from the *Novy Mir* Editorial Staff," 3.

38 Gérard Genette, "Valéry and the Poetics of Language," in *Textual Strategies: Perspectives in Post-Structuralist Criticism*, ed. Josué V. Harari (Ithaca, NY: Cornell University Press, 1979), 359.

39 This apparent paradox should lead us to consider that the two positions (for which Perloff and Vendler may serve as metonyms) are also oppositional without being contradictory.

40 Gérard Genette, *Mimologics*, trans. Thaïs E. Morgan (Lincoln: Nebraska University Press, 1994), 334.

41 Genette, "Valéry and the Poetics of Language," in *Textual Strategies: Perspectives in Post-Structuralist Criticism*, 364.

42 Ibid., 372.

43 Stevens, *Opus Posthumous*, 160.

44 Ibid., 164.

45 Charles Altieri, "Modernist Innovations: A Legacy of the Constructed Reader," in *Modernism, Volume 1*, eds. Astradur Eysteinsson and Vivian Liska (Amsterdam, The Netherlands, and Philadelphia, PA: John Benjamins, 2007), 67.

46 Ibid., 69.

47 Helen Vendler, "The Amassing Harmony," in *On Extended Wings: Wallace Stevens' Longer Poems* (Cambridge, MA: Harvard University Press, 1969), 205, 169.

48 J. Hillis Miller, "Wallace Stevens' Poetry of Being," in *Tropes, Parables, Performatives: Essays on Twentieth-Century Literature* (Durham, NC: Duke University Press, 1991), 37.

49 Although Maeder focuses her analysis on "The Man with the Blue Guitar," she argues that, to a greater or lesser extent, Stevens's use of tercets in his long poems has the same effect (*Wallace Stevens' Experimental Language: The Lion in the Lute* [New York: St Martin's Press, 1999], 196–7).

CHAPTER FOUR

1 Hannah Weiner, "Mostly about the Sentence," in *Hannah Weiner's Open House*, ed. Patrick Durgin (Berkeley: Kenning Editions, 2007), 122.

2 Weiner uses "the words," "the voices," and "the forces" interchangeably to refer to the words and images that she sees. She personifies them, believing

them to have agency. I follow her lead, allowing the words the agency she insists upon. Moreover, the quotations included here from *Clairvoyant Journal* and from the manuscripts of her other clair-style poems have not been corrected or standardized for spelling, punctuation, or grammar.

3 Hannah Weiner, "Silent Teacher," *silent teachers/remembered sequel* (New York: Tender Buttons, 1994), 69.

4 Ron Silliman, "Hannah Weiner Notes" (10 Nov. 1998), Electronic Poetry Center at SUNY Buffalo, http://epc.buffalo.edu/conferences/reports/hannah98-doc.html (accessed 1 July 2009), n.p.

5 Hannah Weiner, "Hannah Weiner at Her Job," *Hannah Weiner's Open House*, 23.

6 Daniel Kane, *All Poets Welcome: The Lower East Side Poetry Scene in the 1960s* (Berkeley and Los Angeles: University of California Press, 2003), 141.

7 Kane, *All Poets Welcome*, 189.

8 Jerome Rothenberg, ed., *Technicians of the Sacred*, Second Edition (Berkeley and Los Angeles,: University of California Press, 1985), 528–9.

9 Jerome Rothenberg and Pierre Joris, eds., *Poems for the Millennium* (Berkeley: University of California Press, 1998).

10 Rothenberg, *Technicians of the Sacred*, xviii–xix.

11 Patrick Durgin, "Introduction," *Hannah Weiner's Open House*, 13.

12 Charles Bernstein, "Hannah Weiner," *Jacket* 12 (July 2000) http://jacketmagazine.com/12/wein-bern.html (accessed 15 March 2009), n.p.

13 Kaplan Harris, Insert for Event Program (A Reading for *Hannah Weiner's Open House*, St Mark's Church, New York City, 28 Nov. 2007).

14 Thom Donavan, "Silent Teacher Remembered: Hannah Weiner's Open House" (20 Dec. 2007), *Fanzine*, http://www.thefanzine.com/articles/features/201/ silent_teacher_remembered-hannah_weiner's_open house/ (accessed 15 March 2009), n.p.

15 Weiner, *Clairvoyant Journal* (New York: Angel Hair Books, 1974).

16 Gertrude Stein, *How to Write* (New York: Dover, 1975), 23.

17 Charles Olson, "Projective Verse," *Collected Prose of Charles Olson*, ed. Donald Allen and Benjamin Friedlander (Berkeley and Los Angeles: University of California Press, 1997), 240.

18 "Dictation and 'A Textbook of Poetry,'" *The House That Jack Built: The Collected Lectures of Jack Spicer*, ed. Peter Gizzi (Middletown, CT: Wesleyan University Press, 1998), 7.

19 Ibid., 64.

20 Hannah Weiner, *Pictures and Early Words, Early and Clairvoyant Journals by Hannah Weiner*, Mandeville Special Collections Library, 2004 [1972]), 15, http://orpheus.ucsd.edu/speccoll/m504/3/index.html (accessed 15 July 2009).

21 Hannah Weiner, *Big Words, Early and Clairvoyant Journals by Hannah Weiner*, Mandeville Special Collections Library, 2004 [1973], 129, http://orpheus.ucsd.edu/speccoll/m504/4/index.html (accessed 15 July 2009).

22 "The reader's ego or expectation is further thrown by the occasional running of words together so that rather than put together the reader must pause and separate the words" (OH, 131–2).

23 Hannnah Weiner, "Silent Teacher," 69.

24 "full of energy and wide awake": Hannah Weiner, *The Fast* (New York: United Artists Books, 1992), 36; "higher mind": PE, 34.

25 "The author isn't the only one with an ego" (OH, 131–2).

26 Hannah Weiner, *Spoke* (Washington: Sun and Moon Press, 1984), 65.

27 Samadhi, which can be translated as "superconscious perception," is the last step on the "Eightfold Path of Yoga, "which leads one to the final goal of Kaivalya (Absoluteness), a term which might be more comprehensibly put as 'realization of the Truth beyond all intellectual apprehension'" (Paramhansa Yogananda, *Autobiography of a Yogi* [Los Angeles: Self-Realization Fellowhip, 1946], reprinted by Project Gutenberg, 2005, n.p.; accessed 20 August 2011).

28 That is, she has not completed the project of showing "the mind," but of developing a clair-style poetics.

29 Hannah Weiner, *The Fast*, 9.

30 Ibid., 24.

31 "Clairvoyant Journal, March" (audio), performed by Hannah Weiner, Sharon Mattlin, and Margaret De Coursey (New York: New Wilderness Audiographics, 1978), *PennSound*, http://writing.upenn.edu/pennsound/x/Weiner.html (accessed 1 August 2009). Mattlin and De Coursey's voices are each in one stereo channel of the recording while Weiner's is in both.

32 "Clairvoyant Journal, May" (audio), performed by Hannah Weiner, Sharon Mattlin, and Rochelle Kraut (New York: New Wilderness Audiographics, 1978), *PennSound*, http://writing.upenn.edu/pennsound/x/Weiner.html (accessed 1 August 2009).

33 Maria Damon, "Page-Mother's Open Heart: Open House/Hannah Weiner," KAURAB *Online: A Bengali poetry webzine*, http://www.kaurab.com/english/books/open-house.html (accessed 15 August 2009), n.p.

34 Bernstein, "Hannah Weiner," *Jacket* 12 (July 2000), http://jacketmagazine.com/12/wein-bern.html (accessed 15 March 2009), n.p.

35 Sharon Mattlin, "Review of *Clairvoyant Journal*," *The Poetry Project Newsletter* (May/June 1979), n.p.

36 Hannah Weiner, *Early and Clairvoyant Journals.*

CHAPTER FIVE

1 Michel Foucault, *Ditos e Escritos III – Estética: Literatura e pintura, música e cinema.* Translated by Inês Autran Dourado Barboda (Rio de Janeiro: Forense Universidade, 2001), 264.

2 Richard Zenith's translation, *113 Galician-Portuguese Troubadour Poems* (Manchester: Carcanet, 1995) is, alas, out of print. It holds the most extensive selection in English of the 1,163 poems. I'm hoping it will one day come back into print again.
3 "An Unsung Literature: Galician-Portuguese Troubadour Poetry," 1 July 2004. Accessed at http://www.poetryinternational.org/ (link via Portugal, then Troubadour) on 9 February 2009.
4 This hokey and historically inaccurate American science-fiction television show that ran in 1966–67 had a great hold on me as a child. Lee Meriwether was playing me, of course, though on *my* clipboard, I wrote poetry.
5 The first Portuguese grammar, by Fernão de Oliveira, dates from 1536. The first Galician grammar in Galician, *Grámatica do idioma galego*, by Manuel Lugris Freire, appeared in 1922.
6 "Reconnecemos o típico desinteresse medieval pela sequência cronológica, substituída amiúde por uma visão simultânea e pictórica dos acontecimentos" (120; the English version is my translation). See Stephen Reckert and Helder Macedo, *Do Cancioneiro de Amigo* (Lisbon: Assirio and Alvim, 1996).
7 And this is entirely possible. Before the expulsion of the Jews from Spain in 1492, Galicia had thriving Jewish communities.
8 Giorgio Agamben, "The Dictation of Poetry," in *The End of the Poem: Studies in Poetics*. Translated by Daniel Heller-Roazen (Stanford: Stanford University Press, 1999), 79.
9 Jacques Derrida, *Mal d'archive: une impression freudienne* (Paris: Galilée, 1995), 60; my translation.

CHAPTER SIX

1 Jackson Mac Low, *22 Light Poems* (Los Angeles: Black Sparrow Press, 1968).
2 Quotations of Mac Low's correspondence are drawn from The Black Sparrow Press archive held at the Bruce Peel Special Collections Library, University of Alberta. The citations identify the file, folder, and document as enumerated in O'Driscoll and Dewinetz's *A Bibliography of the Black Sparrow Press Archive*. Any unconventional grammar or spelling is original with Mac Low.
3 Jackson Mac Low, *Thing of Beauty: New and Selected Works*, ed. Anne Tardos (Berkeley: University of California Press, 2008); Jerome Rothenberg, "Preface," in *Representative Works: 1938–1985* by Jackson Mac Low (New York: Roof Books, 1986), vi.
4 Jackson Mac Low, "Poetry, Chance, Silence, Etc.," in *Claims for Poetry*, ed. Donald Hall (Ann Arbor: University of Michigan Press, 1982), 302.
5 Kevin Bezner, "Jackson Mac Low, Interviewed by Kevin Bezner," *New American Writing* 11 (1993), 117.
6 Jackson Mac Low, "Response to Piombino: A Letter to the Poetics List," *Elec-*

tronic Poetry Center at SUNY Buffalo (February 1998): n.p., http://epc.buffalo.edu/ (accessed 13 July 2010).

It is also possible to challenge (as I have) the public overemphasis on chance in accounts of John Cage's work: "while Cage's texts are silent in the sense that they refuse to speak from the depths of their own structural configuration, his work cannot be said to be entirely void of creative will." See O'Driscoll, "Silent Texts and Empty Words: Structure and Intention in the Writings of John Cage," *Contemporary Literature* 38, no. 4 (1997): 621.

7 Jackson Mac Low, "The Terminology," *Open Letter* 11, no. 3 (2001), 84.

8 Ibid., 87.

9 Charles Bernstein, "Sounds Physical," *BookForum: The Review for Art, Fiction, and Culture* 11, no. 5 (2005): 7.

10 Louis Cabri, "'Rebus Effort Remove Government': Jackson Mac Low, *Why?/ Resistance*, Anarcho-Pacifism," *Crayon* 1 (1997): 45–68; Barrett Watten, "New Meaning and Poetic Vocabulary: From Coleridge to Jackson Mac Low," *Poetics Today* 18, no. 2 (1997): 147–86; Steve McCaffery, *Prior to Meaning: The Protosemantic and Poetics* (Evanston, IL: Northwestern University Press, 2001).

11 Steve McCaffery, *North of Intention: Critical Writings 1973–1986* (New York: Roof Books, 1986), 225.

12 McCaffery, *Prior to Meaning*, 281.

13 The overstatement of the role of chance in Mac Low's poetry is even more evident in popular accounts of his writing career. Despite more than two decades of subtle correctives and outright disavowal on his part, obituaries on the occasion of Mac Low's death in 2004 still emphasize his corpus as governed purely by a poetics of chance. Without equivocation, the *Los Angeles Times* states that "Mac Low used chance operations in making his art" (Mark Swed, "Jackson Mac Low, 82; 'Composer of Poetry' Shaped His Verse into Unconventional Forms, Sounds" *Los Angeles Times* (10 December 2004), http://www.latimes.com (accessed 29 July, 2010), while *The New York Times* describes him as "a poet, composer, and performance artist whose work reveled in what happens when the process of composition is left to carefully calibrated chance" and states that "what united Mr. Mac Low's output was a fascination with randomness" (Margalit Fox, "Jackson Mac Low, 82, Poet and Composer," *New York Times* (10 December 2004): A-39.)

14 Douglas Barbour, *Lyric/Anti-Lyric: Essays on Contemporary Poetry* (Edmonton: NeWest Press, 2001), 7, 19.

15 Ibid., 18–19, 24.

16 Rachel Blau DuPlessis, "Lyric and Experimental Long Poems: Intersections," 41–2; Jacques Derrida, "The Law of Genre," in *Acts of Literature*, ed. Derek Attridge (New York: Routledge, 1992), 225.

17 Patrick Durgin, "Indeterminacies and the Poetics of Critical Values," PhD dissertation (State University of New York at Buffalo, 2004).

18 Consider Tyrus Miller's claim in *Singular Examples: Artistic Politics and the*

Neo-Avant Garde (Evanston, IL: Northwestern University Press, 2009) that the "consequence of Mac Low's methods ... is not that the self is eliminated from the poem, but that its boundaries become less fixed and distinct" (50), or Mac Low's own statement that "I wasn't trying to achieve 'purity.' I merely wanted to let language 'be itself' – for both words' sounds and their intrinsic meanings to be perceived in their own right rather than expressing my own emotions, attitudes, opinions, tastes, etc. I never thought of purity's being involved, except in the sense that the input from the ego was minimized" (Bezner, "Jackson Mac Low, Interviewed by Kevin Bezner," 111).

19 Rand Corporation, *A Million Random Digits with 100,000 Normal Deviates* (Glencoe, IL: Free Press, 1955).

20 Mac Low, "Response to Piombino," n.p.

21 Consider, for example, Mac Low's statement emphasizing intention and choice in a 1992 interview with Kim Rosenfield in "Kim Rosenfield Interviews Jackson Mac Low," *Shiny* 7/8 (1992): "Since late 1954 I've devised a large array of such procedures through which one may write various kinds of texts ... They are all characterized by the fact that my intentional choices mainly determine the basic procedures, while the latter determine the details of the texts, scores, and performances (which certain exceptions, which are left either to my choice or that of the performers)," 20.

22 As Mac Low contends in a symposium with Richard Kostelanetz et al., "every word, every speech sound, seems to me as much a matter of *meaning* as of sound, and that anything uttered, certainly any complete words, but even fragments of words, having meaning ... Every poem is as much meaning as sound and as much sound as meaning" ("A Symposium on Text – Sound," *Precisely: A Critical Journal* 10–12 (1981): 158–9, emphasis original).

23 Quoted in Watten, "New Meaning and Poetic Vocabulary: From Coleridge to Jackson Mac Low," *Poetics Today* 18, no. 2: 180.

24 S.E. Tillman, *A Text-Book of Important Minerals and Rocks,* Third Edition, Revised (New York: John Wiley and Sons, 1908), 88–9, emphasis original.

25 McCaffery, *Prior to Meaning*, 282.

CHAPTER SEVEN

1 Rick Smith and Bruce Lourie, *Slow Death by Rubber Duck: How the Toxic Chemistry of Everyday Life Affects our Health* (Toronto: Alfred A. Knopf Canada, 2009), 4.

2 Smith and Lourie contrast their scientific approach to the so-called "sound science" movement, an industry-funded strategic initiative that often paints academic research counter to industrial interests as self-serving "junk science" (SD, 209). By emphasizing the subjective dimension of their research, the authors undercut this critique and turn personal experience into a political asset instead of a liability.

3 Jarry spells *'pataphysics* with an apostrophe preceding the word in order to "avoid a simple pun." (Alfred Jarry, *Exploits & Opinions of Dr. Faustroll, Pataphysician: A Neo-Scientific Novel*, trans. Simon Watson Taylor [Boston: Exact Change, 1996], 21.) The Toronto Research Group (TRG) distinguishes a Canadian tradition by marking the move from the elision of the single apostrophe to the open quotation of "Pataphysics. The aim of this orthographic shift is to identify "a science of the perpetually open citing." See the Toronto Research Group, *Rational Geomancy: The Kids of the Book-Machine: The Collected Research Reports of the Toronto Research Group 1973–1982*, ed. Steve McCaffery (Vancouver: Talonbooks, 1992), 301.

4 Jarry, *Exploits & Opinions of Dr. Faustroll, Pataphysician,* 21.

5 Karl Jirgens, "A Short History of 'Pataphysics," *Rampike* 5, no. 2 (1983), 9.

6 Kenneth Goldsmith, *Soliloquy* (New York: Granary Books, 2001).

7 Donald Favareau, "The Evolutionary History of Biosemiotics," in *Introduction to Biosemiotics: The New Biological Synthesis*, ed. Marcello Barbieri (Dordrecht, The Netherlands: Springer, 2007), 29.

8 Jesper Hoffmeyer, *Signs of Meaning in the Universe* (1993), trans. Barbara J. Haveland (Bloomington and Indianapolis: Indiana University Press, 1996), vii.

9 Jesper Hoffmeyer, *Biosemiotics: An Examination into the Signs of Life and the Life of Signs*, trans. Jesper Hoffmeyer and Donald Favareau (Scranton, PA: University of Scranton Press, 2008), xvi.

10 Dana Phillips, *The Truth of Ecology: Nature, Culture, and Literature in America* (Oxford and New York: Oxford University Press, 2003), 157.

11 Robert Finch and John Elder, eds., *The Norton Book of Nature Writing* (New York: W.W. Norton and Company, 1990), 26.

12 David Abram, *The Spell of the Sensuous: Perception and Language in a More-Than-Human World* (New York: Vintage Books, 1997).

13 J. Scott Bryson, "Introduction," in *Ecopoetry: A Critical Introduction*, ed. J. Scott Bryson (Salt Lake City: University of Utah Press, 2002), 7–8.

14 Ibid., 7.

15 Christian Bök, *'Pataphysics: The Poetics of an Imaginary Science* (Evanston, IL: Northwestern University Press, 2002), 14.

16 Ibid., 14.

17 Marcello Barbieri, "Editorial," in *Introduction to Biosemiotics*, xi.

18 Bök, *'Pataphysics,* 16.

19 Jakob von Uexküll, "The Theory of Meaning," *Semiotica* 42, no. 1 (1982), 69.

20 Jakob von Uexküll, "A Stroll Through the Worlds of Animals and Men: A Picture Book of Invisible Worlds" (1934), in *Instinctive Behavior: The Development of a Modern Concept*, ed., trans. Claire H. Shiller (New York: International Universities Press, 1957), 25, 28.

21 The functional circle is explicitly recast in hermeneutic terms by Uexküll: "One may even speak of functional circles as meaning circles, whose task lies in the utilization of the meaning-carriers" (SCA, 36). This semiotic dimen-

sion makes a discussion of *Umwelten* especially relevant to culture and the kinds of alternative *Umwelt* building we might associate with 'pataphysics.

22 Thomas A. Sebeok, *Signs: An Introduction to Semiotics*, second edition (Toronto: University of Toronto Press, 2001), 34.

23 "A Stroll Through the Worlds of Animals and Men," 50.

24 Uexküll's poetic formulations, his emphasis on "magic" formations in *Umwelten*, and his insistence on "the over-all plan of nature" imbued his theory with too many mystical elements to be palatable to the majority of contemporary scientists working in a Darwinian paradigm ("A Stroll Through the Worlds of Animals and Men," 42).

25 Jane Bennett, *Vibrant Matter: A Political Ecology of Things* (Durham, NC, and London: Duke University Press, 2010), viii.

26 Wendy Wheeler, *The Whole Creature: Complexity, Biosemiotics and The Evolution of Culture* (London: Lawrence and Wishart, 2006), 127.

27 Stacey Alimo, "MCS Matters: Material Agency in the Science and Practices of Environmental Illness," TOPIA*: Canadian Journal of Cultural Studies* 21 (2009): 9–27, 15.

28 Ibid., 25.

29 Timothy Morton, *Ecology without Nature: Rethinking Environmental Aesthetics* (Cambridge, MA, and London: Harvard University Press, 2007), 125.

30 Back cover of Kenneth Goldsmith's *Traffic* (Los Angeles: Make Now, 2007).

31 Carolyn Merchant, *The Death of Nature: Women, Ecology, and the Scientific Revolution* (San Francisco: Harper and Row, 1989), xxi.

32 Ibid., 39–40.

33 Marjorie Perloff, "Moving Information: On Kenneth Goldsmith's *The Weather*," *Open Letter* 12, no. 7 (2005): 79.

34 Ibid., 79.

35 "Being Boring," in *American Poets in the 21st Century*, ed. Claudia Rankine and Lisa Sewell (Middletown, CT: Wesleyan University Press, 2007), 366.

36 "A Week of Blogs for the Poetry Foundation," in *The Consequence of Innovation: 21st Century Poetics*, ed. Craig Dworkin (New York: Roof Books, 2008), 142.

37 Goldsmith, *Soliloquy*, 131.

38 Craig Douglas Dworkin, "The Imaginary Solution," *Contemporary Literature* 48, no. 1 (2007): 37.

39 An important exception to this is Christopher Schmidt's article on Goldsmith ("The Waste-Management Poetics of Kenneth Goldsmith," *SubStance* 37, no. 2 [2008]: 25–40). What counts as an analog code and a digital code can change depending on the context of assessment. For example, while written language is in general a digital code, more specific rhetorical aspects of language use can be regarded in relative terms as analog. In fact, Schmidt discusses the denotative aspects of language as digital and the connotative figures of speech as being predominantly analog. From this perspective,

Schmidt notes the irony in *Fidget* "that a 'poetic' language that Goldsmith abjures might better capture the analogical dimensions of the body movement than his machinic [digital] antidote" (35).

40 Goldsmith, "Being Boring," 364.
41 Ibid., 361.
42 "*Day* Labour," 177.
43 Molly Schwartzburg, "Encyclopedic Novelties: On Kenneth Goldsmith's Tomes," *Open Letter* 12, no. 7 (2005), 24.
44 Jesper Hoffmeyer, "Code Duality Revisited," *SEED* 2, no. 1 (2002). http://www.library.utoronto.ca/see/SEED/Vol2-1/Hoffmeyer/Hoffmeyer.htm
45 Goldsmith, *Soliloquy*, 328.
46 Dworkin, "The Imaginary Solution," *Contemporary Literature* 48, no.1: 35.
47 "*Day* Labour," 174.
48 Kenneth Goldsmith, *Fidget* (Toronto: Coach House Books, 2000), 15.
49 Schmidt, "The Waste-Management Poetics of Kenneth Goldsmith," 31–2.
50 William Rueckert, "Literature and Ecology: An Experiment in Ecocriticism," in *The Ecocriticism Reader: Landmarks in Literary Ecology,* ed. Cheryll Glotfelty and Harold Fromm (Athens, GA, and London: University of Georgia Press, 1996), 110.
51 Simon Morris, *Kenneth Goldsmith: Sucking on Words* (New York: Pal DVD Video, 2007).
52 Joshua Schuster, "On Kenneth Goldsmith: The Avant-Garde at a Standstill," *Open Letter* 12, no. 7 (2005), 109.
53 Rachel Carson, *Silent Spring: Fortieth Anniversary Edition* (Boston and New York: Mariner Books/Houghton Mifflin, 2002).

CHAPTER EIGHT

1 Harold Bloom, "A.R. Ammons: 'When You Consider the Radiance,'" in *Considering the Radiance: Essays on the Poetry of A.R. Ammons,* eds. David Burak and Roger Gilbert (New York: W.W. Norton, 2005), 45–88.
2 'How a thing will / unfold': Fractal Rhythms in A.R. Ammons's *Briefings*," *Complexities of Motion: New Essays on A.R. Ammons's Long Poems*, ed. Steven P. Schneider (Cranbury, NJ: Associated University Presses, 1999), 80.

Perloff argues that Ammons's *Briefings* shows "a quasi-Oulipean concern" with "mathematical structure" (69): she sets this buried structure against what she calls the poet's Emersonianism. "[W]hether directly or indirectly," she concludes, "his poetry testifies to the fractal geometer's concern for the "morphology of the amorphous" (76).

3 A.R. Ammons, *Garbage* (New York and London: W.W. Norton, 1993), 109.
4 "No matter how much an ice-skater practices, when she hits the ice it's a one-time event ..."; A.R. Ammons, *Set in Motion: Essays, Interviews, and Dialogues*, ed. Zofia Burr (Ann Arbor: University of Michigan Press, 1996), 125.

5 A.R. Ammons, "Saliences," *The Selected Poems, Expanded Edition* (New York and London: W.W. Norton, 1986), 48.

6 In a 24 March 2009 letter to the *Globe and Mail*, the director of the Institute for Resources, Environment and Sustainability at UBC wrote: "Landfills will always burn. Why? Because microbes have evolved to figure out what Canadians apparently don't get: Waste is a resource. Soil microbes will consume landfill waste no matter how hard we try to protect it from their insatiable appetites. The result is greenhouse gases, toxic fumes and groundwater pollution – not to speak of the massive loss of recoverable energy."

7 In an interview with David Lehman in 1994, Ammons remarked: "The garbage heap of used-up language is thrown at the feet of poets, and it is their job to make or revamp a language that will fly again" (*SIM*, 102).

8 In a variant of the "dead pit," Ammons writes: "…there is a mound, / too, in the poet's mind dead language is hauled / off to and burned down on …" (G, 20)

9 Percy Bysshe Shelley, *Shelley's Poetry and Prose*, ed. Donald H. Reiman and Sharon B. Powers (New York and London: W.W. Norton, 1977), 482.

10 Ralph Waldo Emerson, "The Poet," *The Complete Essays and Other Writings*, ed. Brooks Atkinson (New York: Random House, 1950), 329.

11 According to the *OED Online*, the oldest sense of the noun: "the offal of an animal used for food; esp. the entrails" as in (from 1580) "To pulle out the the garbishe or guttes of a thing." The *OED*'s first illustrative quotation is from 1430. It suggests a possible derivation from OF *garbe*, "sheaf."

12 John Ashbery, "In the American Grain," *Considering the Radiance*, 91–2. Bloom, less to the point (for the reasons I mention), notes that "saliences etymologically are out-leapings, 'mind feeding out'" (*Considering the Radiance*, 71).

13 Sidney Landau, *Dictionaries: The Art and Craft of Lexicography*, 2nd ed. (Cambridge: Cambridge University Press, 2001), 217.

14 That said, one can't help but notice the consistency of Ammons's anglophobia in the area of word choice. "The very avoidance betrays the usage he avoids," as Emerson put it; see Ralph Waldo Emerson, "Art," in *Complete Essays and Other Writings*, 306; cited in Richard Poirier's *Poetry and Pragmatism* (Cambridge, MA: Harvard University Press 1992), 16. The (British) word "rubbish" only appears once in this long poem, while there are numerous instances of other words for garbage: "trash," "junk," "waste," "leavings," "throwaways," and so on. There are other equally arresting examples – manifested negatively – of Ammons's control of diction and usage. "Composition," for instance, is a word he studiously avoids, which is surprising given how much he relies upon "disposition" and "exposition" throughout his writings.

15 Ammons, *The Selected Poems, Expanded Edition*, 48. It is a rare sort of speaker who sets in print highly-worked versions of his own utterances and

who, as a result, notices a time "when I stopped using the word *salient* so much and began to use the word *suasion*" (SIM, 104).

16 Ammons recounts that, in the case of *Garbage*, he would type on "a wide roll of adding machine tape and tore off the sections in lengths of a foot or more" (SIM, 125).

17 Hugh Kenner, "Art in a Closed Field," *The Avant-Garde Tradition in Literature*, ed. Richard Kostelanetz (Buffalo, NY: Prometheus Books, 1982), 210.

18 Not to be confused with Charles Olson's notion of composition by field.

19 At several points in this essay I will refer to findings based upon searches of the *Corpus of Contemporary American English* (COCA), the database compiled by Dr Mark Davies of Brigham Young University. Its sources include popular magazines, newspapers, works of fiction (literary and television), academic books and articles, and unscripted speech from television and radio. Other English language corpora include the Brown Corpus, the Lancaster-Oslo-Bergen Corpus, the American National Corpus, the British National Corpus, the Bank of English, and the Oxford English Corpus.

20 According to COCA data collected during 1990–94, across all categories of written or recorded speech, the frequency of "the" (the mostly commonly occurring word in American English) was 56,969.4 per million words; of "spread" 63.9 per million; of "factor" 62.1 per million; of "the overall" 20.5 per million; of "variable" 20.1 per million; of "garbage" 19.2 per million; of "rubbish" 2.1 per million; of "a single thing" 0.33 per million; of "not a single thing" 0.03 per million.

21 Wilhelm von Humboldt, *On Language: On the Diversity of Human Language Construction and its Influence on the Mental Development of the Human Species*, ed. Michael Losonsky, trans. Peter Heath (Cambridge: Cambridge University Press, 1999), 167.

22 "[T]he poem [*Garbage*] / … is about the pre-Socratic idea of the dispositional axis from stone to wind, wind / to stone …" (G, 20).

23 COCA's data base for the 1990–94 period shows that, as Ammons suspected, the phrase "waste disposal" had a much higher frequency of use in the academic literature (4.6 per million), as well as in general (2.5 per million). The phrase "garbage disposal" occurred less frequently and usually with reference to the shredding instrument commonly installed in kitchen sinks (0.4 per million). For that reason, perhaps, "garbage disposal" occurs almost two times more frequently in fictional (0.7 per million) than in other contexts.

24 Landau, *Dictionaries*, 104.

25 See "The Prosody of Anxiety" (SIM, *119*); and also G, 118–20.

26 This reliance is by no means downplayed in an on-line interview with A.S. Bessa, in which Goldsmith tells of his plan for a project he calls a "year-long *Soliloquy*": "[it will be] a documentation of every word that I speak for an entire year – unedited. But it will differ from the first version of *Soliloquy* in that it will take place live over the Internet. I'll be hooked up to a wireless

headset, which will cellularly beam my words to a voice recognition system on a computer that will, in turn, automatically churn my words into web pages" (Bessa, "kenneth goldsmith and as bessa | 6799," *zingmagazine* 11, http://www.zingmagazine.com/zing11/bessa/ [accessed 8 Sept. 2010], n.p.).

27 Since "a fundamental property of language corpora" is that "they represent collections of actual language use as produced by a cross-section of [its] speakers (and/or writers)," the OED database of illustrative sentences is by modern linguistic standards not comprehensive enough to be a first-rate corpus. See Sebastian Hoffman, "Using the OED Quotations Database as a Corpus – a Linguistic Appraisal," *ICAME Journal*, no. 28 (2004), 20.

28 Literary or unconventional utterance appears as infrequently in *Day* or *The Weather* as it does in the desiderata of corpus linguistics. Of course, it may be that Goldsmith's works allude obliquely to exemplary utterance by soliciting the reader to notice the most mundane varieties of usage and collocation.

29 As Benoit Mandelbrot put it in *The Fractal Geometry of Nature* (1982), "Clouds are not spheres, mountains are not cones, coastlines are not circles, and bark is not smooth, nor does lightning travel in a straight line." Cited in Benoit B. Mandelbrot and Richard L. Hudson, *The (Mis)Behaviour of Markets: A Fractal View of Risk, Ruin, and Reward* (New York: Basic Books, 2004), 124.

30 The ten most frequently spoken and written words in American English are: "the," "be," "and," "of," "a," "in," "to" (the preposition), "have," "to" (infinitive particle), and "it." The pronoun "I" is the eleventh most frequently occurring word. "Say," at nineteenth, is the next verb after "be" and "have." "Poem" ranks 2,517 of the top 5,000 words; "garbage" comes in at 3,974 (Mark Davies, "Word Frequency Lists and Dictionary of Contemporary American English," http://www.wordfrequency.info [accessed 8 July 2010]).

31 Mandelbrot takes credit for developing "the mathematical toolkit with which genuine irregularity that goes beyond the fuzziness of a peach can be understood now and, in due time, managed" (*MBM*, 125).

32 Ashbery, "In the American Grain," 90–1.

33 By an apology, for instance. Or by remaining silent when one might have spoken: "I recognize cases / in other words from time to time that I'd rather / see go through than my own …" (G, 56–7).

34 The other side of it, however, is that "this kind of ape will join his fellows in a / dirty street and hack another fellow who has / done ungroupliness to death, axe him right / in the pleading face …" (G, 106).

35 George Kingsley Zipf, *Human Behavior and the Principle of Least Effort: An Introduction to Human Ecology* (Cambridge, MA: Addison Wesley Press, 1949).

36 See, for instance, G, 65.

37 Ralph Waldo Emerson, "Self-Reliance," *Complete Essays and Other Writings*, 148, 150-1. See pages 97, 113–14, 121, 190, 193, 201–2, 218–19, 226–7 and 231 (not an exhaustive list) in Stanley Cavell, *Emerson's Transcendental Etudes*, ed. David Justin Hodge (Stanford: Stanford University Press, 2003).

38 An interesting finding turned up by COCA shows that the emphatic phrase "what the hell kind of" occurs with much greater frequency in fictional or literary use than in ordinary speech, where it almost never occurs. And one can find an inverse effect in the case of certain high frequency words and phrases (e.g. "factor" or "the overall"): literary writers shun these terms.

39 Humboldt: "the single generation impinges ... on its language not even purely, since those coming up and those departing live mingled side by side" (*On Language*, 63).

40 See, however, Steve McCaffery's "Zarathustran 'Pataphysics," a double-columned essay showing what random, accumulating typographical errors will do to the "propositional and explanatory" powers of words; *Prior to Meaning: The Protosemantic and Poetics* (Evanston, IL: Northwestern University Press 2001), 15–30.

CHAPTER NINE

1 Ron Silliman, "The Practice of Art," in *The Art of Practice: 45 Contemporary Poets*, ed. Dennis Barone and Peter Gannick (Elmwood, CT: Potes and Poets Press, 1994), 377.

2 Tom Mandel et al., *The Grand Piano. An Experiment in Collective Autobiography, Part 7: San Francisco, 1975–1980* (Detroit: Mode A, 2008), 152.

3 Craig Douglas Dworkin, "Introduction." At *The UbuWeb Anthology of Conceptual Writing*, http://www.ubu.com/concept/ (accessed 1 April 2009).

4 Jean-François Lyotard, "Answering the Question: What Is Postmodernism?" trans. Régis Durand, in *The Postmodern Condition: A Report on Knowledge* (Minneapolis: University of Minnesota Press, 1984), 77.

5 "When I reach 40, I hope to have cleansed myself of all creativity"; Kenneth Goldsmith, "Uncreativity as a Creative Practice," in *Day* (Calgary: House Press, 2001), unpaginated.

6 Marjorie Perloff, "'Vocable Scriptsigns'": Differential Poetics in Kenneth Goldsmith's *Fidget*" in *Fidget* (Toronto: Coach House Books, 2000), 90.

7 Kenneth Goldsmith, *Fidget*, 47.

8 Rubén Gallo, "*Fidget*'s Body," in *Kenneth Goldsmith and Conceptual Poetics, Open Letter*, 12, no. 7 (Fall 2005): 50–7.

9 Derek Beaulieu, "*Fidgeting* with the Scene of the Crime," in *Kenneth Goldsmith and Conceptual Poetics*, 58–61.

10 Goldsmith, *Fidget*, 84.

11 Quoted in Christian Bök, "Unacknowledged Legislation," in *avant-post: the avant-garde under "post-" conditions*, ed. Louis Armand, (Prague: Litteraria Pragensia, 2006), 189.

12 Ronald Sukenick, *The Death of the Novel and Other Stories* (New York: The Dial Press, 1969).

13 Michel Foucault, *Aesthetics, Method and Epistemology: Essential Works of*

Foucault, 1954–84, volume 2, ed. James D. Faubion (New York: The New York Press, 1998), 148.

14 Joshua Schuster, "On Kenneth Goldsmith: The Avant-Garde at a Standstill," in *Kenneth Goldsmith and Conceptual Poetics*, 102–9.

15 Maurice Blanchot, *The Work of Fire*, trans. Charlotte Mandell (Stanford: Stanford University Press, 1995), 327.

16 In his later critical writings, Goldsmith replaces the term "nutritionless" with "non-creative" or "conceptual." I find it hard not to interpret the idea of "nutritionless" writing as a wry allusion to John Cage's earlier call (circa 1970) for edible texts (first exhibited at Stanford University Art Museum in January 1992): "Inks used for printing or writing should have delicious flavors. Magazines or newspapers read at breakfast should be eaten for lunch. Instead of throwing one's mail in the waste-basket, it should be saved for the dinner-guests. " See John Cage, *M: Writings, '67–'72* (Middletown, CT: Wesleyan University Press, 1973), 115; Cage's lineation not adhered to.

17 Atavistic granted, but Goldsmith's transcriptive method is not manual – he employs assistants equipped with scanners and OCR software.

18 Jan van der Eng, "Introduction," in *Avant-Garde* 5/6, ed. Willem G. Weststeijn (Amsterdam and Atlanta, GA: Rodopi, 1991), 3.

19 Prévert collected the matchboxes during the German occupation. They were displayed "all threaded together so as to form a continuous ribbon that ran along the mantelpiece, climbed the wall, extended to the moulding, and climbed down again next to a door." Quoted in Jacques Lacan, *The Seminar of Jacques Lacan: Book VII: The Ethics of Psychoanalysis, 1959–60*, trans. Dennis Porter (New York: W.W. Norton, 1992), 114.

20 Goldsmith's project of ennui is different from Heideggerian boredom, which, as a basic mood of *Dasein*, involves both abandonment to emptiness and being held in a state of suspense. This hardly applies to Goldsmithian boredom which arises both in the act of "composition" and potentially in the act of reading.

21 Tan Lin, *Heath* (La Laguna, Canary Islands: Zasterle Press, 2007), unpaginated.

22 Jacques Rancière, "The Politics of Literature," *SubStance* 33, no. 1 (2004), 10–24.

23 For Lyotard's discussion of his theory of paganism, see Jean-François Lyotard and Jean-Loup Thébaud, *Just Gaming*, trans. Wlad Godzich (Minneapolis: University of Minnesota Press, 1985). For an effective application of it, see Gerald L. Bruns, *On the Anarchy of Poetry and Philosophy: A Guide for the Unruly* (New York: Fordham University Press, 2006), 133–52.

24 Stéphane Mallarmé, *Mallarmé in Prose*, ed. Mary Ann Caws (New York: New Directions, 2001), 109.

25 Alain Badiou, *Handbook of Inaesthetics*, trans. Alberto Toscano (Stanford: Stanford University Press, 2005), 17.

26 The pertinent passage in Plato is *The Republic* (608b), ed. Elizabeth Hamilton and Huntington Cairns, *The Collected Dialogues of Plato* (Princeton: Princeton University Press, 1989), 833.
27 Robert Duncan, *The Truth & Life of Myth: An Essay in Essential Autobiography* (Fremont, MI: The Sumac Press, 1968), 26.
28 "Art invites us to intellectual consideration, and that not for the purpose of creating art again, but the knowing philosophically what art is." (G.W.F. Hegel, *Aesthetics: Lectures on Fine Art*, trans. T.M. Knox. (Oxford: Clarendon Press, 1975), I: 13.) Blanchot too develops Hegel's insight in his own concept of *désoeuvrement* or unworkability that radically repositions writing as a mode of non-productive inutility. See especially: M. Blanchot, *The Infinite Conversation*, trans. Susan Hampson (Minneapolis: University of Minnesota Press, 1993), 307–13, 351–9, 403.
29 Consider one unpublished and hardly known non-literary endeavor: the obsessively detailed diary of the Rev. Robert Shields of Dayton, Ohio. Shields died in October 2007 at the age of eighty-nine, leaving behind him a personal diary of his final twenty-five years that methodically chronicles his life in five-minute segments of hilarious bathos. The diary comprises thirty-seven million words written on paper and currently occupies ninety-one boxes. Shields described his work as "uninhibited" and "spontaneous" and here are four typical entries quoted from Chuck Shepherd's syndicated column "News of the Weird" in *ArtVoice* 6, no. 46 (15–21 Nov. 2007).

> Aug. 13, 1992. 8.40 a.m. I filled the humidifier basin mounted over the Futura baseboard heater.
> 8.45 a.m. I shaved twice with the Gillette Sensor blade (and) shaved my neck behind both ears, and crossways of my cheeks too.
> July 25, 1993. 7.00 a.m. I cleaned out the tub and scraped my feet with my fingernails to remove layers of dead skin.
> 7.05 a.m. Passed a large, firm stool, and a pint of urine. Used 5 sheets of paper (5).

30 All of Goldsmith's works are available in on-line versions and on various websites.
31 Gene Youngblood, "Life in Counterculture," *Umelec* 2 (2006): 13.
32 Robert Duncan, *A Selected Prose*, ed. Robert J. Bertholf (New York: New Directions, 1995), 161.
33 Jacket blurb by Christian Bök to *Kenneth Goldsmith, Sucking on Words: A Film by Simon Morris* (New York: Pal DVD Video, 2007).
34 Jean Baudrillard, *Symbolic Exchange and Death*, trans. Iain Hamilton Grant (London and Thousand Oaks, CA: Sage Publications, 1993), 202.
35 Baudrillard's argument – laid out in *Symbolic Exchange and Death* and specifically in chapter 6, "The Extermination of the Name of God" – effectively turns Saussure's theory on its head. Instead of paragrammatically embedding the names of deities according to a law that governs the distribu-

tion of consonants and vowels in certain ancient texts, as Saussure concluded, the name is actually morselated, volatized by chains of phonemic doublings whose enantiomorphic relation cancels meaning, exterminates the name.

For more on Saussure's investigations see Jean Starobinski, *Words upon Words*, trans. Olivia Emmet (New Haven: Yale University Press, 1979).

Bibliography

Abram, David. *The Spell of the Sensuous: Perception and Language in a More-Than-Human World.* New York: Vintage Books, 1997.

Adorno, Theodor. "On Lyric Poetry and Society." In *Notes to Literature, Volume One.* Translated by Shierry Weber Nicholsen, 37–54. New York: Columbia University Press, 1991.

Agamben, Giorgio. "The Dictation of Poetry." In *The End of the Poem: Studies in Poetics.* Translated by Daniel Heller-Roazen. Stanford: Stanford University Press, 1999.

Ahearn, Barry. *Zukofsky's "A": An Introduction.* Berkeley: University of California Press, 1983.

Alimo, Stacey. "MCS Matters: Material Agency in the Science and Practices of Environmental Illness." *TOPIA: Canadian Journal of Cultural Studies* 21 (2009): 9–27.

Altieri, Charles. "Taking Lyrics Literally: Teaching Poetry in a Prose Culture." *New Literary History* 32, no. 1 (Winter 2001): 259–81.

– "Modernist Innovations: A Legacy of the Constructed Reader." In *Modernism*, Vol. 1. Edited by A. Eysteinsson and V. Liska, 67–86. Amsterdam, The Netherlands, and Philadelphia: John Benjamins, 2007.

Ammons, A.R. *The Selected Poems, Expanded Edition.* New York and London: W.W. Norton, 1986.

– *Garbage.* New York and London: W.W. Norton, 1993.

– *Set in Motion: Essays, Interviews, and Dialogues.* Edited by Zofia Burr. Ann Arbor: University of Michigan Press, 1996.

Ashbery, John. *Three Poems.* New York: The Viking Press, 1972.

– *Flow Chart.* New York: Alfred A. Knopf, 1991.

– "In the American Grain" [1972]. In *Considering the Radiance: Essays on the Poetry of A.R. Ammons.* Edited by David Burak and Roger Gilbert, 89–94. New York and London: W.W. Norton, 2005.

Badiou, Alain. *Handbook of Inaesthetics.* Translated by Alberto Toscano. Stanford: Stanford University Press, 2005.

Baker, Peter. *Obdurate Brilliance: Exteriority and the Modern Long Poem.* Gainesville: University of Florida Press, 1991.

Bakhtin, Mikhail M. "Discourse in Poetry and Discourse in the Novel." In *The Dialogic Imagination: Four Essays.* Edited by Michael Holquist. Translated by Caryl Emerson and Michael Holquist, 275–300. Austin: University of Texas Press, 1981.

– "From Notes Made in 1970–71." In *Speech Genres and Other Late Essays.* Translated by Vern W. McGee. Edited by Caryl Emerson and Michael Holquist, 132–58. Austin: University of Texas Press, 1986.

– "The Problem of Speech Genres." In *Speech Genres and Other Late Essays.* Translated by Vern W. McGee. Edited by Caryl Emerson and Michael Holquist, 60–102. Austin: University of Texas Press, 1986.

– "The Problem of the Text in Linguistics, Philology, and the Human Sciences: An Experiment in Philosophical Analysis." In *Speech Genres and Other Late Essays.* Translated by Vern W. McGee. Edited by Caryl Emerson and Michael Holquist, 103–31. Austin: University of Texas Press, 1986.

– "Response to a Question from the *Novy Mir* Editorial Staff." In *Speech Genres and Other Late Essays.* Translated by Vern W. McGee. Edited by Caryl Emerson and Michael Holquist, 1–7. Austin: University of Texas Press, 1986.

– "Toward a Methodology for the Human Sciences." In *Speech Genres and Other Late Essays.* Translated by Vern W. McGee. Edited by Caryl Emerson and Michael Holquist, 159–72. Austin: University of Texas Press, 1986.

Barbieri, Marcello. "Editorial." In *Introduction to Biosemiotics: The New Biological Synthesis.* Edited by Marcello Barbieri. Dordrecht, The Netherlands: Springer, 2007.

Barbour, Douglas. "Lyric/Anti-Lyric: Some Notes about a Concept." In *Lyric/Anti-Lyric: Essays on Contemporary Poetry.* Edmonton: NeWest Press, 2001.

Baudrillard, Jean. *Symbolic Exchange and Death.* Translated by Iain Hamilton Grant. London and Thousand Oaks, CA: Sage Publications, 1993.

Beaulieu, Derek. "*Fidgeting* with the Scene of the Crime." In *Kenneth Goldsmith and Conceptual Poetics, Open Letter* 12, no. 7 (Fall 2005): 58–61.

Beja, Morris. *Epiphany in the Modern Novel.* Seattle: University of Washington Press, 1971.

Benjamin, Walter. *The Arcades Project.* Translated by Howard Eiland and Kevin McLaughlin. Cambridge, MA, and London: Belknap Press of Harvard University Press, 1999.

Bennett, Jane. *Vibrant Matter: A Political Ecology of Things.* Durham, NC, and London: Duke University Press, 2010.

Bernstein, Charles. "Hannah Weiner (1928–1997)." At *Hannah Weiner (1928–1997): An Online Tribute, Collected Responses from the Poetics List.* Email sent 12 September 1997. Edited by Loss Pequeño Glazier. *Electronic Poetry Center at SUNY Buffalo.* http://epc.buffalo.edu/authors/weiner/obit-hw.html (accessed 15 April 2009).

– *My Way: Speeches and Poems.* Chicago: University of Chicago Press, 1999.

– "Hannah Weiner." *Jacket* 12 (July 2000). http://jacketmagazine.com/12/wein-bern.html (accessed 15 March 2009).

– "Sounds Physical." *BookForum: The Review for Art, Fiction, & Culture* 11, no. 5 (2005): 7.

Bernstein, Michael André. *The Tale of the Tribe: Ezra Pound and the Modern Verse Epic*. Princeton: Princeton University Press, 1980.

Bessa, A.S. "Kenneth Goldsmith and AS Bessa | 6799." Interview. *Zingmagazine* 11. http://www.zingmagazine.com/zing11/bessa/ (accessed 8 Sept. 2010).

Bezner, Kevin. "Jackson Mac Low, Interviewed by Kevin Bezner." *New American Writing* 11 (1993): 109–24.

Blanchot, Maurice. *The Infinite Conversation*. Translated by Susan Hampson. Minneapolis: University of Minnesota Press, 1993.

– *The Work of Fire*. Translated by Charlotte Mandell. Stanford: Stanford University Press, 1995.

Bloom, Harold. "A.R. Ammons: 'When You Consider the Radiance.'" In *Considering the Radiance: Essays on the Poetry of A.R. Ammons*. Edited by David Burak and Roger Gilbert, 45–88. New York and London: W.W. Norton, 2005.

Bök, Christian. *'Pataphysics: The Poetics of an Imaginary Science*. Evanston, IL: Northwestern University Press, 2002.

–"Unacknowledged Legislation." In *Avant-post: The Avant-garde under "Post-" Conditions*. Edited by Louis Armand, 178–93. Prague: Litteraria Pragensia, 2006.

Booth, Wayne. *The Rhetoric of Fiction*. Chicago and London: University of Chicago Press, 1961.

Bruns, Gerald. *On the Anarchy of Poetry and Philosophy: A Guide for the Unruly*. New York: Fordham University Press, 2006.

Bryson, J. Scott. "Introduction." In *Ecopoetry: A Critical Introduction*. Edited by J. Scott Bryson. Salt Lake City: The University of Utah Press, 2002.

Buell, Lawrence. *The Environmental Imagination: Thoreau, Nature Writing, and the Formation of American Culture*. Cambridge, MA, and London: Harvard University Press, 1995.

– *Writing for an Endangered World: Literature, Culture, and Environment in the U.S. and Beyond*. Cambridge, MA, and London: The Belknap Press of Harvard University Press, 2001.

Cabri, Louis. "'Rebus Effort Remove Government': Jackson Mac Low, *Why?/Resistance*, Anarcho-Pacifism." *Crayon* 1 (1997): 45–68.

Cage, John. *M: Writings, '67–'72*. Middletown, CT: Wesleyan University Press, 1973.

Carson, Rachel. *Silent Spring: Fortieth Anniversary Edition*. Boston and New York: Mariner Books/Houghton Mifflin, 2002.

Castle, Terry. "Do I Like It? Outsider Art." *London Review of Books* 33, No. 15 (28 July 2011): 19–23.

Cavell, Stanley. *Emerson's Transcendental Etudes*. Edited by David Justin Hodge. Stanford: Stanford University Press, 2003.

Corpus of Contemporary American English: 450 million words, 1990–present. (COCA). Compiled by Mark Davies. http://corpus.byu.edu/coca (accessed July 10, 2010).

Costello, Bonnie. "US Modernism I: Moore, Stevens and the Modernist Lyric." In *The Cambridge Companion to Modernist Poetry*. Edited by Alex Davis and Lee M. Jenkins, 163–80. New York: Cambridge University Press, 2007.

Creeley, Robert. *The Collected Essays of Robert Creeley*. Berkeley: University of California Press, 1989.

Culler, Jonathan. "Poetics of the Lyric." In *Structuralist Poetics: Structuralism, Linguistics and the Study of Literature*, 161–88. Ithaca, NY: Cornell University Press, 1975.

– "Apostrophe." In *The Pursuit of Signs: Semiotics, Literature, Deconstruction*, 135–54. Ithaca, NY: Cornell University Press, 1981.

– "Changes in the Study of the Lyric." In *Lyric Poetry: Beyond New Criticism*. Edited by Chaviva Hosek and Patricia Parker, 38–54. Ithaca, NY: Cornell University Press, 1986.

– "Deconstruction and the Lyric." In *Deconstruction is/in America: A New Sense of the Political*. Edited by Anselm Haverkamp, 41–51. New York: New York University Press, 1995.

Damon, Maria. "Page-Mother's Open Heart: Open House/Hannah Weiner." *KAURAB Online: A Bengali poetry webzine*. http://www.kaurab.com/english/books/open-house.html (accessed 15 July 2009).

Davies, Mark. "Word Frequency Lists and Dictionary of Contemporary American English." http://www.wordfrequency.info (accessed 8 July 2010).

Davis, Alex, and Lee M. Jenkins, eds. "Introduction." In *The Cambridge Companion to Modernist Poetry*, 1–10. New York: Cambridge University Press, 2007.

Dembo, L.S. "Louis Zukofsky interviewed by L.S. Dembo (1968)." *Contemporary Literature* 10, no. 2 (Spring 1969): 203–19.

De Quincey, Thomas. "Letters to a Young Man Whose Education Has Been Neglected." In *Collected Writings*, Vol. 13. Edited by David Masson, 9–94. Edinburgh: A. and C. Black, 1896.

Derrida, Jacques. "The Law of Genre." In *Acts of Literature*. Edited by Derek Attridge, 221–52. New York: Routledge, 1992.

– *Mal d'archive: Une impression freudienne*. Paris: Galilée, 1995.

Donavan, Thom. "Silent Teacher Remembered: Hannah Weiner's Open House." *Fanzine*, 20 December 2007. http://www.thefanzine.com/articles/features/201/silent_teacher_remembered-hannah_weiner's_open_house/ (accessed 15 March 2009).

Dubois, Page. *Sappho is Burning*. Chicago: University of Chicago Press, 1995.

Duncan, Robert. *The Truth & Life of Myth: An Essay in Essential Autobiography*. Fremont, MI: The Sumac Press, 1968.

– *A Selected Prose*. Edited by Robert J. Bertholf. New York: New Directions, 1995.

DuPlessis, Rachel Blau. *Genders, Races, and Religious Cultures in Modern American Poetry, 1908–1934*. Cambridge: Cambridge University Press, 2001.

– *Blue Studios: Poetry and Its Cultural Work*. Tuscaloosa: University of Alabama Press, 2006.

– "Oppen from Seventy-five to a Hundred, 1983–2008." *Jacket Magazine* 36 (2008). http://jacketmagazine.com/36/oppen-duplessis.shtml (accessed 1 March 2009).

– "Agency, Social Authorship, and the Political Aura of Contemporary Poetry." *Textual Practice* 23, no. 6 (2009): 945–57.

Durgin, Patrick. "Indeterminacies and the Poetics of Critical Values." PhD dissertation, State University of New York at Buffalo, 2004.

– "Introduction." In *Hannah Weiner's Open House*, 13–19. Berkeley: Kenning Editions, 2007.

Dworkin, Craig Douglas. "The Imaginary Solution." *Contemporary Literature* 48, no. 1 (2007): 29–60.

– "Introduction." *The UbuWeb Anthology of Conceptual Writing*. http://www.ubu.com/concept/ (accessed 1 April 2009).

Easthope, Antony. *Poetry as Discourse*. London: Methuen, 1983.

Eliot, T.S. *Collected Poems, 1909–1962*. London: Faber and Faber, 1963.

Ellmann, Richard, and Charles Feidelson, Jr., eds. *The Modern Tradition: Backgrounds of Modern Literature*. New York: Oxford University Press, 1965.

Emerson, Ralph Waldo. "Art." In *The Complete Essays and Other Writings*. Edited by Brooks Atkinson, 305–15. New York: Random House, 1950.

– "The Poet." In *The Complete Essays and Other Writings*. Edited by Brooks Atkinson, 319–41. New York: Random House, 1950

– "Self-Reliance." In *The Complete Essays and Other Writings*. Edited by Brooks Atkinson, 145–69. New York: Random House, 1950.

Eng, Jan van der, "Introduction." In *Avant-Garde* 5/6. Edited by Willem G. Weststeijn, 3–13. Atlanta, GA: Rodopi B.V., 1991.

Eysteinsson, Astradur, and Vivian Liska. "Introduction: Approaching Modernism." In *Modernism*, vol. 1. Edited by A. Eysteinsson and V. Liska, 1–10. Amsterdam, The Netherlands, and Philadelphia: John Benjamins, 2007.

Favareau, Donald. "The Evolutionary History of Biosemiotics." In *Introduction to Biosemiotics: The New Biological Synthesis*. Edited by Marcello Barbieri, 1–67. Dordrecht, The Netherlands: Springer, 2007.

Finch, Robert, and John Elder, eds. *The Norton Book of Nature Writing*. New York: W.W. Norton, 1990.

Fones, Robert. "A Theory of Snow Prevention." *Open Letter* 6/7 (1980–81): 38–40.

Foucault, Michel. *O que é um autor*. Translated by Antônio F. Cascais e Edmundo Cordeiro. Lisbon: Vega, 1992.

– *Aesthetics, Method and Epistemology: Essential Works of Foucault, 1954–84, Volume 2*. Edited by James D. Faubion. New York: The New York Press, 1998.

– *Ditos e escritos III – Estética: Literatura e pintura, música e cinema*. Translated by Inês Autran Dourado Barboda. Rio de Janeiro: Forense Universidade, 2001.

Fox, Margalit. "Jackson Mac Low, 82, Poet and Composer." *New York Times* (10 December 2004): A–39.

Friedman, Susan Stanford. "Gender and Genre Anxiety: Elizabeth Barrett Browning and H.D. as Epic Poets." *Tulsa Studies in Women's Literature* 5 (1986): 203–28.

– "When a 'Long' Poem is a 'Big' Poem: Self Authorizing Strategies in Women's Twentieth-Century 'Long Poems.'" LIT 2, no. 1 (1990): 9–25.

– "Craving Stories: Narrative and Lyric in Contemporary Theory and Women's Long Poems." In *Feminist Measures: Soundings in Poetry and Theory.* Edited by Lynn Keller and Cristanne Miller, 15–42. Ann Arbor: University of Michigan Press, 1994.

Gallo, Rubén. "*Fidget's* Body." *Open Letter* 12, no. 7 (Fall 2005): 50–7.

Genette, Gérard. "Valéry and the Poetics of Language." In *Textual Strategies: Perspectives in Post-Structuralist Criticism.* Edited by Josué V. Harari, 359–73. Ithaca, NY: Cornell University Press, 1979.

– *The Architext: An Introduction.* Translated by Jane E. Lewin. Berkeley: California University Press, 1992.

– *Mimologics.* Translated by Thaïs E. Morgan. Lincoln: Nebraska University Press, 1994.

Goldsmith, Kenneth. *Fidget.* Toronto: Coach House Books, 2000.

– *Soliloquy.* New York: Granary Books, 2001.

– *Day.* Great Barrington, MA: The Figures, 2003.

– *The Weather.* Los Angeles: Make Now, 2005.

– *Traffic.* Los Angeles: Make Now, 2007.

– "Being Boring." *American Poets in the 21st Century.* Edited by Claudia Rankine and Lisa Sewell, 361–7. Middletown, CT: Wesleyan University Press, 2007.

– "A Week of Blogs for the Poetry Foundation." In *The Consequence of Innovation: 21st Century Poetics.* Edited by Craig Dworkin, 137–50. New York: Roof Books, 2008.

Handelman, Susan A. *The Slayers of Moses: The Emergence of Rabbinic Interpretation in Modern Literary Theory.* Albany, NY: State University of New York Press, 1982.

Harris, Kaplan. "A Reading for *Hannah Weiner's Open House.*" Insert for Event Program. St Mark's Church, New York City. 28 Nov. 2007.

Hegel, G.W.F. *Aesthetics: Lectures on Fine Art.* Translated by T.M. Knox. Oxford: Clarendon Press, 1975.

Hoffmann, Sebastian. "Using the OED Quotations Database as a Corpus – A Linguistic Appraisal." ICAME *Journal: Computers in English Linguistics.* No. 28 (2004): 17–30. *EBSCOHost* (accessed 1 Oct. 2010).

Hoffmeyer, Jesper. *Signs of Meaning in the Universe* (1993). Translated by Barbara J. Haveland. Bloomington and Indianapolis: Indiana University Press, 1996.

– "Code Duality Revisited." *SEED* 2, no. 1 (2002). http://www.library.utoronto.ca/see/SEED/Vol2-1/Hoffmeyer/Hoffmeyer.htm (accessed 15 July 2010).

– *Biosemiotics: An Examination into the Signs of Life and the Life of Signs.* Trans-

lated by Jesper Hoffmeyer and Donald Favareau. Scranton, PA: University of Scranton Press, 2008.
Humboldt, Wilhelm von. *On Language: On the Diversity of Human Language Construction and its Influence on the Mental Development of the Human Species.* Edited by Michael Losonsky. Translated by Peter Heath. Cambridge: Cambridge University Press, 1999.
Jakobson, Roman. "What is Poetry?" In *Language in Literature*, 368–78. Cambridge, MA: Harvard University Press, 1987.
Jarry, Alfred. *Exploits & Opinions of Dr. Faustroll, Pataphysician: A Neo-Scientific Novel.* Translated by Simon Watson Taylor. Introduction by Roger Shattuck. Boston: Exact Change, 1996.
Jirgens, Karl. "A Short History of 'Pataphysics." *Rampike* 5, no. 2 (1983): 8–11.
Johnson, Barbara. *The Feminist Difference: Literature, Psychoanalysis, Race, and Gender*. Cambridge, MA: Harvard University Press, 1998.
Johnson, James Williams. "Lyric." In *The New Princeton Encyclopedia of Poetry and Poetics.* Edited by Alex Preminger and T.V.F. Brogan, 713–27. Princeton: Princeton University Press, 1993.
Kane, Daniel. *All Poets Welcome: The Lower East Side Poetry Scene in the 1960s.* Berkeley and Los Angeles: University of California Press, 2003.
Kaufman, Robert. "A Future for Modernism: Barbara Guest's Recent Poetry." *The American Poetry Review* 29, no. 4 (July/August 2000): 11–16.
– "Aura, Still." *October* 99 (Winter 2002): 45–80.
Kenner, Hugh. "Art in a Closed Field." In *The Avant-Garde Tradition in Literature*. Edited by Richard Kostelanetz, 204–15. Buffalo, NY: Prometheus Books, 1982.
Kostelanetz, Richard, et al. "A Symposium on Text-Sound." *Precisely: A Critical Journal* 10–12 (1981): 145–60. *MLA International Bibliography, EBSCO.* http://ebscohost.com/ (accessed 13 July 2010).
Kristeva, Julia. "Word, Dialogue, and Novel." In *Desire in Language: A Semiotic Approach to Literature and Art.* Edited by Leon S. Roudiez, 64–90. New York: Columbia University Press, 1980.
– "Revolution in Poetic Language." In *The Kristeva Reader*. Edited by Toril Moi, 89–136. New York: Columbia University Press, 1986.
Lacan, Jacques. *The Seminar of Jacques Lacan: Book VII: The Ethics of Psychoanalysis, 1959–60*. Translated by Dennis Porter. New York: W.W. Norton, 1992.
Landau, Sidney. *Dictionaries: The Art and Craft of Lexicography*, 2nd ed. Cambridge: Cambridge University Press, 2001.
Lin, Tan. *Heath*. La Laguna, Canary Islands: Zasterle Press, 2007.
Lyotard, Jean-François. "Answering the Question: What Is Postmodernism?" Translated by Régis Durand. In *The Postmodern Condition: A Report on Knowledge*, 71–82. Minneapolis: University of Minnesota Press, 1984.
– "Representation, Presentation, Unpresentable." In *The Inhuman: Reflections on*

Time. Translated by Geoffrey Bennington and Rachel Bowlby, 109–28. Stanford: Stanford University Press, 1991.

– "The Sublime and the Avant-Garde." In *The Inhuman: Reflections on Time*. Translated by Geoffrey Bennington and Rachel Bowlby, 108–18. Stanford: Stanford University Press, 1991.

Lyotard, Jean-François, and Jean-Loup Thébaud. *Just Gaming*. Translated by Wlad Godzich. Minneapolis: University of Minnesota Press, 1985.

Mac Low, Jackson. *22 Light Poems*. Los Angeles: Black Sparrow Press, 1968.

– "Poetry, Chance, Silence, Etc." In *Claims for Poetry*. Edited by Donald Hall, 296–302. Ann Arbor: University of Michigan Press, 1982.

– "Response to Piombino: A Letter to the Poetics List." *Electronic Poetry Center at SUNY Buffalo*, February 1998. http://epc.buffalo.edu/ (accessed 13 July 2010).

– "The Terminology." *Open Letter* 11, no. 3 (2001): 84–90.

– *Thing of Beauty: New and Selected Works*. Edited by Anne Tardos. Berkeley: University of California Press, 2008.

Mackey, Nathaniel. *Splay Anthem*. New York: New Directions, 2006.

Maeder, Beverly. *Wallace Stevens' Experimental Language: The Lion in the Lute*. New York: St Martin's Press, 1999.

Mallarmé, Stéphane. *Mallarmé in Prose*. Edited by Mary Ann Caws. New York: New Directions, 2001.

Mandel, Tom, Carla Harryman, Barrett Watten, et al. *The Grand Piano. An Experiment in Collective Autobiography, Part 7: San Francisco, 1975–1980*. Detroit: Mode A, 2008.

Mandelbrot, Benoit B., and Richard L. Hudson. *The (Mis)Behaviour of Markets: A Fractal View of Risk, Ruin, and Reward*. New York: Basic Books, 2004.

Mattlin, Sharon. "Review of *Clairvoyant Journal*." *The Poetry Project Newsletter* 67 (May/June 1979), n.p.

McCaffery, Steve. *North of Intention: Critical Writings 1973–1986*. New York: Roof Books, 1986.

– *Prior to Meaning: The Protosemantic and Poetics*. Evanston, IL: Northwestern University Press, 2001.

Merchant, Carolyn. *The Death of Nature: Women, Ecology, and the Scientific Revolution*. San Francisco: Harper and Row, 1989.

Middleton, Peter. "The Longing of the Long Poem." *Jacket Magazine* 40 (Late 2010). http://jacketmagazine.com/40/middleton-long-poem.shtml (accessed 1 Dec. 2011).

Miller, J. Hillis. *Tropes, Parables, Performatives: Essays on Twentieth-Century Literature*. Durham, NC: Duke University Press, 1991.

Miller, Tyrus. *Singular Examples: Artistic Politics and the Neo-Avant-Garde*. Evanston, IL: Northwestern University Press, 2009.

Mohanty, Satya P. *Literary Theory and the Claims of History: Postmodernism, Objectivity, Multicultural Politics*. Ithaca, NY: Cornell University Press, 1997.

Morris, Simon. *Kenneth Goldsmith: Sucking on Words.* Video. New York: Pal DVD Video, 2007.
Morton, Timothy. *Ecology without Nature: Rethinking Environmental Aesthetics.* Cambridge, MA, and London: Harvard University Press, 2007.
Moure, Erín. *Sheep's Vigil by a Fervent Person: A Transelation of Alberto Caeiro / Fernando Pessoa's O Guardador de Rebanhos.* Toronto: House of Anansi Press, 2004.
– *O Cadoiro.* Toronto: House of Anansi Press, 2007.
– "*O Cadoiro* Postface." www.anansi.ca/ocadoiro/postface (accessed 24 Jan. 2012).
Możejko, Edward. "Tracing the Modernist Paradigm: Terminologies of Modernism." In *Modernism*, Vol. 1. Edited by A. Eysteinsson and V. Liska, 11–33. Amsterdam, The Netherlands, and Philadelphia, PA: John Benjamins, 2007.
Nichol, bp. "Rediscovery of the 22-Letter Alphabet: An Archaeological Report." *Open Letter* 6 and 7 (1980–81): 41–7.
Notley, Alice. "Epic and Women Poets." In *Disembodied Poetics: Annals of the Jack Kerouac School.* Edited by Anne Waldman and Andrew Schelling, 103–9. Albuquerque: University of New Mexico Press, 1994.
– "Iovis Omnia Plena." *Chicago Review* 44 (1998): 117–29.
– *Coming After: Essays on Poetry.* Ann Arbor: University of Michigan Press, 2005.
O'Driscoll, Michael, and Jason Dewinetz. "Silent Texts and Empty Words: Structure and Intention in the Writings of John Cage." *Contemporary Literature* 38, no. 4 (1997): 616–39.
– *A Bibliography of the Black Sparrow Press Archive.* Edmonton: University of Alberta Libraries, 2002.
Olson, Charles. "Projective Verse." In *Collected Prose of Charles Olson.* Edited by Donald Allen and Benjamin Friedlander, 239–52. Berkeley and Los Angeles: University of California Press, 1997.
Oxford English Dictionary. OED *Online* (accessed 15 October 2010).
Oppen, George. *Selected Letters of George Oppen.* Edited by Rachel Blau DuPlessis. Durham, NC, and London: Duke University Press, 1990.
– *New Collected Poems.* Edited by Michael Davidson. Preface by Eliot Weinberger. New York: New Directions, 2002.
– *Selected Poems.* Ed. Robert Creeley. New York: New Directions, 2003.
Perloff, Marjorie. *The Poetics of Indeterminacy: Rimbaud to Cage.* Princeton: Princeton University Press, 1981.
– *Dance of the Intellect: Studies in the Poetry of the Pound Tradition.* Cambridge: Cambridge University Press, 1985.
– "Revolving in Crystal: The Supreme Fiction and the Impasse of Modernist Lyric." In *Wallace Stevens: The Poetics of Modernism.* Edited by Albert Gelpi, 41–64. New York: Cambridge University Press, 1985.
– *Radical Artifice: Writing Poetry in the Age of Media.* Chicago: University of Chicago Press, 1991.

– "Visionary Company." *Boston Review* 23, no. 3–4 (Summer 1998). http://bostonreview.net/BR23.3/perloff.html (accessed 18 August 2003).
– "'How a thing will / unfold': Fractal Rhythms in A.R. Ammons's *Briefings.*" In *Complexities of Motion: New Essays on A.R. Ammons's Long Poems*. Edited by Steven P. Schneider, 68–82. Cranbury, NJ: Associated University Presses, 1999.
– "'Vocable Scriptsigns': Differential Poetics in Kenneth Goldsmith's *Fidget.*" In *Fidget,* 89–107. Toronto: Coach House Books, 2000.
– *21st-Century Modernism: The "New" Poetics.* Malden, MA: Blackwell Publishers Inc., 2002.
– "A Conversation with Kenneth Goldsmith." *Jacket Magazine*, 21 (February 2003). http://jacketmagazine.com/21/perl-gold-iv.html (accessed 14 September 2010).
– *The Vienna Paradox: A Memoir.* New York: New Directions, 2003.
– *Differentials: Poetry, Poetics, Pedagogy.* Tuscaloosa: The University of Alabama Press, 2004.
– "Moving Information: On Kenneth Goldsmith's *The Weather.*" *Open Letter* 12, no. 7 (2005): 75–85.
– *Unoriginal Genius: Poetry by Other Means in the New Century*. Chicago: University of Chicago Press, 2010.
Phillips, Dana. *The Truth of Ecology: Nature, Culture, and Literature in America.* Oxford and New York: Oxford University Press, 2003.
Plato. *The Collected Dialogues of Plato*. Edited by Elizabeth Hamilton and Huntington Cairns. Princeton: Princeton University Press, 1989.
Poe, Edgar Allan. *Poems and Essays on Poetry*. Edited by C.H. Sisson. New York: Routledge, 2003.
Poirier, Richard. *Poetry and Pragmatism*. Cambridge, MA: Harvard University Press, 1992.
Pope, Alexander. *The Dunciad in Four Books*. Edited by Valerie Rumbold. Harlow, United Kingdom, and New York: Longman, 1999.
– "An Essay on Man in Four Epistles." *The Major Works.* Edited by Pat Rogers. Oxford: Oxford University Press, 2006.
Pound, Ezra. *ABC of Reading* (1934). New York: New Directions, 1960.
– *Instigations* (1920). Freeport, NY: Books for Libraries Press, 1967.
– *The Cantos*. New York: New Directions, 1986.
Prince, Ruth E.C. "A New Way of Being: Helen Vendler on Poetry Past and Future." Interview. In *Radcliffe Quarterly* (Winter 2000): 1–6.
Puttenham, George. *The Arte of English Poesie* (1589). A Facsimile Reproduction. Kent, OH: Kent State University Press, 1970.
Rainey, Lawrence. "Pound or Eliot: Whose Era?" In *The Cambridge Companion to Modernist Poetry*. Edited by Alex Davis and Lee M. Jenkins, 87–113. New York: Cambridge University Press, 2007.
Rancière, Jacques. "The Politics of Literature." *SubStance* 33, no. 1 (2004): 10–24.
Rand Corporation. *A Million Random Digits with 100,000 Normal Deviates.* Glencoe, IL: Free Press, 1955.

Reckert, Stephen, and Helder Macedo. *Do Cancioneiro de Amigo*. Lisbon: Assirio and Alvim, 1996.

Rosenfield, Kim. "Kim Rosenfield Interviews Jackson Mac Low." *Shiny* 7/8 (1992): 5–25.

Rothenberg, Jerome (ed). *Technicians of the Sacred*, Second Edition. Berkeley and Los Angeles: University of California Press, 1985.

– "Preface." In *Representative Works: 1938–1985*, v–x. By Jackson Mac Low. New York: Roof Books, 1986.

– and Pierre Joris, eds. *Poems for the Millennium*. Berkeley: University of California Press, 1998.

Rueckert, William. "Literature and Ecology: An Experiment in Ecocriticism." In *The Ecocriticism Reader: Landmarks in Literary Ecology*. Edited by Cheryll Glotfelty and Harold Fromm, 105–23. Athens, GA, and London: University of Georgia Press, 1996.

Saramago, José. *All The Names*. Translated by Margaret Jull Costa. San Diego and New York: Harcourt, 1999.

Schmidt, Christopher. "The Waste-Management Poetics of Kenneth Goldsmith." *SubStance* 37, no. 2 (2008): 25–40.

Sholes, Robert. "Introduction." In *The Architext: An Introduction*. By Gérard Genette, i–ix. Berkeley: University of California Press, 1992.

Schwartzburg, Molly. "Encyclopedic Novelties: On Kenneth Goldsmith's Tomes." *Open Letter* 12, no. 7 (2005): 21–35.

Schuster, Joshua. "On Kenneth Goldsmith: The Avant-Garde at a Standstill." In *Kenneth Goldsmith and Conceptual Poetics, Open Letter* 12, no. 7 (Fall 2005): 102–9.

Sebeok, Thomas A. *Signs: An Introduction to Semiotics*, Second Edition. Toronto: University of Toronto Press, 2001.

Shelley, Percy Bysshe. "A Defense of Poetry." In *Shelley's Poetry and Prose*. Edited by Donald H. Reiman and Sharon B. Powers. New York and London: W.W. Norton, 1977.

Shepherd, Chuck. "News of the Weird." *Artvoice* 6, no. 46 (Nov. 15–21, 2007): 5.

Shoptaw, John. *On the Outside Looking Out: John Ashbery's Poetry*. Cambridge, MA: Harvard University Press, 1994.

Silliman, Ron. "I Wanted to Write Sentences: Decision Making in the American Longpoem." *Sagetrieb* 11, no. 1–2 (1992): 11–20.

– "The Practice of Art." In *The Art of Practice: 45 Contemporary Poets*. Edited by Dennis Barone and Peter Gannick. Elmwood, CT: Potes and Poets Press, 1994.

– "Hannah Weiner Notes." *Electronic Poetry Center at SUNY Buffalo*. 10 November 1998. http://epc.buffalo.edu/conferences/reports/hannah98-doc.html (accessed 1 July 2009).

– "'As to Violin Music': Time in the Longpoem." *Jacket Magazine* 27 (April 2005). http://www.jacketmagazine.com/27/silliman.html (accessed 3 May 2008).

– *The Age of Huts (compleat)*. Berkeley, CA: University of California Press, 2007.

– *The Alphabet.* Tuscaloosa: University of Alabama Press, 2008.

Smith, Rick, and Bruce Lourie. *Slow Death by Rubber Duck: How the Toxic Chemistry of Everyday Life Affects our Health.* Toronto: Alfred A. Knopf Canada, 2009.

Spicer, Jack. *The House that Jack Built: The Collected Lectures of Jack Spicer.* Edited by Peter Gizzi. Middletown, CT: Wesleyan University Press, 1998.

Starobinski, Jean. *Words upon Words.* Translated by Olivia Emmet. New Haven: Yale University Press, 1979.

Stein, Gertrude. *Tender Buttons.* In *Selected Writings of Gertrude Stein.* Edited by Carl Van Vechten, 459–509. New York: The Modern Library, 1962.

– *How to Write.* New York: Dover Publications., 1975.

– "Patriarchal Poetry." In *The Yale Gertrude Stein: Selections with an Introduction by Richard Kostelanetz,* 106–46. New Haven, CT: Yale University Press, 1980.

Stevens, Wallace. *The Collected Poems of Wallace Stevens.* New York: Vintage Books / Random House, 1990.

– *Opus Posthumous.* Edited by Milton J. Bates. New York: Vintage Books, 1990.

Sukenick, Ronald. *The Death of the Novel and Other Stories.* New York: The Dial Press, 1969.

Swed, Mark. "Jackson Mac Low, 82; 'Composer of Poetry' Shaped His Verse into Unconventional Forms, Sounds." *Los Angeles Times* (10 December 2004). http://www.latimes.com (accessed 29 July, 2010).

Tigges, Wim. "The Significance of Trivial Things: Towards a Typology of Literary Epiphanies." In *Moments of Moment: Aspects of the Literary Epiphany.* Edited by Wim Tigges, 11–36. Amsterdam, The Netherlands: Rodopi B.V., 1999.

Tillman, S.E. *A Text-Book of Important Minerals and Rocks.* Third Edition, Revised. New York: John Wiley and Sons, 1908.

Todorov, Tzvetan. *Mikhail Bakhtin: The Dialogical Principle.* Translated by Wlad Godzich. Minneapolis: The University of Minnesota Press, 1984.

Toronto Research Group. *Rational Geomancy: The Kids of the Book-Machine: The Collected Research Reports of the Toronto Research Group 1973–1982.* Edited by Steve McCaffery. Vancouver: Talonbooks, 1992.

Tzara, Tristan. "To Make a Dadaist Poem." In *Poems for the Millennium, Volume One.* Edited by Jerome Rothenberg and Pierre Joris, 302. Berkeley: University of California Press, 1995.

UbuWeb. www.ubu.com (accessed 1 Dec. 2011).

Uexküll, Jakob von. "A Stroll through the Worlds of Animals and Men: A Picture Book of Invisible Worlds" (1934). In *Instinctive Behavior: The Development of a Modern Concept.* Edited and translated by Claire H. Shiller, 5–80. New York: International Universities Press, 1957.

– "The Theory of Meaning" (1940). *Semiotica* 42, no. 1 (1982): 25–82.

Vendler, Helen. "The Amassing Harmony." In *On Extended Wings: Wallace Stevens' Longer Poems,* 168–205. Cambridge, MA: Harvard University Press, 1969.

– "A Life of Learning." *American Council of Learned Societies* Occasional Paper

No. 50. http://www.acls.org/Publications/OP/Haskins/2001_HelenVendler.pdf (accessed 13 July 2003).

Watten, Barrett. "New Meaning and Poetic Vocabulary: From Coleridge to Jackson Mac Low." *Poetics Today* 18, no. 2 (1997): 147–86.

Webster's Third New International Dictionary of the English Language, unabridged. Springfield, MA: Merriam-Webster, 1993.

Weiner, Hannah. *Clairvoyant Journal*. New York: Angel Hair Books, 1974.

– "Clairvoyant Journal, March." Audio. Performed by Hannah Weiner, Sharon Mattlin, and Margaret De Coursey. New York: New Wilderness Audiographics, 1978. Available at *PennSound*, http://writing.upenn.edu/pennsound/x/Weiner.html (accessed 1 August 2009).

– "Clairvoyant Journal, May." Audio. Performed by Hannah Weiner, Sharon Mattlin, and Rochelle Kraut. New York: New Wilderness Audiographics, 1978. Available at *PennSound*, http://writing.upenn.edu/pennsound/x/Weiner.html (accessed 1 August 2009).

– *Spoke*. Washington: Sun and Moon Press, 1984.

– "Forum." *The Politics of Poetic Form: Poetry and Public Policy*. Edited by Charles Bernstein, 226–7. New York: Roof, 1990.

– *The Fast*. New York: United Artists Books, 1992.

– "Silent Teacher." In *silent teachers/remembered sequel*, 69. New York: Tender Buttons, 1994.

– "Big Words" (1973). In *Early and Clairvoyant Journals by Hannah Weiner*. San Diego: Mandeville Special Collections Library, Geisel Library, University of California, 2004. http://orpheus.ucsd.edu/speccoll/m504/4/index.html (accessed 15 July 2009).

– "Clairvoyant Journal" (1974). In *Early and Clairvoyant Journals by Hannah Weiner*. San Diego: Mandeville Special Collections Library, Geisel Library, University of California, 2004. http://orpheus.ucsd.edu/speccoll/m504/5/index.html (accessed 15 July 2009).

– "Pictures and Early Words" (1972). In *Early and Clairvoyant Journals by Hannah Weiner*. San Diego: Mandeville Special Collections Library, Geisel Library, University of California, 2004. http://orpheus.ucsd.edu/speccoll/m504/3/index.html (accessed 15 July 2009).

– "Hannah Weiner at Her Job." In *Hannah Weiner's Open House*. Edited by Patrick Durgin, 23. Berkeley: Kenning Editions, 2007.

– "Mostly about the Sentence." In *Hannah Weiner's Open House*. Edited by Patrick Durgin, 122–35. Berkeley: Kenning Editions, 2007.

– "The words in CAPITALS and underlines are words I see." In *Hannah Weiner's Open House*. Edited by Patrick Durgin, 63–4. Berkeley: Kenning Editions, 2007.

Wellek, René, and Austin Warren. "Euphony, Rhythm, and Metre." In *The Structure of Verse: Modern Essays on Prosody*. Edited by Harvey Gross, 21–41. Greenwich, CT: Fawcett Books, 1966.

Wershler-Henry, Darren. *The Tapeworm Foundry: andor the dangerous prevalence of imagination*. Toronto: House of Anansi, 2000.

Wheeler, Wendy. *The Whole Creature: Complexity, Biosemiotics and The Evolution of Culture*. London: Lawrence and Wishart, 2006.

Wieners, John. *The Hotel Wentley Poems: Original Versions*. San Francisco: David Haselwood, 1965.

Williams, Raymond. *Politics of Modernism: Against the New Conformists*. Edited by Tony Pinkney. Brooklyn, NY: Verso Books, 2007.

Williams, William Carlos. *The Collected Poems of William Carlos Williams, Volume I, 1909–1939*. Edited by A. Walton Litz and Christopher MacGowan. New York: New Directions, 1986.

– *The Collected Poems of William Carlos Williams, Volume II, 1939–1962*. Edited by Christopher MacGowan. New York: New Directions, 1988.

– *Paterson*. Revised edition, prepared by Christopher MacGowan. New York: New Directions, 1992.

Yogananda, Paramhansa. *Autobiography of a Yogi* (1946). Los Angeles: Self-Realization Fellowship. Reprinted in *Project Gutenberg*, 2005. http://www.gutenberg.org/etext/7452 (accessed 1 July 2009).

Youngblood, Gene. "Life in Counterculture." *Umelec* 2 (2006): 13.

Zenith, Richard, trans. *113 Galician-Portuguese Troubadour Poems*. Manchester: Carcanet, 1995.

Zima, Peter V. "The Subject, the Beautiful and the Sublime." In *Modernism*, Vol. 1. Edited by A. Eysteinsson and V. Liska, 143–53. Amsterdam, The Netherlands, and Philadelphia, PA: John Benjamins Publishing, 2007.

Zipf, George Kingsley. *Human Behavior and the Principle of Least Effort: An Introduction to Human Ecology*. Cambridge, MA: Addison Wesley Press, 1949.

Zukofsky, Louis. *ALL the collected short poems, 1923–64*. New York: W.W. Norton, 1971.

– *"A"*. Berkeley: University of California Press, 1978.

– *Collected Fiction*. Elmwood Park, IL: Dalkey Archive Press, 1989.

– *Complete Short Poetry*. Baltimore: Johns Hopkins University Press, 1991.

– *Prepositions+: The Collected Critical Essays*. Additional prose edited and introduced by Mark Scroggins. Middletown, CT: Wesleyan University Press, 2000.

– *Louis Zukofsky: Selected Poems*. Edited by Charles Bernstein. New York: Library of America, 2006.

Contributors

ADAM DICKINSON teaches poetry and poetics in the English Department at Brock University in St Catharines, Ontario. His scholarly writing has appeared most recently in publications such as *ISLE: Interdisciplinary Studies in Literature and Environment*, *Rhizomes: Cultural Studies in Emerging Knowledge*, and *Canadian Poetry*. He is the author of *Kingdom, Phylum*, which was a finalist for the 2007 Trillium Book Award for Poetry. His third book of poetry, *The Polymers*, is forthcoming in 2013.

KERRY DOYLE teaches poetry and literary studies at York University in Toronto.

RACHEL BLAU DUPLESSIS, professor (emerita) of English at Temple University, is a prominent scholar of women's writing, feminist criticism, and innovative poetries as well as a poet and essayist with more than twenty books to her credit. Her critical works include a feminist "trilogy": the influential *The Pink Guitar: Writing as Feminist Practice* (1990), *Blue Studios: Poetry and Its Cultural Work* (2006), and *Purple Passages: Pound, Eliot, Zukofsky, Olson, Creeley and the Ends of Patriarchal Poetry* (2012). She is the editor of *The Selected Letters of George Oppen* (1990), and co-editor of several anthologies of criticism and memoir. Her ongoing long poem project, begun in 1986, includes, most recently, *Torques: Drafts 58–76*, *Pitch: Drafts 77–95*, and *The Collage Poems of Drafts.*

STEVE MCCAFFERY currently holds the David Gray Chair of Poetry and Letters at SUNY Buffalo. His critical writings include *North of Intention* (1986), *Prior to Meaning* (2001), and *The Darkness of the Present: Poetics, Anachrony and the Anomaly* (2012). His collections of poetry include *Dr. Sadhu's Muffins* (1974), *Panopticon* (1984), *The Black Debt* (1989), *The Theory of Sediment* (1991) and the retrospective *Seven Pages Missing* (2000). In the 1970s, with bpNichol, Paul Dutton, and Rafael Barreto-Rivera, McCaffery was a member of the Four Horsemen, an influential performance and sound poetry group. McCaffery also collaborated with Nichol in the Toronto Research Group (TRG), whose writings appeared in the journal *Open Letter* through the late 1970s and the 1980s and are collected in *Rational Geomancy* (1992).

ERÍN MOURE, a past winner of the Governor General's Award and a three-time finalist for the Griffin Poetry Prize, is one of Canada's most respected poets. In her recent *O Resplandor* (2010) and – with Oana Avasilichioaei – *Expeditions of a Chimæra* (2009), poetry is hybrid and emerges in translation and collaboration. Moure has translated Nicole Brossard (with Robert Majzels) and Louise Dupré from French, Chus Pato and Rosalía de Castro from Galician, Andrés Ajens from Chilean Spanish, and Fernando Pessoa from Portuguese. The essays collected in *My Beloved Wager* (2009) are a chronicle of twenty-five years of writing practice. *The Unmemntioable*, a poetic investigation into subjectivity and experience in western Ukraine and Alberta, appeared in 2012.

MICHAEL O'DRISCOLL, Associate Professor of English at the University of Alberta and Editor of *ESC: English Studies in Canada*, has published on figures such as Derrida, Foucault, Whitman, Pound, and Cage in *Mosaic*, *ESC*, *SLI*, and *Contemporary Literature*. He is co-editor of *After Poststructuralism: Writing the Intellectual History of Theory* (2002) and co-author of *A Bibliography of the Black Sparrow Press* (2003). He is currently at work on two major projects: *A Poetics of the Archive* is a study of archive theory and radical poetics; *Margins: The Black Sparrow Press and Contemporary American Poetry* is a history of one of the most important avant-garde publishers in late twentieth-century America.

JENNIFER RUSSO is an Assistant Professor at Montclair State University in New Jersey. She received her PhD from the City University of New York Graduate Center. Her essay on Hannah Weiner's political poetry of the 1980s was included in a recent issue of the journal *Wild Orchid*. She is currently writing about the poetry of artist and American Indian Movement activist Jimmie Durham.

J. MARK SMITH teaches nineteenth- and twentieth-century literature in the English Department at Grant MacEwan University in Edmonton, Alberta. His essays on Romantic and modernist poetry and poetics have appeared in *ELH*, *European Romantic Review*, *Texas Studies in Literature and Language*, *Paideuma*, and *Studies in Romanticism*.

Index